Partisan Priorities

Americans consistently name Republicans as the party better at handling issues such as national security and crime, while they trust Democrats on issues such as education and the environment – a phenomenon called "issue ownership." *Partisan Priorities* investigates the origins of issue ownership, showing that in fact the parties deliver neither superior performance nor popular policies on the issues they "own." Rather, Patrick J. Egan finds that Republicans and Democrats simply prioritize their owned issues with lawmaking and government spending when they are in power. Because the parties tend to be particularly ideologically rigid on the issues they own, politicians actually tend to ignore citizens' preferences when crafting policy on these issues. Thus, issue ownership distorts the relationship between citizens' preferences and public policies.

Patrick J. Egan is Assistant Professor of Politics and Public Policy at New York University. He is coeditor of *Public Opinion and Constitutional Controversy* (with Nathaniel Persily and Jack Citrin, 2008). *Partisan Priorities* is based on his dissertation, which won the Carl Albert Award for best dissertation in legislative studies from the Legislative Studies Section of the American Political Science Association. In 2012, Professor Egan won the NYU Golden Dozen Award in recognition of his outstanding contribution to learning in the classroom. Before entering academia, he served as an Assistant Deputy Mayor of Policy and Planning in the office of Philadelphia Mayor Edward Rendell.

Partisan Priorities

*How Issue Ownership Drives and
Distorts American Politics*

PATRICK J. EGAN

New York University

CAMBRIDGE
UNIVERSITY PRESS

CAMBRIDGE
UNIVERSITY PRESS

32 Avenue of the Americas, New York, NY 10013–2473, USA

Cambridge University Press is part of the University of Cambridge.

It furthers the University's mission by disseminating knowledge in the pursuit of education, learning, and research at the highest international levels of excellence.

www.cambridge.org
Information on this title: www.cambridge.org/9781107617278

First published 2013

Printed in the United States of America

A catalog record for this publication is available from the British Library.

Library of Congress Cataloging in Publication data
Egan, Patrick J.
Partisan priorities : how issue ownership drives and distorts American politics / Patrick J. Egan.
    pages   cm
Includes bibliographical references and index.
ISBN 978-1-107-04258-2 (hardback)
1. Political parties – United States – Platforms.   2. United States – Politics and government – 21st century.   I. Title.
JK2255.E44   2013
320.97309′05–dc23   2013009958

ISBN 978-1-107-04258-2 Hardback
ISBN 978-1-107-61727-8 Paperback

In memory of my aunt Mary C. Hackett (1925–2011),
the first woman to hold a cabinet-level position in the
Rhode Island state government – and a steadfast partisan
with inspiring priorities.

Contents

Acknowledgments

I am grateful to those who helped me bring this book to its conclusion and to those who accompanied me on the journey. *Partisan Priorities* began as my dissertation at the University of California, Berkeley – a very fruitful, collegial, and enjoyable place to earn a PhD in political science. I first and foremost thank Henry Brady, who not only chaired my dissertation but at several critical junctures provided me with the encouragement and opportunities to obtain the skills I needed to make this project what it is. Throughout, Henry was an ideal mentor: at once critical and caring, holding me to high standards with kindness and concern. A student could simply not ask for more from an advisor, and I can only hope that I am making similar contributions to the intellectual lives of those whom I teach.

I next thank Bruce Cain and Laura Stoker, each of whom played important roles in this project and in my development as a scholar. Laura was the first to bring the notion of issue ownership to my attention during a series of weekly dissertation meetings we held together. So much of what I know about statistics and research design rests upon an intellectual foundation built by Laura – in classes that I first completed as a student and, later, that I taught as her assistant. For his part, Bruce took me under his wing early on at Berkeley's Institute of Governmental Studies (IGS). He advised me throughout this project and in particular helped me think about how to make these ideas relevant to a wider audience. Additional Berkeley faculty who contributed to this project in ways large and small included Rui de

Figueiredo, John Ellwood, Bob Powell, Jas Sekhon, Merrill Shanks, Rob Van Houweling, and Margaret Weir. Jack Citrin belongs on the preceding list, but deserves special mention as a mentor, *macher*, and coconspirator.

After Berkeley, other institutions and people helped bring this book to completion. I acknowledge the Center for the Study of Democratic Politics at Princeton University's Woodrow Wilson School, where I worked on this project as a visiting scholar. There, I received thorough and generous advice on this work from Chris Achen, Larry Bartels, Ted Carmines, Marty Gilens, Dan Gingerich, Karen Long Jusko, Adam Meirowitz, Tali Mendelberg, Tasha Philpot, Bob Putnam, and Jessica Trounstine – and was cheered on by Michele Epstein. This book has benefited tremendously from the support – intellectual, logistical, and collegial – I have received from each and every one of my fellow faculty members in New York University's Politics Department. For comments and conversations about this project in particular I thank Neal Beck, Jon Eguia, Sandy Gordon, Mik Laver, Larry Mead, Becky Morton, Jonathan Nagler, David Stasavage, and Josh Tucker. Financial resources from the Politics Department and from NYU's Goddard Junior Faculty Fellowship made it possible to complete this book.

It is appropriate that a book focusing so much on government spending properly acknowledge the public funding that indirectly made it possible. The ways in which this book brings empirical work and formal models together reflect an approach in political science known as Empirical Implications of Theoretical Models (EITM). I am appreciative of the training I received from the National Science Foundation–funded EITM Initiative and grateful to the political scientists who dreamed up and spearheaded this program. I also owe a great debt to the archives of opinion surveys – many maintained in one way or another with the help of government dollars – that serve as incomparably valuable, publicly available resources on over-time trends in Americans' attitudes on politics and public affairs. These include the American National Election Studies, the National Annenberg Election Survey, the General Social Survey of the National Opinion Research Center, surveys conducted by the Pew Research Center, and the collections of the Roper Center Public Opinion Archives at the University of Connecticut.

I am appreciative of the feedback I have received on this book from many other individuals and audiences over the years, including seminars at George Washington, the Harris School, Harvard, MIT, Michigan, Minnesota, Stanford, Temple, and Vanderbilt. Conversations with Jamie Druckman, Stephen Jessee, Rick Valelly, and Chris Wlezien were particularly valuable as this project entered its final phases. I also thank the anonymous reviewers – those identified by both Cambridge and another press – for extensive, thoughtful comments on the manuscript that made this book considerably better. My editor Robert Dreesen and the production teams at Cambridge and Newgen Knowledge Works have been fantastic partners in the Herculean effort of getting this book into print.

Since we first met when I was a master's student at the Woodrow Wilson School more than fifteen years ago, Doug Arnold has been a trusted mentor who I am now honored to call my friend. Doug's insight and encouragement – and the detailed comments he provided after reading the entire manuscript – were critical to bringing this project to its fruition. Mentors of every stripe, past and present, have left their indelible marks on me; their legacies may be found within these pages. They include Joy Charlton, Donna Cooper, Nan Feyler, Walt Odets, Eric Rofes, Ken Sherrill, and Lisa Shulock.

My extended family – my parents, brothers and sister, in-laws, nieces and nephews – have supported me with their love and enthusiasm, and have even suffered occasional conversations about the ideas presented here. Fantastic, dedicated friends – especially Chris Bartlett, all the Edens, Ronda Goldfein and David Lee Preston, Bill Heinzen, Kimee Kimura, Valerie Koscelnik, Megan Mullin, Abe Newman, Fred Wherry, and Tom Wilson Weinberg – have walked with me on this journey and made it enjoyable. Finally, I thank my partner Ken Harmon for his unconditional love for me, his indefatigable faith in me, and the joy he has shared with me at every stage of this book's progress – and now, happily, its completion.

I

Introduction

In March 2012, the Republican-controlled House of Representatives passed a budget resolution that in some sense was decades in the making. Crafted by House Budget Committee Chair Paul Ryan (R-WI), the plan spelled out cuts to the tax rates paid by many Americans and proposed the consolidation of taxpayers into just two income brackets. The corporate income tax rate would be reduced, too. Although the cuts would be accompanied by reforms designed to broaden the tax base and end distortions and loopholes, total government revenues over the next ten years would still be $2 trillion less than projected by the budget released a month earlier by Democratic President Barack Obama (House Budget Committee 2012).

The budget reflected an alliance between the Republican Party and anti-tax activists that by 2012 had spanned almost forty years. Long ago, Republican fiscal policy had been firmly anchored in the principle of balancing budgets rather than shrinking revenues. But this changed in the 1970s (Karol 2009). The marquee event signaling the party's embrace of the tax cut agenda was California's Proposition 13, which wrote strict limits on property-tax increases into the state's constitution when it was approved overwhelmingly by voters in 1978. The initiative's champion was Howard Jarvis, an activist who had been working hand in hand with state Republicans to craft tax limitation measures since the late 1960s. He found a natural partner in Governor

Ronald Reagan, who had sponsored a failed statewide measure to reduce income taxes as far back as 1973 (Sears and Citrin 1982).

Similar change came to the Republican Party outside of California in the 1970s. On the same day as the passage of Prop. 13, liberal Republican Senator Clifford Case of New Jersey was upset in his primary race by Jeffrey Bell – himself an activist for fiscal conservatism and a former aide to Gov. Reagan. And in Congress, Republican legislators were coalescing around a bill introduced by Sen. William Roth (R-DE) and Rep. Jack Kemp (R-NY) proposing to cut tax rates by about 30 percent across the board. Given little chance of passage when introduced in 1977, just four years later the proposal became the centerpiece of the sweeping tax cuts that Reagan pushed through Congress after Republicans captured the presidency and the Senate in the 1980 elections.

In seizing ownership of the issue of taxation in the 1970s, the Republican Party responded to a national consensus that until then political elites had never quite explicitly addressed: Americans want to pay lower federal income taxes. In 1947, the Gallup Poll began asking what has become a standard survey item about how Americans feel about their individual tax burden: "Do you consider the amount of federal income tax you have to pay as too high, about right, or too low?" In the sixty-five times in which this question appeared on national polls through 2010, in only a handful of instances did the share of Americans saying their taxes are "too high" fall below a majority (Bowman and Rugg 2010).

Four times after Reagan's ascendancy to the presidency – in 1981, 1986, 2001, and 2003 – Republicans spearheaded sweeping overhauls to the tax code that included substantial cuts in income tax rates and other taxes. A notable exception to the party's tax-cutting fervor was the deficit reduction package agreed to by President George H. W. Bush in 1990, a bipartisan bill including tax hikes and spending cuts. The bill left conservatives up in arms; when Bush lost his bid for reelection in 1992, they pointed to this apostasy as the reason for his defeat. The party would not make the same mistake again. As noted approvingly by conservative Ramesh Ponnuru in 2012, not one Republican in ̄   had voted for a broad-based tax increase since then (Ponnuru   nericans took note: between 1981 and 2012, surveys found   s consistently rating the Republican Party as significantly better able to "handle" the issue of taxes than the Democrats. Even Democratic President Bill Clinton's efforts to cut taxes for families with children and for the working poor in the mid-1990s did little to place a dent in the Republican Party's domination of the issue.

If the budget passed by the House Republicans in 2012 was decades in the making, the Patient Protection and Affordable Care Act was the culmination of the work of generations. With its enactment in March 2010, Democrats achieved their long-held goal of extending health care coverage to nearly every American. It was a prize that Democratic presidents from Harry Truman to Bill Clinton had tried and failed to attain. President Barack Obama signed the bill into law on March 23 at a raucous ceremony in the White House East Room that was packed to the rafters with Democratic lawmakers and activists. Standing just over Obama's right shoulder was Victoria Reggie Kennedy – widow of Massachusetts Democrat Edward Kennedy, the passionate advocate of health care legislation, who died in 2009 after a forty-seven-year career in the U.S. Senate. Kennedy was part of a constellation of Democratic leaders whose commitment to the issue meant that nearly all of the major expansions of health care coverage at the federal level occurred under the party's watch. These included the creation of the Medicare and Medicaid programs, spearheaded by another Democratic president, Lyndon Johnson, in 1965; the Health Insurance Portability and Accountability Act of 1996; and a significant expansion of the Children's Health Insurance Program, or CHIP, in 1997.

Of the members of the Democratic coalition's efforts to expand health care coverage, one of the most critical elements was the labor movement. The AFL-CIO, for example, played an important role in organizing support for the establishment of Medicare in the 1960s. Through the decades, unions often also acted as health care's ideological gatekeeper. They helped kill a national health insurance plan in the mid-1970s for not going far enough toward universal coverage (despite its being cosponsored by Senator Kennedy); similar kinds of labor critiques led to a splintering of liberal support for Clinton's failed health plan in the early 1990s (Hoffman 2009). In 2008, health care was at the top of the list of issues motivating support for Democrats from labor groups such as the Service Employees International Union

(SEIU), which spent more than $16 million to support Obama in his campaign against Republican John McCain (Ortiz 2008).

The Democratic Party's association with the issue of health care was buoyed by a broad consensus among Americans that government resources and effort should be directed toward making health care affordable and effective. Since 1973, the General Social Survey (GSS) has asked Americans whether we spend "too much," "too little," or "about the right amount" of money on "improving and protecting the nation's health." In every one of the twenty-seven surveys administered by the GSS through 2010, a majority of Americans said we spend "too little." Since 1994, the Pew Research Center has asked Americans about their priorities for the president and Congress in the upcoming year; in every survey through 2012, a majority of Americans ranked health care–related concerns as a "top priority." As a result, the Democratic Party's dedication to health care made an indelible impression on the American public. Since 1945, when the Gallup Poll asked its national sample which party would better handle "improving the health of the people," Americans had long told pollsters they believed the Democrats to be the party better able to handle the health care issue – usually by double-digit margins over the Republicans. The Democrats' ownership of health care remained little changed even after a Republican-controlled Congress passed President George W. Bush's expansion of the Medicare program to cover the cost of prescription drugs for seniors in 2003.

Despite being about two different parties and two different issues, these stories bear obvious similarities. In poll after poll, survey research finds broad consensuses among Americans that – all things being equal – they endorse the goals of low taxes and improved health care. For decades, these issues have stood at or near the top of the list of priorities of the Republican and Democratic parties. Their prioritization is sustained by powerful activists who are so influential in party politics that it is difficult to tell where their domains end and those of their parties begin. And their clout yields results: in the four decades beginning with the 1970s, most of the major legislation cutting taxes passed because of Republican efforts; most of the landmark laws on health care were the work of Democrats. Last but not least, these issues are important political assets for the two parties: surveys conducted over the same period of time show that Americans consistently credit Republicans as better able to handle taxes and Democrats as better able to handle health care.

The two vignettes illustrate the kind of politics and policy making that accompany a set of issues found at the center stage of American politics. I call these *consensus issues*, and what these issues have in common is that – even in our era of partisan and ideological polarization – there in fact exist broad national consensuses regarding the ultimate goals associated with them. On health care, most Americans – including most conservatives – want to live in a society where people live longer, healthier lives at lower cost to the economy. The same is true for taxes, where most Americans (including liberals) want to pay lower taxes in a simplified, transparent fashion. These issues join others – such as the environment, crime, national security, and education – around which there is national agreement regarding ultimate end states. In one way or another, political scientists have been classifying issues like these together since at least Donald Stokes's introduction of the term "valence issues" five decades ago (Stokes 1963). But unlike previous work, here I set out clear criteria for categorizing these issues and identify similarities in public opinion across them. Americans of all ideological stripes think that the federal government is responsible for achieving each of these goals. They also agree to a remarkable extent that federal dollars should be spent on attaining these goals (including lower taxes, if we consider tax reduction as the "spending" of federal funds). Of course, there are obvious contradictions here, as constraints on government resources and lawmakers' attention prevent a simultaneous pursuit of all of these goals. Nevertheless, Americans agree that they are all important, and that responsibility for achieving them rests on the shoulders of the federal government.

Consensus issues engender a particular kind of politics. It is the politics of *issue ownership*: the long-term positive associations that exist between individual consensus issues and America's two political parties. Taxes join issues such as national security and crime as consensus issues that are "owned" by the Republican Party. Th ⌐ not only health care but also other consensus issues ¦ and the environment. Issue ownership has long intr politics: the term has had a place in the political scie it was introduced by British scholars Ian Budge and

1983. The concept gained widespread attention among Americans with the 1996 publication of John Petrocik's pathbreaking study on issue ownership in the United States. A primary contribution of this line of scholarship has been to identify a valid way to measure the positive associations voters make between parties and issues with survey questions that abstract beyond specific policies and instead focus squarely on the parties' reputations for solving problems. To determine which party owns a particular issue, scholars have generally looked to the party that the majority of Americans name when they are asked a survey question such as "which party is better able to handle issue X?" More than 6,000 questions like these have appeared on national public opinion surveys over the past four decades. Much of the scholarship on issue ownership has been devoted to in-depth investigations of the hypothesis that political campaigns are battles between parties to raise the salience of the issues they own. As we shall see, political scientists' findings regarding this conjecture are mixed. Evidence that the parties emphasize different sets of issues as predicted by issue-ownership theory has been counterbalanced by research demonstrating that candidate messages instead tend to converge on issues that are important to the electorate.

Understanding how issue ownership shapes candidate messaging strategy is interesting and important, with tremendous empirical and normative consequences for the meanings we ascribe to campaigns and elections. But the literature's focus on campaigns has meant that a series of basic questions about issue ownership has gone unaddressed. Most glaringly, political scientists have been remarkably vague about what issue ownership actually means – that is, what causes parties to own issues in the first place. Many scholars have essentially thrown up their hands, defining issue ownership with the same hazy language used in the survey questions: voters' perceptions that one party is better able to "handle" a particular issue than the other. Researchers who have ventured tangible explanations for issue ownership have offered three possible sources for the enduring associations voters make between parties and issues. Some assume that issue ownership arises because Americans agree with the *policies* of the parties that own issues – for example, the tax cuts in the budget passed by the House Republicans in 2012, or the health care policies put in place by the Democrats' Affordable Care Act. Others have inferred that when

Americans say one party is better able to handle an issue, it is because that party has turned in a superior *performance* on the issue. Finally, still others have speculated that issue ownership finds its origins in the parties' issue *priorities* – such as the fact that tax cuts generally happen under Republicans and health care legislation under Democrats. Enfolded within the mystery of the meaning of issue ownership are three additional important questions. First, for what set of issues is the concept of issue ownership analytically germane? Second, is the parties' ownership of issues stable or transitory? Third, for all the attention given to issue ownership's role in campaigns, does it correspond with how the parties actually govern?

This final question signals that there may be much more at stake than previously surmised by scholars of issue ownership. The vignettes presented here about taxes and health care suggest that issue ownership in fact does tell us something about how the parties govern when they gain power in Washington. If this is the case, then the relevance of issue ownership extends far beyond the study of campaigns and elections. It can also yield important insights about political parties, citizens' preferences, and public policy. This raises more questions: Are voters assigning ownership to the parties accurately? Are the parties good stewards of the issues they own? Can voters keep the parties accountable on the issues they own?

In the chapters to follow, I explore all of these questions by undertaking a comprehensive investigation of the role of issue ownership in American politics. I begin by demarcating the notion of "consensus issues" in detail, and show that there is a surprisingly broad consensus among Americans – liberals and conservatives alike – for government spending and action on a wide range of consensus goals. I argue that the concept of issue ownership will be of limited relevance beyond these kinds of issues. Parties can unambiguously improve their reputations to the extent that they can associate themselves with consensus goals such as clean air, safe streets, and good schools. But the same is decidedly not true for divisive issues such as abortion, gay rights, or guns, on which no consensus on goals exists – and thus no partisan stance exists that burnishes a party's image in the same universal, clear-cut fashion as is possible with consensus issues.

I then carefully unpack each of the three hypotheses offered for the origins of issue ownership with simple spatial models showing how any or all of the explanations in the literature could logically comport with the electoral advantages accorded to owning salient issues in elections. As none of these possibilities can be ruled out a priori, identifying the source of issue ownership requires empirical investigation. I begin this by developing estimates of over-time issue ownership with a dataset consisting of the thousands of questions on issue ownership appearing on public opinion surveys over the past forty years. These decade-by-decade figures show that ownership on most issues has proven remarkably resistant to change: for the most part, the issues owned by the parties in the 1970s are the same ones they own today.

I proceed by testing each of the three issue-ownership hypotheses with data drawn from the domains of public opinion and public policy. I reject the first two hypotheses by showing that Republicans and Democrats deliver neither popular policies nor superior performance on their owned issues. Survey data show that Americans do not particularly like the policies of parties on the issues they own: for example, over the past few decades, the typical voter has actually been more likely to agree with the Republicans on jobs policy and with the Democrats on foreign policy. Objective indicators of national conditions on the parties' owned issues do not improve in any detectable ways when they are in power, and most Americans pay too little attention to these indicators to assign proper credit or blame to parties for their performance.

However, a series of tests provides decisive support for the priorities hypothesis. Surveys of Democratic and Republican partisans conducted over the past forty years – from the elites to the rank and file – show that they consistently list their parties' owned issues as higher priorities than other issues. When the parties come to power in Washington, these priorities are reflected in how they govern. Specifically, lawmaking and budgetary data show that the parties do exactly what Americans want them to do on their owned issues: enact major legislation and spend federal dollars designed to address consensus goals on the issues they own. These are the efforts Americans are recognizing when they respond to opinion surveys: year in and year out, they name the Democrats and Republicans as better able to "handle" the issues that the respective parties prioritize.

These analyses allow me to arrive at a conceptually clear, empirically documented definition of issue ownership. *Issue ownership* describes the long-term positive associations between political parties and particular consensus issues in the public's mind – associations created and reinforced by the parties' commitments to prioritizing these issues with government spending and lawmaking.

With this definition in hand, we might conclude that issue ownership is a benign – or even beneficial – aspect of American politics. But the complete picture is not so sanguine. In this book, I also show that issue ownership weakens the relationship between citizens' preferences and public policies. Because party activists are especially ideologically rigid on their owned issues, the parties' lawmakers are significantly less responsive to shifts in public opinion in their policy making and spending allocations on these issues. Thus in addition to being an important driver of American politics, issue ownership also plays a distortionary role in our nation's public affairs. To see this, let us return to the two stories with which this chapter began.

Republicans, Taxes, and the Pledge

The budget passed by the GOP-led House in the spring of 2012 arrived amid a troubling increase in the size of the nation's deficit and nearly unprecedented levels of income inequality. For these and other reasons, polls indicated that the public overwhelmingly favored tax increases on the wealthiest Americans. For example, a CNN survey of American adults conducted that April found 72 percent favored requiring those making $1 million or more per year to pay at least 30 percent of their income in taxes. This was the so-called Buffett rule, named after its well-known proponent investment mogul Warren Buffett.

Yet the Republicans – the party that had owned the issue of taxes for the past forty years – refused to consider popular tax increases such as these. In fact, by most eyes, the party's budget did just the opposite. Its consolidation of tax brackets meant that the income tax rates paid by the wealthiest Americans would actually fall from 35 percent to 25 percent. Although the GOP budget also called for reforms that would simplify the tax system by ending many deductions and thus ultimately be revenue-neutral, it did not say what these reforms would be. Many independent analysts argued that closing the biggest loopholes – including eliminating the deductions for interest paid on home mortgages and ending the practice of shielding premiums paid for employer-provided health insurance from taxation – would in fact further shift tax burdens from the rich to the middle and upper-middle classes (e.g., Gravelle and Hungerford 2012; Toder and Baneman 2012).

Behind the party's resistance to any kind of tax increases were the very same activists who had propelled Republicans to ownership of the issue of taxes in the first place. By 2012, the anti-tax movement had matured into a set of powerful, immensely influential interest groups based in Washington, including a think tank (the Heritage Foundation), a political action committee (the Club for Growth), and – most prominently of all – the lobbying group Americans for Tax Reform (ATR). Founded at the behest of Ronald Reagan, ATR was best known for its Taxpayer Protection Pledge. Grover Norquist, ATR's powerful leader, devised the "Pledge" (as it became known in GOP circles) shortly after the group's founding in 1986. It committed its signatories to "oppose any and all efforts to increase the marginal income tax rates for individuals and/or businesses" and required that any revenues gained from changes to tax deductions or credits be offset by reductions to taxes elsewhere. Thus the plan released by Paul Ryan and the House Republicans in the spring of 2012 reflected the near hegemony that the anti-tax movement enjoyed within the ranks of Republican elected officials. Of the 242 Republicans serving in the House of Representatives in 2012, all but 6 had signed the pledge; the same was true for all but 7 GOP senators (Americans for Tax Reform 2012).

For the few Republicans who wavered on taxes, there could be grave penalties. That May, Indiana Senator Richard Lugar – one of the few Republican legislators to forgo signing the pledge – became the latest to face the consequences of challenging the party's anti-tax orthodoxy. The senator's six-term incumbency came to an end after he was defeated by his Republican primary challenger, state treasurer (and enthusiastic pledge-signer) Richard Mourdock. Lugar began the race with a comfortable lead. But in the months leading up to the primary, the Club for Growth spent an estimated $1.7 million against Lugar (Sunlight Foundation 2012). Other conservative groups piled on, and the distinguished senator's numbers went into free fall. Just one week before the election, Norquist endorsed Mourdock. Lugar's refusal to sign the pledge, said Norquist, meant that he wanted "to leave the door open to tax increases in the future." In making his endorsement, Norquist also settled old scores, taking Lugar to task for his work on the Bush tax hike of 1990 (Litvan 2012). In the end, the margin of Lugar's loss – more than twenty percentage points – was monumental for an incumbent, and it was certainly attributable to more than the opposition of anti-tax interest groups. But his defeat further thinned the ranks of Republicans willing to stand up to Norquist and his allies, and it sent a strong signal that these advocates would brook no dissent in the pursuit of their agenda.

Democrats, Health Care, and Organized Labor

The happy day for Democrats that would take place when President Obama signed the Affordable Care Act in the East Room in March 2010 was difficult for them to envision just two months earlier. That January, all of the trends seemed to be moving in the wrong direction on health care reform. Republican Scott Brown had just triumphed in the special election to fill the U.S. Senate seat left open by Kennedy's death. With Brown's win, Democrats no longer held the sixty seats necessary to overcome a filibuster to pass legislation in the Senate. And Republicans were sure to use the tactic to block the passage of Obama's health care law, which had consumed much of his first year in office. In his ride to victory in one of the most Democratic states in the country, Brown had been unequivocal in his opposition to the bill. "I could be the 41st senator that could stop the Obama proposal that's being pushed right now through Congress," he declared (Viser 2009). Meanwhile, public opinion remained solidly against the health care plan. A Pew Research Center poll that January found 48 percent of Americans opposing the health care bills being discussed in Congress with just 39 percent in favor, numbers that had held relatively steady since Obama first outlined his vision for reform in a joint congressional session the previous September.

An anxious White House began exploring the idea of scaling back the health care law. A revised bill, suggested Chief of Staff Rahm Emanuel, could focus primarily on the more politically popular idea of insuring children. But House Speaker Nancy Pelosi (D-CA) – long associated with the most liberal elements of the Democratic Party – had nothing but disdain for the idea, and she needed only two words to make her displeasure clear. "Kiddie care," she called it. Pelosi wanted to go forward. "We'll never have a better majority in your presidency in numbers than we've got right now," she told the president. "We can make this work" (Stolberg, Zeleny, and Hulse 2010). Less than two months later, Pelosi had her wish. Through a series of arcane legislative maneuvers that defied description by even the most seasoned of Washington observers, the Speaker – along with Senate Majority Leader Harry Reid (D-NV) – successfully steamrolled the bill through Congress. Ignoring public opinion, the party and its activists accomplished one of its most cherished goals.

Two years passed, the November 2012 elections loomed – and the public's attitudes toward the Affordable Care Act had changed very little. Although some elements of the law were popular, by May 2012 the share of Americans viewing the overall bill favorably had remained around 40 percent for over a year. As they looked forward to the elections, many Democratic lawmakers distanced themselves from health care reform – particularly the eleven remaining in the House who had cast votes against the bill two years earlier. This lack of loyalty did not sit well with organized labor. That spring, it trained its sights on two House Democrats from Pennsylvania who had voted against the health care bill: Representatives Jason Altmire and Tim Holden. Both incumbents survived tough challenges in the 2010 congressional elections in swing constituencies. But now both had been placed into new districts by redistricting – and both faced liberal challengers in their respective Democratic primaries. Labor unions pounced, and health care was at the center of their attack. Holden was "pummeled" by his challenger, lawyer Matt Cartwright, for his vote against the health care law. Altmire's opponent, fellow Democratic representative Mark Critz, had the help of "an army of organized labor supporters" as well as the endorsement of former President Bill Clinton (Weisman 2012; see also Clark and Itkowitz 2012; Maher 2012). In April, both Altmire and Holden went down to defeat.

Thus the very same forces that lead parties to prioritize issues – and therefore to own them – also exercise their considerable power to force party elected officials to be ideologically pure on these issues. In 2012, an election cycle in which issue activists would be expected to stockpile scarce ad dollars and volunteer hours to support their parties in November, they instead devoted considerable resources to throwing their co-partisans out of office. In some cases, this kind of fratricide had disastrous results for the parties. In November 2012, Richard Mourdock was routed by his general-election opponent Democrat Joe Donnelly, causing the loss of what had been considered a safe Senate seat for Republicans in Indiana. Mark Critz lost the conservative-leaning Western Pennsylvania district where he staged his primary victory against Jason Altmire by just three percentage points to Republican Keith Rothfus; it is not unreasonable to speculate that the more moderate Altmire might have emerged the winner. These stories illustrate how issue ownership distorts American politics. They are cautionary tales for incumbents who fail to toe the ideological line on their parties' owned issues: unlike Representatives Altmire and Holden and Senator Lugar, most incumbents conform. Furthermore, those who embrace and advance the orthodoxy on their parties' owned issues are often rewarded with elevated status and power, as evidenced by Paul Ryan's nomination as the Republicans' vice presidential candidate in 2012. As a consequence, elected officials pay less attention to the public's preferences on their parties' owned issues than on other issues.

In sum, the politics of issue ownership present a trade-off to American voters. On the one hand, Americans like how owning parties prioritize particular consensus issues and thus devote government resources toward achieving the goals associated with these issues. But on the other, Americans are often unsatisfied with the ideologically rigid policies the parties adopt in pursuit of those goals. Investigating this trade-off is a chief purpose of this book. Along the way, we will gain new insights regarding enduring questions in the scholarly study of American politics. To understand issue ownership's role in public affairs is to better understand the relationship between citizen opinion and public policy, the consequences of partisan polarization, and the structure of the debates regarding some of the most important issues on our nation's political landscape.

THE PLAN OF THE BOOK

I proceed in the following chapter by introducing the concept of "consensus issues" and explaining why it is for this set of issues that the phenomenon of issue ownership is analytically relevant. The chapter defines consensus issues as those having to do with shared goals such as clean air and water, a low crime rate, a nation safe from its enemies, and a well-educated populace. Many voters who appreciate a party's prioritization of a particular goal can nevertheless disagree with the party's policies on that issue. This explains why issue ownership can persist in spite of a party's unpopular policies. Chapter 3 reviews previous scholarship on issue ownership and shows that there is a remarkable degree of ambiguity in the literature about what the concept means analytically and what it means in the minds of voters. The chapter presents simple spatial models showing how any or all of the three hypotheses offered by scholars regarding the source of issue ownership – that it derives from policies, performance, or priorities – are logically possible, and thus these hypotheses must be adjudicated by empirical analyses. It then begins this process by presenting definitive estimates of which parties owned which issues between 1970 and 2010 – ownership that on most issues persisted remarkably unchanged over the course of decades. Using these estimates, the chapter then confirms and expands previous work showing that parties whose owned issues are salient in presidential campaigns are more likely to win elections.

Chapter 4 and Chapter 5, respectively, rule out two of the issue-ownership hypotheses and provide overwhelming evidence for the third. Chapter 4 rejects the policy hypothesis by showing that Americans consider themselves no closer to the parties' policies on the issues they own than the issues they do not. It then rejects the performance hypothesis by showing that parties' ownership of most issues is completely unrelated to whether conditions on those issues actually improve when they hold power in Washington. Chapter 5 turns to the priorities hypothesis and shows, in test after test, that the parties prioritize different sets of issues, and these priorities are strongly correlated with issue ownership. Surveys of party activists show that their concerns about the nation's most important problem consistently correspond with the issues their parties own. Surveys of Democratic and Republican voters show that rank-and-file partisans echo the same priorities as their leaders. Finally, the chapter demonstrates that major legislation is more likely to be enacted on Democratic and Republican issues to the extent that those parties are in control in Washington, and that the parties direct government dollars toward programs and agencies devoted to their priorities.

The empirical finding that issue ownership derives from party priorities is the basis for the key assumption of a theory presented in Chapter 6 that is based upon a spatial model incorporating issue ownership. The model yields the prediction that parties offer policies that are more ideologically extreme on their parties' owned issues than on other issues. Two empirical analyses then confirm the model's predictions. A study of constituency opinion and roll call votes in Congress shows that legislators are less responsive to district opinion on the issues their parties own than on the issues they do not. A second analysis finds that when a party is in power, federal spending is less responsive to the public's preferences on issues owned by the party than on other issues. Chapter 7 concludes by discussing how the book's results illuminate our understanding of the structure of public issues, the effects of citizen opinion on policy, and the role that parties play in government's pursuit of fundamental national goals. It also considers the implications of these findings for our evaluation of the effectiveness of the American democratic system's ability to represent the public's preferences.

Readers interested in additional details about the analyses presented in this book are encouraged to visit my professional website, where they will find an appendix with supplementary material along with replication data and code.

2

Consensus Issues

Amid Polarization, Shared Goals

This chapter sets the stage for the rest of the book by demarcating the set of issues for which the concept of issue ownership is analytically relevant. These "consensus issues" have to do with shared *goals* on which surveys consistently show broad consensuses exist among Americans – liberals and conservatives alike – for spending and government action. Because of the universal popularity of these goals, neither party can afford to be explicitly against achieving them. Rather, the parties are differentiated in three ways: they disagree about which consensus goals should be *priorities*, they disagree about how well those in government have *performed* in pursuit of those goals, and they disagree about which *policies* are best suited to achieving the goals.

The remainder of the chapter discusses theoretical and empirical criteria for determining whether an issue qualifies as a consensus issue. It introduces the *ceteris paribus* criterion – the idea that, all things being equal, Americans must support government action and spending on a consensus goal in order for the debates associated with it to be considered a consensus issue. It then delves more deeply into the distinction between priorities and policies, and shows how common it is for voters to find a party's prioritization of a consensus issue to be appealing while being opposed to key policy stances the party takes on the issue. The chapter then shows that Americans' expressed support for multiple national priorities does not take into account the obvious trade-offs of time and resources that make it impossible for the government to pursue them all simultaneously. Thus, the Democratic and

Republican parties lose very few votes because of their ownership of particular consensus issues. Because this is not true for the positions the parties take on non-consensus issues such as abortion, gay rights, or gun rights, the analytical relevance of the concept of issue ownership is largely limited to understanding the politics of consensus issues.

PRELIMINARIES

Defining Terms

In this book, *goals* are defined as end states: the ultimate outputs of a governing process. By contrast, *policies* are defined as the instruments – often, but not necessarily, laws – used to achieve goals. No Child Left Behind, a federal law championed by President George W. Bush that was passed in 2001, is an example of a policy enacted in pursuit of the goal of improved education for America's students. The Freedom of Access to Clinic Entrances Act signed by President Clinton in 1994 – which made it a federal crime to use violence against those seeking or providing abortions and other reproductive health services – is a policy designed to achieve the goal of guaranteeing access to abortion. As these examples attest, not all goals are equally popular, and not everyone would agree about the policies best designed to achieve certain goals. These two points are key to the book's argument and will be explored in detail in the pages to come.

A few additional definitions are needed. In this book, *performance* is defined in a straightforward way as the extent to which a goal is being achieved. Debates about performance encompass the credit or blame assigned with regard to progress on the goal, and expectations about how well those seeking control of the government would succeed in advancing toward the goal. Performance is thus considered in both retrospective and prospective terms. *Priorities* are defined as commitments to deploying scarce time, resources, and political capital to address goals. In deciding what to do while in office, those who govern face these and other constraints requiring that they determine which goals should be pursued first. Thus elected officials' decisions about priorities can be just as important as the policies they ultimately pursue (e.g., Baumgartner and Jones 1993; Jones, Larsen-Price and Wilkerson 2009; Light 1998; Sulkin 2005).

This leaves a final definition on the table: what, exactly, is an *issue*? As will be seen, many of the classic treatments of this topic in fact disagree on this question. In this book, an issue is defined as a *related set of public debates about a goal* – including the extent to which the goal is desirable, the policies best suited for achieving it, and the performance on the goal of those running the government, as well as how much the goal should be prioritized compared to others.

The Terms in Context: Abortion and Education

With these terms in hand, let us return to the two issues of abortion and education. Americans fundamentally disagree about the "goal" in the abortion issue – a disagreement so profound that it is more appropriate to use the rather infelicitous phrase "desired end state" instead of "goal." An ABC News/*Washington Post* survey of American adults in July 2011 found that 54 percent of Americans believed that abortion should be legal in "all" or "most cases," while 45 percent believed it should be illegal in all or most cases. These results are largely echoed by other surveys and reflect a persistent national divide (Luks and Salamone 2008).

Because the degree to which abortion should be accessible is in permanent dispute, debates about policies, performance, and priorities on the abortion issue are almost impossible to disentangle from those about the desired end state. The major debates over abortion *policies* – such as parental and spousal notification laws, allowing or banning Medicaid coverage of abortion procedures, and regulation of abortion providers – all have to do with expanding or restricting abortion access at the margins. How a voter judges an incumbent's *performance* on the abortion issue will largely depend on where she or he stands on the pro-life to pro-choice continuum and whether the incumbent has made access to abortion easier or more difficult. The same can be said for *prioritization*: it is nonsensical for a voter to support the devoting of scarce government resources and attention to the abortion issue unless it will move conditions toward the end state she or he prefers. So although the abortion issue may nominally include debates about policies, performance, and priorities, in the end most of these aspects of the issue boil down to disagreement about the *goal*: to what extent should abortion be legally available?

By contrast, the education issue can be fairly characterized as being focused on a goal around which there is a strong national consensus. Nearly all Americans are in accord with the goal of a populace that has the skills and knowledge needed to succeed at the workplace and participate as full citizens in the nation's democracy – and they largely agree that this is the government's responsibility. (The universal popularity of this goal is attested to by the fact that no public opinion surveys find it worthwhile to include questions about whether the goal is desirable.) Rather than focusing on the desirability of the goal, the education issue incorporates debates about which *policies* – including charter schools, teacher tenure, school vouchers, funding equalization, and mandatory tests – are most likely to lead to the achievement of the goal, how well government is *performing* at progressing toward this goal, and the extent to which this goal should be *prioritized* compared to other uses of government resources and attention. In this regard, the issue of education could not be more different than the issue of abortion. Education debates are not about the desirability of the goal of an educated citizenry; they are about policies, performance, and priorities with regard to this goal.

CONSENSUS ISSUES

Issues such as education, which concern a goal around which there is a strong national consensus, will be the primary focus of this book. As will be shown, the distinctions among polices, performance and priorities on these issues are key to understanding the origins and consequences of issue ownership. In this book, these issues will be called *consensus issues*. The goals themselves will often be referred to as *consensus goals*. Such issues make up a large share of the nation's political agenda; as shown in Figure 2.1, consensus issues typically make up more than 80 percent of the issues named by Americans as the nation's "most important problem" during presidential election years. Even amid the din of our nation's increasingly polarized politics, there are many goals upon which most Americans still agree. Conservatives and liberals alike want to live in a nation safe from its enemies, with clean air and water, a budget in balance, and a low crime rate. The general desirability of these goals is attested to by the fact that incumbents like to claim credit for progress toward these goals – and challengers are

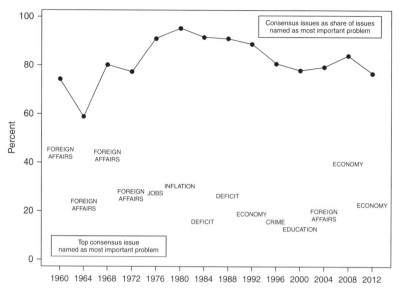

FIGURE 2.1. Consensus issues on the nation's agenda, 1960–2012.
Source: American National Election Studies (1960–2000), Gallup (2004–2012).

quick to lay blame for failing to meet them. Taking credit and casting blame are restricted to no ideology or party. In election campaigns, Republican governors boast about rising test scores in their states' schools; Democratic mayors point proudly to declining crime rates in their cities.

Identifying Consensus Issues

The ceteris paribus *criterion.* To determine whether an issue qualifies as a consensus issue, identify the goal at the center of the issue, and then apply what I will call the *ceteris paribus* criterion: "Is there a consensus that the goal is (1) desirable and (2) the responsibility of government, all other things being equal?" The *ceteris paribus* approach is critical for identifying consensus issues because it analytically isolates the goal in question from rival considerations that are often implicitly associated with it. For example, liberals may be reluctant to voice support for reductions in crime because they object to harsh sentences or the cost of incarceration. Conservatives may resist calls for improving schools because they foresee a consequent hike in taxes. By phrasing the question in the context of *ceteris paribus*, evaluation is focused on the goal itself, rather than any trade-offs required for it to be accomplished. All things being equal, few liberals want to live in a society with a high crime rate – and not many conservatives prefer a nation of poorly educated citizens. Liberals and conservatives alike look to the government to make progress toward crime and education goals. (Even conservatives who advocate putting public schools under private control wish to do so with government-funded subsidies.)

Application of the *ceteris paribus* approach to issues on the national agenda rules out many that cannot be considered consensus issues. A great number of these fall into the category of controversies usually deemed "social issues," such as the abortion issue discussed in the previous section (Egan 2011). Should religious expression be forbidden, permitted, or encouraged in public schools? Should gays have the right to marry and adopt children, or should government policy reflect traditional notions of family? Other non-consensus issues have to do with broader disagreements about the role of government, visions of a just society, and intergroup competition. Should economic inequality be reduced or tolerated? Is society better off with labor unions, or do they restrict free enterprise too much? Should government guarantee a minimum standard of living for all citizens, or is that not its responsibility? Should government provide protection and resources for specific constituencies, such as racial minorities and religious groups? In debates such as these, the goals themselves – the end states – are in dispute. These issues thus all fail the *ceteris paribus* criterion: all things being equal, at this writing there is *no* national consensus about end states such as the level of acceptance of gays and lesbians, the amount of inequality, or the prevalence of labor unions.

Thus consensus goals are all what economists call "goods": there is broad agreement that, all things being equal, more of the ultimate goal (such as clean air or student skills) is preferred to less.[1] The first two diagrams in Figure 2.2 illustrate this condition. They are the hypothetical distributions of citizens' preferred outcomes (or "ideal points")

---

[1] Consensus goals need not necessarily be *public* goods as defined by economists. Many goals fail to meet the public goods criteria of nonrivalrousness and nonexcludability but are nevertheless consensus goals (such as literacy, education, and public safety).

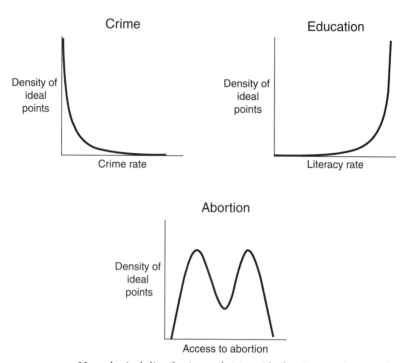

FIGURE 2.2. Hypothetical distributions of citizen ideal points on three goals.

on two consensus issues (crime and education). The distributions of ideal points in both diagrams are highly skewed: all things being equal, just about all citizens prefer a crime rate of zero and a literacy rate of 100 percent. By contrast, on non-consensus issues, there is no agreement about whether more or less of the outcome (such as access to abortion, government endorsement of traditional families, or inequality) is better. This is shown in the final diagram in Figure 2.2, which displays a hypothetical distribution of ideal points on a non-consensus issue (in this case, access to abortion). In this distribution, the ideal points are bimodal (with pro-life and pro-choice voters outnumbering those in between). To the extent there is a consensus at all, it is that most ideal points are in the middle of the distribution. That is, there are very few voters who would ban legal abortion in all circumstances (such as when a woman's life is threatened by her pregnancy) or who would allow legal abortion in all cases (such as for selection of the sex of the fetus). In sum, opinion on an issue such as abortion is structured in a fundamentally different way than it is on consensus issues such as education and crime.

Empirical evidence: support for government action and spending. To be clear, whether an issue counts as a consensus issue is to be determined empirically rather than stipulated a priori. For example, an issue such as education seems intuitively to qualify as a consensus issue to those living in the present-day United States. But throughout much of American history, no consensus existed about whether the goal of an educated populace was desirable; if it was the responsibility of government; and if so, who qualified for such an education. Two empirical questions that can be asked about a goal to determine whether it meets the *ceteris paribus* criterion are the levels of general agreement among Americans that (1) government should do something about the goal, and (2) government funds should be spent in pursuit of the goal.

We might expect this set of issues to be small in number given an American political culture that is unusually skeptical about government's ability to solve problems (Pew Global Attitudes Project 2003). But in fact, the list of national goals that qualify as consensus issues is actually quite lengthy. Strong evidence of Americans' endorsement of a broad range of consensus goals can be found by examining survey data from what most observers would consider to be a low point in the public's support for government action and spending: the period just before and after the 2010 congressional elections. During this span, approval of President Barack Obama and the Democratic-controlled Congress plummeted, and the limited-government Tea Party movement gained strength and momentum. The elections held in November 2010 swept Republicans into power in the House of Representatives with a net gain of sixty-three seats and severely reduced the Democrats' majority in the Senate. Surveys of voters on Election Day found that by a 56 to 38 percent margin, voters thought government was "doing too many things better left to businesses and individuals" rather than that it should "do more to solve problems" – an eighteen-point gap that was the largest on record since the question was first placed on exit polls in 1994 (National Election Pool Exit Poll 2010). *Congressional Quarterly*'s postelection analysis reflected the conventional wisdom that a main reason for the Republican victories was "a broad sense that the federal government was overreaching under the Democrats" (Congressional Quarterly 2011). Indeed, by one measure, the national government had grown bigger than at any time since World War II: as a share of GDP, federal outlays during the prior two fiscal years averaged 24.7 percent, a level not seen since the Truman administration (White House Office of Management and Budget 2012a: Table 1.3). Research by political scientists finding that American public opinion reacts to government activity as would a "thermostat" – demanding more government intervention when government contracts, and less when government expands – would therefore lead us to expect support for bigger government to be especially low at this time (Wlezien 1995; Soroka and Wlezien 2010).

Thus the national environment in 2010 and 2011 would seem to be particularly inhospitable to the notion that government should be taking action and spending public dollars to solve the nation's problems. Nevertheless, survey data from this period demonstrate that this is exactly what vast majorities of Americans wanted. Since it began in the 1970s, the biennial General Social Survey (GSS) has been asking representative samples of American adults whether they think spending on a series of national problems is "too little," "too much," or "about right." In 2010, the GSS was fielded from March through August. Table 2.1 displays responses to this battery of questions among GSS respondents who reported voting in the 2008 presidential election. Even at that moment, a remarkable consensus existed regarding spending on many national problems.[2] On no issue did support for cutting spending amount to more than one in three voters, and majorities of voters supported increased spending on every issue in the table save one: the military. And there was nothing particularly unusual about 2010, or for that matter the GSS. Year in and year out over the past four decades, the GSS has found high levels of support for spending on the consensus goals listed here. Similar results are obtained from similar questions posed in surveys fielded by other organizations, including the American National Election Studies and the Pew Research Center.

Americans not only like spending money on a broad range of consensus goals; they also consistently look to Washington to address these goals. Table 2.2 presents data from an annual survey conducted

---

[2] The table includes responses to the GSS question on taxation – which, *ceteris paribus*, everyone would like to be as low and simple as possible – and thus is classified as a consensus issue in this book. This decision is justified later in this section.

TABLE 2.1. *Voters' support for spending on selected consensus goals, 2010*

Goal	On this problem, we are currently spending...		
	too little	about right	too much
improving education	76%	17%	7%
developing alternative energy	67%	25%	8%
assistance to the poor	66%	24%	10%
taxes (reverse-coded)*	52%	46%	2%
Social Security	57%	34%	9%
halting rising crime rate	56%	36%	8%
protecting the environment	60%	27%	13%
dealing with drug addiction	53%	36%	11%
improving health	59%	19%	22%
military, armaments, and defense	28%	38%	34%

Source: General Social Survey.

Question wording: We are faced with many problems in this country, none of which can be solved easily or inexpensively. I'm going to name some of these problems, and for each one I'd like you to tell me whether you think we're spending too much money on it, too little money, or about the right amount ... [read items]

*Question wording for taxes: Do you consider the amount of federal income tax which you have to pay as too high, about right, or too low? (For comparability purposes, responses to this question are reverse-coded: "too high" responses are reported in table in the "too little" column; "too low" responses in the "too much" column.)

Sample: American adults reporting voting in the 2008 presidential election. Data are weighted. N's range from 663 to 1,378. In some cases, responses were combined for two survey items with similar question wording. See this book's online appendix for details.

by Pew on Americans' priorities for the president and Congress. The data displayed here come from the Pew survey fielded in early January 2011, just six weeks after the congressional elections. Respondents were given a series of possible priorities for Obama and the new Congress, and for each were asked to say whether it should be a "top priority, important but lower priority, not too important, or should it not be done." Table 2.2 displays responses among those reporting voting in the 2010 elections – a group that supported Republican congressional candidates by a 53–47 point margin. Once again, despite the fact that the survey was fielded during a high-water mark of Americans' skepticism about government's ability to solve problems, a strong consensus existed that Washington should do exactly that. Given the

TABLE 2.2. *Voters' priorities for the President and Congress on selected consensus goals, January 2011*

Goal	% of voters naming goal as…			
	top priority	important but lower priority	not too important	should not be done
Improving the job situation	87%	12%	0%	1%
Strengthening the nation's economy	87%	11%	1%	1%
Defending the country from future terrorist attacks	73%	23%	3%	1%
Reducing the budget deficit	70%	27%	2%	1%
Taking steps to make the Social Security system financially sound	69%	25%	5%	1%
Improving the educational system	63%	29%	6%	2%
Taking steps to make the Medicare system financially sound	61%	32%	5%	2%
Reducing health care costs	60%	30%	5%	5%
Dealing with the problems of poor and needy people	51%	37%	10%	2%
Dealing with the nation's energy problem	51%	38%	9%	2%
Strengthening the U.S. military	49%	34%	12%	4%
Dealing with the issue of illegal immigration	47%	38%	11%	4%
Reducing crime	41%	44%	11%	3%
Changing the federal income tax system to make it simpler	40%	38%	15%	6%
Dealing with global trade issues	38%	45%	14%	3%
Protecting the environment	37%	45%	14%	4%

Source: Pew Research Center.

<u>Question wording</u>: I'd like to ask you about priorities for President Obama and Congress this year. As I read from a list, tell me if you think each should be a top priority, important but lower priority, not too important or should it not be done. (First,) should [INSERT ITEM] be a top priority, important but lower priority, not too important, or should it not be done?

<u>Sample</u>: American adults reporting voting in the 2010 Congressional elections. Data are weighted. N's range from 516 to 541 per question; each respondent was asked half of items via a split-sample design.

Republican tilt of these voters, it is perhaps not surprising that chief concerns of conservatives – such as the deficit, terrorism, the military, immigration, and taxes – were named as "top priorities" by pluralities of these voters. But so were liberal concerns such as education, health care, Social Security, and poverty. Just as notable is that fact that the share of Americans saying that work on these goals "should not be done" was quite low, reaching no higher than the single digits on every one of the sixteen issues listed here.

The GSS and Pew items are helpful in identifying consensus issues for two reasons. First, they are all phrased in terms of goals – or in a few cases such as Medicare and Social Security, very popular programs closely linked to goals – rather than policies. Second, the questions are asked in a *ceteris paribus* fashion. Participants in the GSS were not asked to consider trade-offs among various types of spending or whether they would be willing to raise taxes or increase the deficit in order to achieve the spending increases they desire. Similarly, Pew respondents were allowed to name as many issues to be a "top priority" for the incoming Congress as they liked, rather than having to consider that elected officials might face constraints with regard to time, resources, or attention in solving these problems. (A Congress able to address all ten of the problems listed as "top priorities" by majorities of American voters in Table 2.2 during its two-year session would be a very productive legislature indeed!) Thus although these questions may be nominally about priorities, they are more accurately considered indicators of how strongly the notion of government action on consensus goals appeals to the American public – all things being equal.

Taxes and the deficit as consensus issues. This book will consider two important issues on the agenda – the deficit and taxes – as consensus issues. This may give some readers pause: after all, both issues have to do with goals regarding the government itself, rather than (as the examples of consensus issues that have been mentioned thus far) goals that might be achieved through government action. Nevertheless, they meet the *ceteris paribus* test. All things being equal, Americans would like to live in a nation that is in surplus, rather than deficit. And if there were no trade-offs in terms of reduced government services, just about every American would like to pay low taxes in a simple, straightforward fashion. Survey data demonstrate that Americans support that government attention and resources be devoted to deficits and taxes in ways similar to other consensus goals. Table 2.2, for example, shows that Americans clearly consider these two issues as high priorities for government action. Table 2.1 shows that – if the definition of "spending" is expanded to include all net government outflows – Americans can also be considered to support government "spending" on taxes. Americans consistently say that their own taxes are "too high": 52 percent of the GSS sample in 2010 agreed with this statement; only 2 percent said they were "too low." Unfortunately, whether Americans support "spending" on the deficit is a matter difficult to discern with survey data, because survey questions about the deficit are rarely posed in a *ceteris paribus* fashion: instead, they ask what Americans would be willing to trade off – in terms of increased taxes and reduced government spending – in order to reduce it. Despite this lack of evidence, it is sensible to treat deficit reduction as a consensus goal.

Two non-consensus issues: inequality and immigration. Two final examples illustrate the differences between consensus issues and non-consensus issues. Consider two sets of closely related issues: first, poverty and inequality, and second, unauthorized immigration and immigration. In both sets of issues, the former is the consensus issue, the latter is not. To see why, apply the *ceteris paribus* criterion to these two issues. If cost were no barrier, most Americans (even most conservatives) would prefer that no one live in poverty. Putting aside the question of legal immigration, most Americans (even most liberals) would prefer that the level of *unauthorized* immigration to the country be zero. The national consensuses regarding these two issues are reflected in survey data. Table 2.1 shows that 90 percent of American voters in 2010 believed we should be spending no less than we currently do on "assistance to the poor." Although the GSS does not ask about spending preferences regarding unauthorized immigration, the American National Election Studies (ANES) did so in 2008. That survey found that 87 percent of voters favored keeping federal spending on "tightening border security to prevent illegal immigration" at no less than current levels. Likewise, Table 2.2 shows that "dealing with the problems of poor and needy people" and "dealing with illegal immigration" were top priorities of pluralities of Americans in 2011.

TABLE 2.3. *Opinion on two non-consensus goals, 2010*

Government should reduce income inequality (GSS, May–August 2010)		Immigration to the U.S. (CBS News/*New York Times*, April 2010)	
	percent		percent
Strongly agree	7	Welcome ALL immigrants	33
Agree	23	Welcome SOME immigrants, but not others	34
Neither	18	Cannot afford to open	27
Disagree	32	doors to ANY newcomers	
Strongly disagree	20	Unsure	6
Total	100	Total	100
N = 1,370		*N* = 1,079	

Question wording:

Inequality: Do you agree or disagree ... it is the responsibility of the government to reduce the differences in income between people with high incomes and those with low incomes.

Immigration: Which comes closer to your opinion? America should always welcome all immigrants. OR, America should always welcome some immigrants, but not others. OR, America cannot afford to open its doors to any newcomers.

Samples: American adults.

However, no such consensus exists over inequality and legal immigration. As shown in Table 2.3, Americans are divided on whether it is government's responsibility to reduce income differences. (If anything, opinion leans against the idea.) When asked about the extent to which the United States should welcome new immigrants, opinion is as divided as can be, with about a third of Americans each favoring allowing entry to all, some, and no new immigrants. The high levels of disagreement in opinion on these non-consensus issues reflect deep differences in basic values. This kind of division can exist alongside of the agreement expressed by Americans on closely related consensus issues.

Comparison with Other Issue Typologies

This book is by no means the first to note the similarities found among the issues I am calling consensus issues. However, there are some important distinctions between the classification scheme presented here and those of past work. At first glance, consensus issues appear to be similar to those identified as "valence issues" by Donald E. Stokes fifty years ago in his article "Spatial Models of Party Competition." Valence issues, wrote Stokes, are those that involve "some condition that is positively or negatively valued by the electorate," such as economic prosperity or American prestige abroad. He contrasted valence issues with "position issues," which have to do with debates over "government actions from a set of alternatives" (Stokes 1963: 373). Similarly, Warren E. Miller and J. Merrill Shanks introduce their discussion of retrospective voting in *The New American Voter* by describing issues that are "based on a broad consensus ... concerning those circumstances or conditions that are desirable (such as a strong economy) or undesirable (such as pollution)." They contrast these with issues involving "some kind of conflict or disagreement within the society" (Miller and Shanks 1996: 370).

Crucially, both of these classification schemes categorize related debates as separate issues – in the case of Stokes, "valence" and "position" issues; for Miller and Shanks, "consensual" and "conflict" issues. For example, Stokes considered the "problem of Korea" a valence issue in the 1952 presidential election – an issue used by Republicans to pin the Democrats with the unpopular "war party" moniker. But Stokes contended that "position issues lurk behind many valence issues," and in the case of Korea the position issue was whether the United States should escalate the conflict, maintain the status quo, or withdraw (1963: 373). Similarly, Miller and Shanks write that the "topics or 'problems' that are emphasized in a campaign often involve a combination of *both* kinds of issues" – that is, both consensus and conflict issues (1996: 370).

The typology used in this book takes an approach to classifying issues that has a crucial difference: it treats related debates such as these as aspects of the *same* issue. In this framework, the Korean War debates that Stokes separated into valence and position issues are considered simply to be different aspects of the larger consensus issue of foreign affairs. By my classification scheme, the criticism leveled by Eisenhower over Korea in the 1952 elections was about the Democrats' *performance* on the issue of foreign affairs; the question of which strategy should be pursued on the war was a debate about *policy* on the issue of foreign affairs.

In sum, what is new here is that I consider debates about policies, performance, and priorities regarding a consensus goal to be aspects of the same consensus issue. Thus my approach is somewhat more aligned with the critique of Stokes by James E. Alt, who notes that "every issue has, or can have, both valence and position aspects" (Alt 1979: 10).[3] The justification for taking this approach is evident from the previous chapter's discussions of the issues of taxes and health care: the parties' policies, priorities, and performance regarding any consensus goal are intimately tied together. Thus much more analytical purchase is gained when these debates are considered aspects of the same issue, as they are in this book.

PRIORITIES AND POLICIES

At the core of the book's argument is that issue ownership on consensus issues is linked closely with the parties' *priorities* but that issue ownership is often associated with unpopular *policies*. To illuminate the differences between these two concepts, here I undertake a preliminary tour of survey data to show how this is possible.

Partisan Priorities

Although Americans generally like the idea of government taking action on consensus goals with spending and legislation, not all goals can be pursued simultaneously. The constraints on government dollars, policy-makers' time and attention, as well as other scarce resources require that choices be made about how to allocate these resources toward achieving different goals (Baumgartner and Jones 1993; Jones, Larsen-Price and Wilkerson 2009). Unfortunately, poll respondents are rarely asked to explicitly allocate resources in such a fashion (although

---

[3] See also Morris P. Fiorina's distinction between *ends* – which he divides into two types: "consensual" and "controversial" – and the *means* by which society arrives at those ends (Fiorina 1981, 17–19). R. Douglas Arnold makes a similar distinction between what he calls *outcome* preferences and *policy* preferences (Arnold 1990: 17). A conceptualization of valence that is closer to the notion of consensus issues introduced here is offered by Frank R. Baumgartner and Bryan D. Jones, who write that valence issues involve "important decisions about what solutions are most appropriate to combat a uniformly agreed-upon problem" (Baumgartner and Jones 1993: 150).

TABLE 2.4. *Support for spending on selected consensus goals*
by party identification, 2010

Goal	% supporting spending increase – % supporting spending decrease		
	Republicans	Democrats	Difference
military*	18.5	−28.2	46.7
taxes (reverse–coded)*	56.9	43.6	13.3
halting rising crime rate	49.9	43.8	6.1
alternative energy*	47.1	64.6	−17.6
Social Security*	37.2	55.7	−18.5
drug addiction*	30.9	50.5	−19.5
improving education*	55.5	79.3	−23.8
environment*	21.3	67.6	−46.3
assistance to the poor*	28.5	74.8	−46.3
health*	8.2	61.0	−52.9

Source: General Social Survey.

Question Wording: See Table 2.1.

Sample: American adults. Data are weighted. N's range from 787 to 1,609.

*Differences between Republicans and Democrats are statistically significant at $p < .05$.

a few instances of these kinds of surveys are discussed in the next section). However, we can learn something about respondents' priorities by examining their relative rankings of different consensus goals, and seeing how this relative support varies across the population.

The questions motivating this book lead us to be particularly interested in how support for different consensus goals differs along party lines. This is seen in Tables 2.4 and 2.5, where the survey data examined earlier in the chapter on Americans' support for government spending and government priorities are now broken down by voters' party identification. Entries in Table 2.4 are the shares of Republicans and Democrats in the 2010 GSS saying the nation is spending "too little" on each consensus goal minus the share saying it is spending "too much." The goals are listed from those with the highest relative support among Republicans to those most popular with Democrats. For example, the first row of the table shows that among Republicans, supporters of an increase in military spending outnumber those supporting a cut in spending by nineteen percentage points. By contrast,

TABLE 2.5. *Priorities on selected consensus goals
by party identification, 2011*

Goal	% naming goal as a "top priority"		
	Republicans	Democrats	Difference
Dealing with the issue of illegal immigration*	58.7	36.7	22.0
Reducing the budget deficit*	71.5	59.9	11.5
Strengthening the U.S. military	47.9	39.6	8.3
Changing the federal income tax system to make it simpler	40.0	32.2	7.7
Defending the country from future terrorist attacks*	77.8	70.8	7.0
Strengthening the nation's economy	87.5	87.5	<0.1
Taking steps to make the Social Security system financially sound	66.1	67.1	−1.0
Improving the job situation	85.5	86.6	−1.1
Reducing crime	41.6	45.3	−3.7
Taking steps to make the Medicare system financially sound*	55.4	65.1	−9.7
Dealing with global trade issues*	26.6	40.4	−13.8
Dealing with the nation's energy problem*	42.6	56.6	−14.0
Protecting the environment*	27.5	50.7	−23.2
Dealing with the problems of poor and needy people*	38.1	62.2	−24.0
Reducing health care costs*	48.2	73.3	−25.0
Improving the educational system*	52.0	77.2	−25.2

Source: Pew Research Center.

Question wording: See Table 2.2.

Sample: American adults. Data are weighted. N's range from 654 to 676.

*Differences between Republicans and Democrats are statistically significant at $p < .05$.

among Democrats, supporters of a spending cut outnumber those supporting an increase by twenty-eight points. This forty-seven–point swing in support for military spending makes it the issue whose relative popularity is highest among Republicans, placing it at the top of the table. By contrast, the fifty-three–point difference in support for spending on health care between Democrats and Republicans makes this goal the highest in relative popularity among Democrats, and thus it is listed in the final row of the table. A line is drawn separating the goals that are more popular with Republicans from those more popular with Democrats. Data on Americans' priorities from the 2011 Pew survey are revisited in a similar fashion in Table 2.5. Entries in this table are the shares of Republicans and Democrats calling each of the goals a "top priority," and the goals are ranked by the share of Republicans naming the goal as a top priority minus the share of Democrats. The table thus provides a sense of the relative prioritization of each goal among partisans, with unauthorized immigration garnering the greatest level of relative support from Republicans and education from Democrats. Again, a line is drawn in the table dividing the goals more popular with Republicans from those more popular with Democrats.

This examination of how partisans rank the need for government spending and action on consensus goals yields three observations. First, the differences in relative priorities among Democrats and Republicans are generally substantial and statistically significant. With regard to spending on consensus issues, the differences in priorities between partisans in Table 2.4 exceed ten percentage points – and are statistically significant – on all but one issue: crime. Regarding priorities to be taken by the government in Washington, partisan differences are greater than five points on twelve of the sixteen goals listed in Table 2.5. Second, regardless of the deep partisan disagreements over the nation's priorities, a substantial amount of consensus nevertheless exists between Democrats and Republicans that government spending and action are needed to address these goals. Even in the heyday of the ascendance of Tea Party values in 2010, Republicans preferred increasing spending on every goal listed in Table 2.4, including spending on typically liberal issues such as the environment, poverty, education, and health care. With the exception of military spending, the same was true for Democrats. Similarly, Table 2.5 shows that majorities of Republicans named the traditionally liberal concerns of Social Security, education, and Medicare as top priorities for the president and Congress. Majorities of Democrats said that defending the nation from terrorism and reducing the deficit – goals usually associated with conservatives – should be top priorities. The implications of these consensuses for campaigns and elections are worth noting: all things being equal, a candidate who promises to increase spending on education should win more votes – even from Republicans – than one committed to cutting school spending. A candidate who declares her "top priority" to be defending the country from terrorism should be more popular – even among Democrats – than an opponent who counters that it is a lower priority.

Finally, the relative prioritization of consensus goals among Republicans and Democrats previews a finding that will be documented thoroughly in the following chapters: the parties' priorities correspond overwhelmingly with issue ownership. The issues prioritized most by Republicans – such as immigration, taxes, the military, and terrorism – are among the issues Americans are most likely to say they trust the Republican Party to better handle than the Democrats. The goals ranked highest as priorities by Democrats – including education, the environment, and poverty – correspond with the Democratic Party's owned issues.

Popular Priorities, Unpopular Policies

Some readers may find it difficult to see much of a difference between policies and priorities – particularly when priorities are discussed in terms of government resources. Shouldn't one's preference regarding devoting scarce resources to a particular issue be considered a policy preference? But the difference between these two concepts is substantial: although individual priorities enjoy near-universal popularity across most consensus issues, many individual policies on these issues do not.

Survey data on four issues illustrate the difficult choices many Americans face between parties' policies on the one hand and priorities (as indicated by their support for federal spending on consensus goals) on the other. We have seen that substantial majorities of Americans support spending on assistance to the poor and on the environment (issues prioritized by Democrats) as well as terrorism

TABLE 2.6. *Priorities and policies*
Cell entries are total percentages.

a. Poverty

		PRIORITY: National spending on assistance to the poor			
		too little	about right	too much	Total
POLICY:	Agree	25.0	3.7	0.2	28.9
Government should reduce income inequality	Neither agree nor disagree	14.2	1.4	1.4	17.0
	Disagree	27.7	18.3	8.1	54.1
	Total	66.9	23.3	9.7	100.0

Source: General Social Survey, 2010.

Question wording:

Priority: We are faced with many problems in this country, none of which can be solved easily or inexpensively. I'm going to name some of these problems, and for each one I'd like you to tell me whether you think we're spending too much money on it, too little money, or about the right amount ... assistance to the poor.

Policy: Do you agree or disagree ... it is the responsibility of the government to reduce the differences in income between people with high incomes and those with low incomes.

Sample: American adults reporting voting in the 2008 presidential election. Data are weighted. $N = 444$.

and unauthorized immigration (issues prioritized by Republicans). However, as shown in Table 2.6, large shares of voters do not support the policies promoted on these issues by the parties that prioritize them. The traditionally Democratic priority of directing national spending toward poverty reduction is quite popular: in 2010, about two in three voters thought funding should be increased from current levels. But among these voters, a substantial proportion also opposed a basic principle guiding Democratic Party policies on this issue: that government should reduce income differences between the wealthy and the poor. About 28 percent of all American voters (indicated in the table by the shaded cell) found themselves in this position in 2010. The same is true on the environment, where 41 percent of voters in 2010 both favored an increase in government spending and simultaneously

TABLE 2.6. *Priorities and policies (continued)*
Cell entries are total percentages.

b. Environment

		PRIORITY: National spending on the environment			
		too little	about right	too much	total
POLICY: Poorer countries should make less effort than rich countries on environment	Agree	9.5	3.9	1.5	14.9
	Neither agree nor disagree	9.0	3.8	1.5	14.4
	Disagree	41.1	19.4	10.2	70.8
	Total	59.6	27.1	13.3	100.0

Source: General Social Survey, 2010.

Question wording:

Priority: We are faced with many problems in this country, none of which can be solved easily or inexpensively. I'm going to name some of these problems, and for each one I'd like you to tell me whether you think we're spending too much money on it, too little money, or about the right amount ... [SPLIT: HALF SAMPLE:] Improving and protecting the environment. [HALF SAMPLE:] The environment. [Responses did not differ substantially and are combined.]

Policy: How much do you agree or disagree with each of these statements? ... Poorer countries should be expected to make less effort than richer countries to protect the environment.

Sample: American adults reporting voting in the 2008 presidential election. Data are weighted. N = 926.

opposed the key provision of the Democratic-supported Kyoto treaty on climate change: that rich countries should sacrifice more than poor countries to reduce greenhouse gases.

Similar patterns are found on the two Republican issues. In 2008, 16 percent of voters both favored an increase in federal spending on the war on terrorism while opposing the torture of suspected terrorists – a policy for fighting terrorism that has found some support among Republican party leaders and was explicitly banned by Democrat Barack Obama shortly after he became president in 2009. On the issue of unauthorized immigration, a majority of voters in 2008 supported increasing federal spending on border security. But

TABLE 2.6. *Priorities and policies (continued)*
Cell entries are total percentages.

c. Terrorism

| | | PRIORITY: Federal spending on the war on terrorism | | | |
		Increased	Kept about the same	Decreased	Total
POLICY: U.S.	Favor	10.6	9.4	4.3	24.3
government torturing suspected	Neither favor nor oppose	6.5	9.1	5.3	20.9
terrorists to get information	Oppose	16.3	21.4	17.1	54.8
	Total	33.4	39.9	26.7	100.0

Source: American National Election Studies, 2008.

Question wording:

Priority: If you had a say in making up the federal budget this year...Should federal spending on the war on terrorism be INCREASED, DECREASED, or kept ABOUT THE SAME?

Policy: Do you FAVOR, OPPOSE, or NEITHER FAVOR NOR OPPOSE the U.S. government torturing people, who are suspected of being terrorists, to try to get information?

Sample: American adults reporting voting in the 2008 presidential election. Data are weighted. $N = 1,547$.

many of these voters also supported creating a path to citizenship for illegal immigrants, meaning that 23 percent of the electorate favored a traditional Republican priority while supporting a policy on the same issue that was opposed by most Republican leaders at the time.

Thus there are indeed crucial differences between policies and priorities. The politics of issue ownership can force many American voters to choose whether they will support a party that both prioritizes goals they like and promotes policies they do not. These voters vastly outnumber those in the opposite circumstances. A comparison of the shaded cells in Table 2.6 with their counterparts in the upper-right corners of the individual tables indicate that very few voters disagree with parties' priorities while agreeing with their policies. These four issues are meant to be merely illustrative of the kind

TABLE 2.6. *Priorities and policies (continued)*
Cell entries are total percentages.

d. Unauthorized immigration

		PRIORITY: Federal spending on border security to prevent illegal immigration			
		Increased	Kept about the same	Decreased	Total
POLICY: Path to citizenship for illegal immigrants	Oppose	27.3	6.1	0.4	33.7
	Neither favor nor oppose	8.6	6.4	0.6	15.6
	Favor	22.7	17.1	10.9	50.6
	Total	58.6	29.6	11.9	100.0

Source: American National Election Studies, 2008.

Question wording:

Priority: If you had a say in making up the federal budget this year … Should federal spending on tightening border security to prevent illegal immigration be INCREASED, DECREASED, or kept ABOUT THE SAME?

Policy: Do you FAVOR, OPPOSE, or NEITHER FAVOR NOR OPPOSE the U.S. government making it possible for illegal immigrants to become U.S. citizens?

Sample: American adults reporting voting in the 2008 presidential election. Data are weighted. $N = 780$.

of politics engendered by consensus issues rather than exhaustive of the entire domain of priorities and policies. More comprehensive examinations of these relationships will be presented throughout this book.

THE LOW SALIENCE OF TRADE-OFFS AMONG CONSENSUS GOALS

Using data drawn from multiple opinion surveys, I have demonstrated the near-universal appeal among the American public of a broad set of national goals. Much of the evidence comes from responses to survey questions about federal spending and government priorities, which indicate high levels of support for the pursuit of a wide range of consensus goals among Republicans and Democrats alike. A question raised by these data is why voters' responses to these questions fail to take into account any constraints on government funds or other resources. As will be shown, under the right circumstances Americans are indeed capable of analyzing and understanding the trade-offs that exist among different consensus goals; however, these circumstances rarely arise in the give-and-take of national politics. Here I explore in detail the low salience of trade-offs among consensus goals, as it has important implications for our understanding of how issue ownership works in American politics.

First, to confirm just how little the public considers constraints on the simultaneous pursuit of multiple consensus goals, let us return to the spending and priorities surveys once more. Among the consensus goals listed in the GSS data presented in Table 2.1, there is one – lower taxes – whose fulfillment unambiguously results in reduced revenues flowing to the federal government. Thus if Americans' responses to these questions were to reflect some minimal level of accounting for the trade-offs among different goals, we would expect those saying their taxes are "too high" to be less supportive of increases in government spending than those saying their taxes were "about right" or "too low." Similarly, among the goals listed in the Pew data in Table 2.2, there is one – reducing the deficit – that in 2011 would require some cuts in federal spending in order to be achieved. (Even prominent liberal advocates agreed at the time that closing the deficit solely with tax increases was unrealistic.[4]) So if voters were taking the trade-offs required to achieve these goals into account in some minimal fashion, those listing deficit reduction as a "top priority" should have named fewer goals as top priorities than those ranking deficit reduction as less important.

As seen in Table 2.7 and in Table 2.8, in neither case – tax reduction nor deficit reduction – did Americans' responses to these questions meet a minimal standard of the awareness of constraints on government resources. In Table 2.7, GSS respondents are broken down by the proportion of the consensus goals listed in Table 2.1 (excluding taxation) on which they favored an increase in federal spending minus

---

[4] See, for example, federal budget plans for FY 2012 proposed by the Congressional Progressive Caucus (2011) and the liberal Center on Budget and Policy Priorities (Greenstein 2011).

TABLE 2.7. *The low salience of trade-offs among priorities: Opinion on taxes and spending, 2010*

Spending preferences	Opinion of own federal income taxes			Total
	too high (N = 631)	about right (N = 578)	too low (N = 23)	
supports more cuts than increases	9.8	8.5	2.4	9.1
supports equal number of cuts and increases	4.6	5.5	8.8	5.1
supports more increases than cuts	85.6	86.0	88.7	85.8
Total	100.0	100.0	100.0	100.0

Source: General Social Survey.

Pearson's F (corrected for survey design): .536; $p = .69$

Question wording: See Table 2.1.

Sample: American adults. Data are weighted. N=1,232.

the proportion on which they favored a decrease in spending.[5] As shown in the final column of the table, 86 percent of Americans supported increasing spending on more programs than they favored cutting in 2010. Remarkably, no discernible relationship existed between respondents' attitudes about taxes and their opinion on federal spending. Those who thought their taxes were "too high" were just as supportive of increasing federal spending as those saying their taxes were "about right." (As shown in the table, the GSS respondents saying their taxes were "too low" were so few in number that their responses do not have much effect on the overall relationship between opinion on taxes and spending.)[6]

[5] Spending and priorities items were administered to GSS and Pew respondents in a randomized split-form fashion, and thus not all participants had the opportunity to respond to all items. These tables therefore report preferences on spending and priorities in terms of proportions rather than absolute numbers of programs or goals.

[6] One concern with this analysis is that because lower income people may both perceive their tax burdens as heavier and voice higher support for spending, income may

TABLE 2.8. *The low salience of trade-offs among priorities:*
Opinion on the deficit and other national priorities, 2011

	% of non-deficit goals named as a "top priority"	
	Deficit named as "top priority"	Deficit not named as "top priority"
All respondents	57.5	43.6
Republicans	52.7	46.0
Independents	59.2	40.9
Democrats	62.2	42.9

Source: Pew Research Center.

Question wording: See Table 2.2.

Sample: American adults. Data are weighted. N=737.

The lack of salience of the trade-offs required to achieve consensus goals persists in the Pew 2011 dataset of national priorities, as shown in Table 2.8. Here, respondents are categorized by whether they named reducing the deficit as a "top priority." Cell entries are the percentage of non-deficit goals – all of which require government revenue – they also named as "top priorities." Here we find the exact opposite of the relationship we would expect between prioritization of the deficit and other goals requiring national spending if constraints on government resources were being taken into account in respondents' answers. As shown in the first row of the table, those naming the deficit as a top priority actually listed a *greater* number of other goals as top priorities than those who did not believe reducing the deficit was a top priority. To ensure that this relationship is not an artifact of the set of priorities offered to Pew respondents, the table divides the sample by party identification.[7] As shown this relationship persists among Republicans, Independents, and Democrats: among each of these groups, those

be suppressing a relationship between attitudes on taxes and spending. However, an analysis in which all respondents were first matched on income continued to find no evidence of such a relationship, failing to reject the null at *p*=.52. (This required combining the small number of respondents saying their taxes were "too low" with those assessing their tax burden as "about right.")

[7] It is possible, for example, that by circumstance the set of priorities offered by Pew in 2011 might appeal particularly to Republicans (who are also more likely to prioritize reducing the deficit as a national goal).

prioritizing deficit reduction were more likely to list other goals as top priorities.[8]

Why Aren't Trade-Offs More Salient?

One reaction to these results is to pin the blame for their apparent nonsensicality on Americans' lack of knowledge and engagement in politics, which has been well documented by political scientists (e.g., Delli Karpini and Keeter 1997). Although Americans' ignorance is probably part of the reason for these opinion patterns, additional insight has been provided by a series of papers exploring the more nuanced explanation that these responses have to do with the issue-by-issue fashion in which these questions are posed to survey participants. Poll respondents are rarely asked to explicitly consider the constraints that prevent the simultaneous pursuit of increased spending on government programs, tax relief, and deficit reduction – perhaps because such questions are difficult to ask in a telephone survey. But the few studies that have done so have found that most Americans express preferences that accurately take into account the trade-offs required. For example, in 1995 the ANES asked respondents where they stood on all possible trade-offs among four consensus goals: tax reduction, deficit reduction, spending on domestic programs such as Medicare and education, and spending on national defense. John Mark Hansen's analysis of responses to these questions found preferences to generally reflect rationality criteria such as consistency and transitivity (Hansen 1998; see also Lacy 2001). Putting each of these trade-offs to ANES participants in a pair-wise fashion required two batteries of six survey questions each. This considerable commitment of survey time may be one reason such questions so rarely appear on national polls.

A complementary approach is taken by William Jacoby (2000). He contrasts the issue-by-issue way in which the survey questions analyzed here frame government spending with those that frame government spending in a more general way. He focuses on a question that appears regularly on the ANES in which respondents

---

[8] Among each of the three groups, differences were significant at $p < .05$ (two-tailed test).

indicate their spending preferences by placing themselves on a scale ranging from "government should provide many fewer services; reduce spending a lot" to "government should provide many more services; increase spending a lot." The ANES also includes a battery of issue-by-issue spending questions that are very similar to those analyzed here.

Jacoby's comparison of responses to the two types of questions finds that a large share of Americans simultaneously express support for spending cuts in response to the general question while also saying they favor spending increases in response to the issue-specific questions. Jacoby notes that the general and specific frames mimic the rhetorical strategies employed by the parties when they discuss the federal budget. Republicans, he writes, "tend to discuss the issue in broad, general terms," whereas Democrats "emphasize specific programs and affected constituencies" (Jacoby 2000: 752). He notes that other researchers (including Sears and Citrin 1982 and Feldman and Zaller 1992) as well as activists, pollsters, and journalists have all made similar observations. A related point is made by James A. Stimson, who writes that this rhetoric is particularly resonant among those who identify as conservative but nevertheless support increases in spending on a broad range of consensus goals (including education, health care, and the environment). Stimson estimates that nearly a quarter of Americans belong to this category of "conflicted conservatives," and that national elections often hinge on their votes (Stimson 2004: 84–95; see also Ellis and Stimson 2012).

Trade-Offs and the Incentives of Politicians

These observations – that Democratic calls for spending increases are met with Republican generalities about the size of government – yield an important conclusion. Americans are hardly ever exposed to explicit proposals to cut federal spending on particular consensus goals or to reduce their importance on the list of the nation's priorities. To do so is simply bad politics, as illustrated by the fact that some of the most prominent examples of these kinds of moves are associated with spectacularly unsuccessful candidates. "Let's tell the truth," declared Walter Mondale in his speech accepting the Democratic Party's presidential nomination to take on President Ronald Reagan in 1984. "Mr. Reagan will raise taxes, and so will I.... He won't tell you. I just did" (American Presidency Project 2012). In 1995, future Republican presidential nominee Bob Dole echoed Speaker Newt Gingrich and other Republicans in the House of Representatives in calling for the abolishment of the U.S. Department of Education (Roth 1995). Although both Dole and Mondale faced strong headwinds in their quests for the presidency, neither helped himself with these statements. Both candidates found their own words used against them by their opponents.

Of course, Republicans and Democrats do propose and successfully enact spending cuts on consensus issues. But when they do so, they often describe these actions in ways that obscure the fact that spending is actually being reduced on popular goals. One tactic, as Stimson notes, is to claim that new spending can be supported not by substantive cuts in other programs but rather "that giant reservoir...called 'waste, fraud and abuse.'" (Stimson 2004: 92). A second tactic is to minimize the share of current voters affected by a cost-cutting measure. Examples of this strategy include Barack Obama's proposal in his 2012 State of the Union address to raise taxes (only on millionaires), and the bill passed by House Republicans in 2011 to reduce Medicare costs (only for those whose eligibility for the program was at least ten years off). A final strategy to elide the fact that spending cuts are taking place is simply not to talk about them very much. For example, Obama's fiscal year 2013 budget proposal projected that national security discretionary spending (adjusted for population growth and inflation) would fall from the $905 billion spent in 2011 to $667 billion in 2022 – a major source of deficit reduction (White House Office of Management and Budget 2012b: 239). But it would be easy to miss this in the president's budget message, which devoted a mere seven sentences (out of seven single-spaced pages) to explicit descriptions of these cuts. Sure enough, these descriptions promised Americans that many of the cuts would come from "outdated Cold War–era systems" as well as "unnecessary and lower-priority programs." (White House Office of Management and Budget 2012b: 3–4). At the same time Obama's budget was released, his likely Republican challenger Mitt Romney was promising to cut spending to 20 percent of GDP if elected. But those looking for details about these cuts in Romney's stump speech during the

2012 Republican primary season were likely to be disappointed. As reported by the *Washington Post*, "the only specific cuts [Romney] mentions are the relatively small savings that would be obtained by ending federal subsidies to Amtrak, the National Endowment for the Arts and the National Endowment for the Humanities" (Tumulty and Rucker 2012).

The upshot is that in the give-and-take of national political discourse, Americans are rarely encouraged to consider trade-offs among specific consensus goals. It is not that the public is incapable of doing so: the innovative public opinion surveys such as those analyzed by Hansen show that under the right conditions, most Americans can accurately take these trade-offs into account. But such conditions hardly ever arise in U.S. politics, because neither of the ways that the parties frame debates about national priorities raises the salience of such explicit trade-offs. Few votes are won by taking what can be perceived as a stance against a particular consensus goal, whether it be a liberal priority such as education or health care or a conservative concern such as national defense or tax reduction. Although real trade-offs exist among consensus goals, their near-universal popularity means that these goals are only rarely explicitly pitted against one another by politicians. The result is that – even when antigovernment sentiment peaks as it did in 2010 and 2011 – Americans' evaluations of consensus goals do not take into account the fact that an increase in effort on one goal inevitably requires a reduction in effort on another.

CONSENSUS ISSUES AND ISSUE OWNERSHIP

This chapter has offered evidence for two key claims about American opinion on consensus issues, and together they suggest that the concept of issue ownership has particular analytical relevance for our understanding of the politics of these kinds of issues. The first claim is that vast majorities of Americans want government spending and effort to be directed toward a broad range of consensus goals. The second claim is that circumstances rarely arise that raise the salience of the trade-offs required among these consensus goals.

Put together, these claims lead to the conclusion that a party's or candidate's association with government spending and action on a particular consensus goal has virtually no political downside. When resource allocation is framed on an issue-by-issue basis, the typical voter favors lower taxes, deficit reduction, and more spending ... on virtually everything! As shown by the diagrams in Figure 2.2, the parties' incentives are therefore to be associated as closely as possible with goals such as a low crime rate and high literacy rate – for that is where the votes are. To the extent that a party can successfully own a particular consensus issue through its commitments to achieving a goal through government spending and effort, it wins votes. Documenting why parties own issues and exploring how issue ownership affects the actions parties take when they control government are thus crucial for understanding the politics of consensus issues.

By contrast, issue ownership is *not* a very helpful concept for understanding the politics of non-consensus issues. As shown in the diagram in Figure 2.2 depicting preferences over access to abortion, the distribution of preferences over outcomes on a non-consensus issue has no skew. Where in this space should a party locate if it is to "own" the issue of abortion? There is no obvious answer to this question. To be sure, some think of the Democrats as "owning" the non-consensus issue of, say, gay rights – and the Republicans as owning the issue of gun rights. The problem with this analogy is that on both of these issues, there exists an opposing position for the other party to "own." Republicans are champions of the traditional family; Democrats are advocates for gun control. Rather than owning these issues altogether, the parties simply "own" different locations in the outcome space.

The reason the notion of issue ownership has limited relevance for our understanding of non-consensus issues is that whether one assigns ownership of one of these issues to a political party should boil down to whether one agrees with the party's policies on the issue. The distinctions among policies, priorities, and performance that can be so important for consensus issues hardly exist at all for non-consensus issues. To the extent that a voter says she thinks one party or another is better able to handle a non-consensus issue such as abortion, it is likely that this is simply because she agrees with that party's policies on abortion. (Chapter 4 presents evidence suggesting that this is exactly the case.) By contrast, on consensus issues, large shares of voters can agree with a party's prioritization of the issue while disagreeing with its policies.

By drawing a bright line around the set of issues for which issue ownership is analytically relevant, I am refining the concept of issue ownership in ways that correspond to some extent with previous scholarship and depart from it in other ways. The next chapter explores these ideas in detail.

3

The Meaning and Measure of Issue Ownership

To anyone who follows American politics, the association of specific issues with either the Democratic or Republican party makes a certain intuitive sense. The idea that Americans would trust the Republican Party to better "handle" the issue of taxes than the Democrats while putting their faith in the Democrats on the issue of health care is unsurprising. However, the reasons for these associations and thus their ultimate meaning remain remarkably vague despite decades of scholarship on the topic of issue ownership. The goals of this and the next two chapters are to bring clarity to the meaning of issue ownership by developing theoretically precise hypotheses about the concept; generating improved estimates of the parties' reputations over time, and using these estimates to test the hypotheses with data on American public opinion and public policy.

MEASURING THE ASSOCIATIONS BETWEEN PARTIES AND ISSUES

How do we translate the intuition that there exist long-term associations between parties and issues in the public's mind into quantifiable measures? The study of issue ownership is based largely on survey questions first identified as valid measures by John Petrocik in his pathbreaking article "Issue Ownership in Presidential Elections" (Petrocik 1996). These questions take the following form: "Which political party, the Democrats or the Republicans, do you trust to do a better job handling ... [issue X]?" Closely related questions ask Americans which party they think is better able to "deal with" a certain issue or "do a better job" on it.

Questions such as these had appeared on public opinion surveys for decades, but until Petrocik's work they had drawn little attention from scholars. Prior approaches had analyzed survey questions in which respondents said whether they wanted government to either "do something" about specific issues or to "stay out" of them, and then identified whether the Democrats or Republicans were more likely to "do what you want" on each issue (RePass 1971). Other approaches relied upon subjective coding of official party platforms (Budge and Farlie 1983). The superiority of the "handling" questions to previous measures derives from their generality. Like many items on surveys about politics and public affairs, these questions ask respondents to provide issue-specific evaluations of the Democratic and Republican parties. What distinguishes these questions is that they refrain from asking respondents to state which party they agree with on policies. As Petrocik wrote, they do not "ask *what* policies will be pursued, but [rather] *which* party will more successfully resolve the problem" (Petrocik 1996: 831).

Issue ownership questions have been asked on just about every topic on the agenda of American politics. A few questions – particularly those about the economy and foreign policy – have been asked on a regular basis since World War II. Most others do not appear consistently in surveys until the 1970s. Many questions are included in surveys only as the issues with which they deal become salient, and thus their appearance in polls traces the rise and decline of these issues on the national agenda. The questions are not limited just to the parties themselves; they are also asked about presidents and presidential candidates. For example, in May 1979 an ABC News/Harris Survey asked registered voters, "If you had to choose between Reagan and Carter for president in 1980, which one do you feel ... would do a better job of reducing inflation?" Others have to do with the parties in Congress. In August 2006, CNN asked its national adult sample, "Do you think the Republicans in Congress or the Democrats in Congress would do a better job of dealing with ... health care?" In many surveys, the same question is asked about a battery of issues. For example, a Pew Research Center survey conducted in March 2011 asked respondents to rate the two parties' abilities to handle eight different issues, including Social Security, foreign policy, and health care.

WHAT IS ISSUE OWNERSHIP?

The admirable generalness of the survey questions Petrocik identified to measure issue ownership has proved to be both a blessing and a curse for scholars. The measures have the advantage of tapping the linkages voters make between parties and issues that transcend particular policy debates or political campaigns. But the abstract nature of these items has also contributed to a conceptual vagueness about what issue ownership actually means in the first place. Fundamental questions about the concept remain unsettled despite the hundreds of scholarly articles that have discussed this topic. The pioneers of issue-ownership research provided little guidance about whether policy, performance, or prioritization might cause a party to gain and maintain an advantage at "handling" a particular issue. Subsequent work has done little to resolve this ambiguity, and much of this scholarship has simply conflated the concept of issue ownership with its measure. In addition, considerable disagreement exists about the extent to which issue ownership is stable over time and exactly how it affects campaign strategy and election outcomes.

Where Does Issue Ownership Come From?

Does issue ownership derive from voters' assessments of a party's policies, performance, or priorities? The answers to this question provided by political scientists have been all over the map. Comparative politics scholars Ian Budge and Dennis Farlie – the first researchers to use the term "issue ownership" in their book *Explaining and Predicting Elections* (1983) – surmised that ownership might arise from a party's history of prioritizing an issue at the behest of the different constituencies that make up the core of the party's activists. But they also suggested that issue ownership might be affected by a party's performance on an issue. For example, the advantage they found for Republicans on foreign affairs, they speculated, might be because they "in fact devote more care to international developments than Democrats" (Budge and Farlie 1983: 25).

Petrocik improved on earlier work by providing an explicit definition of issue ownership, which he wrote accrues to parties or candidates when the public assesses they can better "handle" a particular
issue than their opponents. This language – which echoes the survey
questions we now use to measure issue ownership – would suggest that
issue ownership therefore lies in the parties' performance on issues.[1]
But a close reading of Petrocik's definition shows that it actually incorporates notions of both performance and priorities. By "handling,"
Petrocik writes that he means

"... *the ability to resolve a problem* of concern to voters. It is a reputation
for policy and program interests, produced by a history of attention, initiative
and innovation toward these problems, which leads voters to believe that one
of the parties (and its candidates) is *more sincere and committed to doing
something* about them."

(Petrocik 1996, 826; emphasis added)

Certainly, the "ability to resolve a problem" can mean nothing else
than voters' assessments of the parties' relative performance on an
issue. But being "more sincere and committed to doing something"
about these problems has more to do with priorities.[2] These distinctions are important: whereas the latter meaning implies that voters
should reward the parties for mere effort on a particular issue, the
former interpretation suggests that ownership only accrues to parties
that deliver actual results. This definition thus implies that a party's
efforts and results may both contribute to issue ownership.

Petrocik's definition becomes clearer as he proceeds to describe
the sources of issue ownership, which he says is conferred by either
the "record of the incumbent" or the "constituencies of the parties."
Issues falling into the first category are those such as the economy,
foreign policy, and ethical behavior that are clearly linked to either
"good times" or the "demonstration that the incumbent party cannot
do its job" (Petrocik 1996: 827). Petrocik calls these issues "performance issues" and argues that a party's ownership of them is usually
only short-term. By contrast, ownership based on issues linked with

---

[1] For example, the first set of definitions offered for "handle" by the Oxford English
Dictionary is found under the category "to manipulate, manage" (OED Online
2011).

[2] This meaning in fact corresponds to the second set of definitions for "handle" offered
by the OED, listed under the category "to deal with, treat" (OED Online 2011).

a party's constituencies is for the long term because these constituencies shift so slowly, and because constituency cleavages are reinforced by the parties' relative focus on their key issues.[3] But this stipulation still leaves important questions unanswered, because ownership of constituency-based issues could conceivably be due to any or all of policies, performance, or priorities. Consider for example the environment, an issue that overwhelming numbers of Americans believe the Democrats can better handle than the Republicans. Environmentalists are today a key constituency of the Democratic Party.[4] But we do not know if the Democrats' ownership occurs because environmentalists push the Democrats to pursue environmental *policies* preferred by voters, that these activists have provided the Democratic Party with expertise to *perform* better than Republicans on achieving environmental goals, or if these activists pressure Democrats to *prioritize* environmental issues over other national problems.

How Stable Is Issue Ownership?

A related question left unanswered by the literature is the extent to which issue ownership is steady or instead changes hands between the parties over time. The early treatments by Budge and Farlie and Petrocik conceptualized issue ownership as more-or-less fixed. Evidence for the stability of issue ownership is provided by the finding that the public has consistently associated specific traits with the parties' presidential candidates over the past few decades (Hayes 2005). These trait associations – including "empathetic" and "compassionate" with Democratic candidates, and "moral" and "strong leader" with Republicans – on their face seem related to the Democrats' ownership of issues such as poverty and Social Security and the Republicans' ownership of crime and national security. However, in recent research some scholars have encouraged a reassessment of the stability of issue ownership, arguing

---

[3] Petrocik makes clear that he does not think these issues are about redistribution of "divisible benefits" to narrow constituencies, but rather about "sociotropic" concerns that benefit all of society (Petrocik 1996: 828) – a notion very similar to that of consensus issues as they are defined in this book.

[4] For example, in the 2010 GSS, 13 percent of those identifying as strong Democrats named the environment as one of the two most important issues facing America compared to just 5 percent of strong Republicans.

that it can be affected by shifts in the public's partisanship and ideological mood (Pope and Woon 2009) and the parties' relative records on specific issues (Goble and Holm 2008, Sides 2006). A related body of work investigates attempts by candidates to "trespass" on an opposing party's owned issues, such as Bill Clinton's efforts to mitigate the Republicans' traditional advantage on fighting crime (Holian 2004; see also Ansolabehere and Iyengar 1994; Kaufmann 2004; Norpoth and Buchanan 1992; Sellers 1998). Understanding the extent to which issue ownership changes with time should help us better understand the source from which issue ownership ultimately derives. A finding that the parties' ownership of issues was relatively stable would seem to be rooted in the parties' priorities, which could be expected to change no more quickly than the composition of issue activists who make up the parties' coalitions. By contrast, if issue ownership is in fact volatile, then we might look to the parties' changing policies or fluctuating levels of performance on different issues for an explanation.

How Does Issue Ownership Help Parties Win Elections?

The bulk of the scholarly research on issue ownership has focused on documenting the efforts by parties to raise the salience of their owned issues during campaigns and the impact of these efforts on elections. Although much of the research on these questions has yielded mixed results, there do appear to be meaningful relationships among issue ownership, issue salience, campaign strategy, and voting. But because of the ambiguity about what issue ownership actually means, no scholarly consensus exists regarding exactly why we would expect issue ownership to help parties win elections.

Research on issue ownership and elections has examined two main hypotheses. The first is that campaigns are battles between parties to raise the salience of the issues they own. The second is that when a party's owned issues are salient in a particular election season, it earns more votes and is therefore more likely to emerge the victor. These two claims were first stipulated in Budge and Farlie's "saliency theory," which holds that campaigns do not feature debates about how to best solve the most pressing issues of the day, but instead consist of competing efforts by parties to raise the salience of the issues they own. A social democratic party should be expected to focus its campaign on issues such as the public safety net; by contrast, a center-right party might emphasize low taxes. In country-by-country analyses, Budge and Farlie found suggestive evidence that parties attempt to steer campaigns toward their owned issues, and discovered significant correlations between the extent to which a party's owned issues were salient and its vote share in national elections. Petrocik's work identified similar themes in American politics. His analyses of presidential campaigns and elections in the United States found that the candidates and their surrogates labor to generate media coverage of their party's owned issues during campaigns and that the party that succeeds more in these efforts wins a significant advantage in aggregate vote share.

Much of the subsequent empirical work on issue ownership has focused on examining whether candidates actually emphasize their owned issues in their campaigns for office. This research – which includes content analysis of news coverage, candidate advertising, press releases, and websites – has yielded quite mixed results. Those finding the divergent strategies predicted by issue-ownership theory (including Druckman, Kifer, and Parkin 2009; Page 1978; Simon 2002; Spilotes and Vavreck 2002) are counterbalanced by scholars demonstrating that candidate messages instead tend to converge on issues that are important to the electorate (Ansolabehere and Iyengar 1994; Damore 2004, 2005; Dulio and Trumbore 2009; Kaplan, Park, and Ridout 2006; Sides 2006; Sigelman and Buell 2004). Much less investigation has been conducted exploring the hypothesis that issue ownership and issue salience affect election results. A strong relationship exists between the extent to which issues dominate the content of presidential campaigns and whether voters mention Republican- or Democratic-owned issues as important problems facing the country, and whether the balance of these voter mentions favors the Democrats or Republicans is a strong predictor of which party's candidate will win the election (Petrocik, Benoit, and Hansen 2003). However, other research suggests that these effects may well be minimal in races for the House and Senate (Sides 2007).

In sum, proponents of the idea that issue ownership plays a meaningful role in elections hold that campaigns have more to do with what William H. Riker called "heresthetics" (defining the election on issues on which voters already agree with the candidate) rather than persuasion (changing voters' minds to agree with the candidate's positions on issues) (Riker 1983). Formal models of campaigns that incorporate

e ownership largely predict that candidates should emphasize their
ned issues in their campaigns and platforms and that candidates
who are more successful at doing so should win (Feld and Grofman
2001; Hammond and Humes 1993; Krasa and Polborn 2010; Riker
1983; Simon 2002). Successful campaigns are theorized to increase
the extent to which voters weigh a party's owned issues when casting
their votes – a "priming" strategy that should lead to more favorable
evaluations of the party's candidates (Iyengar and Kinder 1987; Miller
and Krosnick 2000). But a mystery remains: what is it about issue
ownership that would help parties win elections? If the parties gain
an advantage with messages that lead voters to weigh one issue more
than another, from where does this advantage derive? We are left with
the same puzzle with which we began.

MODELS OF ISSUE OWNERSHIP

Rather than empirically investigating the question of the origins of
issue ownership, scholars have usually simply stipulated their answers
to it. Here I show the limitations of such an approach using simple
two-dimensional spatial models of elections. The models illustrate how
all three of the possible explanations for issue ownership – policy, performance, or priorities – could in theory explain the relationships thought
to exist among issue salience, issue ownership, and election results.
These models incorporate the key assumption of the issue-ownership
literature that in the short term, candidates' platforms and reputations
are fixed, as are voters' preferences. Thus the only meaningful change in
voters' assessments that can occur as the result of a campaign is heres-
thetic: a shift in the relative importance attached by voters to different
issues. I vastly simplify the problem of modeling electoral competition in
more than one dimension by reducing the electorate to a single "typical"
voter, V. The insights yielded by this approach are substantively similar
to those that emerge from models incorporating continuums of voters.[5]
Each of the analyses considers a hypothetical competition between the

---

[5] Models of multidimensional policy spaces employing continuums of voters can
make formal analyses of even simple aspects of electoral competition in more
than one dimension quite complex. (For examples see Coughlin 1992, Krasa and
Polborn 2010, Lindbeck and Weibull 1987, 1993, and Roemer 2001.) Krasa and
Polborn's model of a continuum of voters in a model of a multidimensional allocation of resources is discussed further below.

two parties on health care (owned by the Democrats) and domestic security (owned by the Republicans). As will be seen, the analyses show that the policy, performance, and priorities explanations for issue ownership are all theoretically possible.

Policy

The diagrams in Figure 3.1 illustrate the implications of considering issue ownership as a policy advantage. In this scenario, the Democrats and Republicans have left- and right-wing policy platforms on both health care and domestic security, placing them in the lower-left and upper-right quadrants of the policy space. In this conceptualization, the Democrats "own" health care because V has liberal policy preferences on this issue, putting her closer on this dimension to the Democrats' platform (D).[6] However, V prefers conservative policies on domestic security, locating her closer to the Republicans (R) on this dimension. Her ideal point is thus located in the upper-left quadrant of the policy space. The ellipses around V's ideal point in each diagram are indifference curves. Each curve represents a set of policies from which V derives equal utility (and thus is indifferent among them); policies located on curves closer to V's ideal point bring V more utility than policies on curves that are farther away.

Note that D and R are located the same distance from V's ideal point. Thus if V cared equally about the two issues, she would be indifferent between the two candidates. This is why the relative salience of the two issues is so important. The top diagram depicts an election in which health care issues are salient, as indicated by the narrow indifference curves around V's ideal point. V weighs the parties' positions on health care more and thus elects D. The bottom diagram shows what happens when domestic security issues are salient: V weighs the parties' positions on this dimension more heavily (as indicated by wide indifference curves) and thus elects R. Issue ownership is conceived this way in models developed by Feld and Grofman (2001), Hammond and Humes (1993) and Simon (2002). In some respects, this conceptualization is also the basis of Riker's original notion of heresthetics (Riker 1983, 1986).

---

[6] The voter is referred to here with female pronouns, the parties with male pronouns.

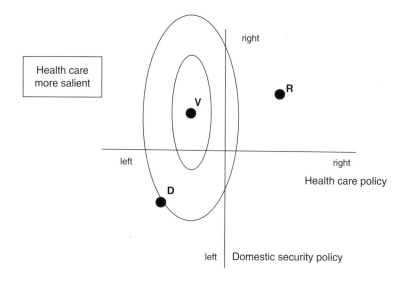

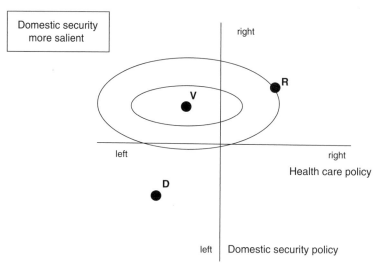

FIGURE 3.1. Issue ownership as a policy advantage.

Performance

In Figure 3.2, issue ownership is modeled as a performance advantage, in that the parties are conceived as better able to achieve national goals on the issues that they own. Instead of a policy space, the diagrams in Figure 3.2 depict a performance space: the axes are the levels

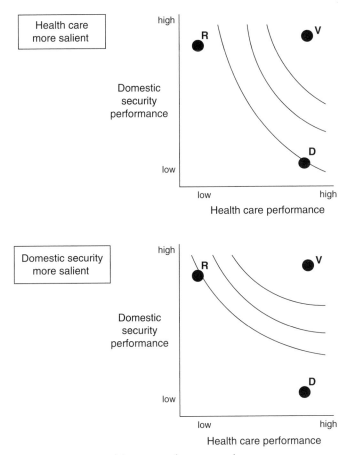

FIGURE 3.2. Issue ownership as a performance advantage.

of progress voters expect the parties will make toward the consensus goals of health care and domestic security. Ideally, voters would like to elect a party that could deliver high performance on both issues, placing *V*'s ideal point at the upper-right corner of the performance space. *D* is expected to perform better on health care than domestic security, placing him in the lower-right corner of the space. By contrast, *R* is expected to deliver a relatively stronger performance on domestic security, placing him in the upper-left corner.

V's choice is again determined by the relative level of salience of the two goals. In the top diagram, she considers health care a more important problem – as indicated by the sharply sloped indifference curves around her ideal point. She thus elects *D*. In the bottom diagram, she cares more about domestic security (as reflected in flatter indifference curves). She therefore elects *R*. Issue ownership is conceived this way in a model developed by Krasa and Polborn (2010) in which two candidates are each more competent at delivering outcomes on one of two dimensions. In their model, competition occurs over how much money or effort candidates will allocate to each dimension if elected (and thus, as discussed below, the model is also about priorities as well as performance). In equilibrium, candidates promise to provide more of the good on which they have a performance advantage. [7]

Priorities

Finally, Figure 3.3 illustrates the competition for *V*'s support that arises when issue ownership is derived from the relative priorities that the parties place on issues. The diagrams depict a priority space, with the axes now the level of priority – that is, commitments of scarce government resources and attention – to be placed on the goals of health care and domestic security. The constraints that prohibit a simultaneous, all-out pursuit of both goals are represented in the diagram by a diagonal dashed line, the budget constraint.

In the top diagram in Figure 3.3, *D*'s and *R*'s varying priorities over the two goals are represented by two sets of indifference curves. *R*'s indifference curves are only slightly sloped, indicating that Republicans are willing to give up a fair amount of attention to health care in order to direct just a bit more government resources toward domestic security. *D* is just the opposite: his steeply sloped indifference curves reflect the fact that Democrats value the pursuit of health care goals much more highly than domestic security. The parties' utilities are maximized at the points where their indifference curves are tangent to the budget constraint. Although both parties are subject to the same constraint, they prefer sharply different allocations of resources. *R*'s utility is maximized when most resources are

---

[7] Krasa and Polborn's model thus takes a different approach than "valence models" in which candidates have fixed locations on a single generic performance dimension and can shift their positions on one or more policy dimensions (such as Ansolabehere and Snyder 2000, Aragones and Palfrey 2002, and Groseclose 2001).

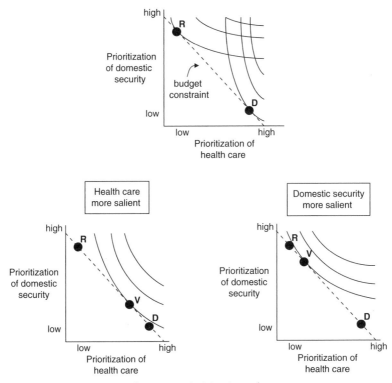

FIGURE 3.3. Issue ownership as a prioritization advantage.

devoted to domestic security; *D* prefers that the bulk of resources be committed to health care.

The two diagrams at the bottom of Figure 3.3 again illustrate two elections in which health care is salient (in the left diagram) and one in which domestic security is salient (right diagram). When the salience of health care is high (and thus *V*'s indifference curves look more like *D*'s than *R*'s), *V* prefers making health care a higher priority than domestic security. This places her closer to *D* on the budget constraint line than *R*. The opposite occurs when the security issue is salient: *V*'s preferred allocation is now closer to that promised by *R*. Of the formal models of issue ownership, only Krasa and Polborn (2010) have considered the possibility that candidates might allocate resources differently toward different issues. In their model, priorities and performance are intertwined: as discussed above, voters want candidates to prioritize the issues on which they have a performance advantage. But as noted by Krasa and Polborn, this performance advantage may in turn be due to prioritization, as a party that prioritizes a consensus goal may attract members who are particularly competent at delivering performance on that goal.

The implication to be drawn from these simple models is clear: any of the three factors that scholars have assumed to be explanations for issue ownership are possible in that they logically comport with the basic elements of issue ownership theory. In fact, none of the explanations rules any of the others out, as any or all of them could be at work simultaneously. Here we have reached the limits of the extent to which purely deductive reasoning can assist in our efforts to identify the origins of issue ownership. It is instead necessary to turn to empirical analysis.

A COMPREHENSIVE DATASET ON ISSUE OWNERSHIP

The first step in deciphering the meaning of issue ownership is to determine in a definitive fashion which parties have owned which issues over time. The basis of this book's exploration of issue ownership will be a dataset I have assembled that consists of every ownership question posed to representative national samples of Americans since 1970. The questions come from the Roper Center Public Opinion Archives, a truly magisterial online database of opinion surveys housed at the University of Connecticut. To be included in my issue ownership dataset, survey questions had to meet two criteria. First, the phrases or words "better job," "handle," "dealing with," or "which political party" had to appear in the text of the survey question. The survey questions that met this criterion were then examined to ensure that they were true measures of issue ownership in that they asked generically about associations between issues and parties. Second, the question had to be put to a representative sample of American adults or registered voters. "Likely voter" samples and exit polls were thus ruled out. Polls that asked respondents to name the nation's most important problem and then asked respondents to rate which party would be best at handling that problem (and thus did not obtain representative samples of the population regarding each issue) were ruled out as well. This process identified a total of 6,101 survey questions appearing on national surveys fielded from January 1970 through July 2011.

Coding of Issues

Survey questions were coded by issue automatically with a text-matching algorithm that searched for key search terms in the survey questions.[8] For example, any question that included the terms "environment" or "pollution" was categorized as pertaining to the issue of the environment; questions with the terms "cost of living," "food prices," "high prices," "interest rates," or "prices down" were categorized as having to do with the issue of inflation. Where appropriate, questions were coded for multiple issues. A first pass of the questions identified no fewer than 112 different issue categories – including which party could best handle controversies ranging from abortion to welfare, military conflicts from Central America to Vietnam, and looking out for the needs of groups from the young to the elderly.

To facilitate analysis, similar issues were grouped together. Generally, this process was straightforward. The most notable set of judgment calls had to do with distinguishing among the three issues of the military, foreign affairs, and domestic security. Questions pertaining specifically to military conflicts and the nation's preparation for them were grouped together as "military." Questions having to do clearly with diplomacy – such as those about arms treaties and "keeping us out of war" – were classified as "foreign affairs." Finally, questions having to do with homeland security, terrorism, and border control were classified as "domestic security." In some cases, surveys asked about "dealing with [country X]." Where the United States's relationship with the country involved an armed conflict or the threat of one, these questions were categorized as both "military" and "foreign affairs," as our relationships involved both military and diplomatic action. (These countries included Afghanistan, Korea, Kosovo, Iran, and Iraq.) Where the United States's relationship with the country did not involve an armed conflict (such as those pertaining to our relationship with Japan, or the economic boycott against

---

[8] The full list of search terms and issues may be found in this book's online appendix.

South Africa), these questions were categorized only as "foreign' affairs."

Selection of Issues for Analysis

In keeping with this book's focus on consensus issues, three broad categories of questions were excluded from the analysis.[9] The first had to do with the extent to which respondents ascribed various characteristics to parties or candidates, including their ethicalness and their ability to manage the government, and whether they "care about people like you." A second set of questions put aside had to do with the parties' abilities to look out for the interests of discrete constituency groups such as farmers, small businesses, seniors, or minorities. The third category of excluded questions consisted of issues that fail to meet the *ceteris paribus* criterion. These were generally social issues, such as gay rights, abortion, gun control, and moral values. Questions about non-social issues that failed to meet the *ceteris paribus* criterion included items about economic inequality, questions about the courts and the judiciary, and questions about the federal budget or federal spending (unless they mentioned the consensus goal of reducing the federal deficit). Finally, any issue that did not appear on at least twenty-five questions in the dataset since 1970 was considered a relatively insignificant aspect of the national agenda and was thus excluded from analysis.

The analysis does incorporate questions about two issues that do not meet the *ceteris paribus* criterion perfectly, and thus their inclusion merits some explanation. First, a category is included for all questions having to do with international trade. In one sense, Americans lack a consensus around international trade because of material conflicts between those who benefit from protectionism (for example, workers in domestic industries threatened by international competition) and those who by contrast benefit from trade liberalization (including industries that rely heavily on exports, as well as consumers who enjoy lower prices because of the availability of less-expensive imported goods). However, a consensus does exist around increasing exports

---

[9] As explained below, all questions excluded from analysis nevertheless remained in the dataset in order to yield more precise estimates of the quantities of interest.

and maintaining international competitiveness. Therefore this issue is included in the analysis. Second, all questions having to do with immigration – whether or not they mentioned *unauthorized* immigration – were grouped together and included in the analysis. As discussed in Chapter 2, consensus is scant among Americans regarding the goals of the nation's immigration policy. However, limiting the analysis to questions focused on unauthorized immigration would leave questions about this topic remaining in the dataset for only five years (from 2006 through 2010). Furthermore, given that the debate on this topic over the past few decades has focused predominantly on unauthorized immigration, it is likely that most Americans would respond to a generic question on this issue by calling to mind the notion of unauthorized immigration. Thus all of these questions were grouped together.

Application of all of these criteria yielded a universe of seventeen consensus issues to be analyzed. They are listed in Table 3.1. Thanks to the sheer volume of the survey data available in the Roper Archive, this list is remarkably comprehensive and generally reflects the range of consensus issues identified in the previous chapter. As shown in the right-hand column of Table 3.1, many of the issues are represented in the dataset by literally hundreds of questions, allowing for the generation of highly precise estimates. Thus assembled, the issue ownership dataset provides an unprecedented opportunity to assess the relative reputations of the parties on consensus issues and the extent to which ownership has persisted or changed over time.

Estimation Strategy

Unlike previous research that has examined the trajectory of issue ownership, my focus is on the parties' *relative* strength on the range of issues. Thus the question of interest here is not simply whether pluralities of Americans rate one party or another as better able to handle particular issues, which has guided the approach of many previous estimates (e.g., Petrocik 1996; Sides 2006; Pope and Woon 2009). In order to investigate if issue ownership changes over time and to determine if it is associated with election results after accounting for other influences, it is necessary to control for any contem-

TABLE 3.1. *Consensus issues included in issue ownership dataset*

Issue	Included topics	Number of survey questions since 1970
crime	drugs, violence	191
deficit		246
domestic security	terrorism, border security	380
economy	prosperity, stock market	862
education		300
energy	foreign oil, gas prices	138
environment	global warming	173
foreign affairs	alliances, disarmament	857
health care	Medicare, Medicaid	639
immigration	border security	107
inflation	high prices	86
jobs	unemployment, wages	253
military		587
poverty	welfare, homelessness	116
Social Security		233
taxes	Internal Revenue Service	380
trade		37

poraneous factors that affect the public's assessment of parties and candidates.

To do so, I adopt a straightforward estimation strategy using Ordinary Least Squares (OLS) that treats the aggregate responses to the issue-ownership questions in the dataset as a time series (Erikson and Wlezien 1999). The unit of analysis is the survey question, and the dependent variable is the share of Americans naming the Republican Party as a percentage of all respondents saying one of the two parties is better able to handle the issue than the other. Indicator variables are included in the regression for each of the seventeen issues listed in Table 3.1, and the model is estimated without an intercept term. Therefore by construction the coefficients on the issue indicator variables are estimates of the Republican Party's issue-ownership advantage (or disadvantage) on these seventeen issues.

The specification includes a comprehensive set of controls chosen to account as much as possible for factors that may be correlated with issue ownership and thus could bias the estimates. As has been shown by previous work, issue ownership responses are highly

TABLE 3.2. *Party ownership of consensus issues, 1970–2011*
Republican ownership (if negative, Democratic ownership) in percentage points.

Issue	1970s	1980s	1990s	2000s	average
domestic security	2.3	26.5***	12.8***	16.3***	14.5***
military	4.8	15.1***	23.7***	11.9***	13.9***
immigration		4.2*	16.9***	4.5***	8.5***
inflation	3.5	19.8***	14.0***	-3.3	8.5*
crime	7.6*	4.2	5.9***	8.5***	6.6*
foreign affairs	7.1*	3.7*	16.8***	-3.7*	6.0*
trade		1.2	-0.5	13.8***	4.8
taxes	1.8	4.4	7.6***	1.8*	3.9*
deficit		3.0+	4.7**	-0.4	2.4
economy	-5.4*	9.1***	2.5	-3.2***	0.8
energy	1.5	0.2		-9.5***	-2.6*
education	-12.1**	-10.2***	-12.5***	-6.9***	-10.4***
jobs	-15.2***	-12.5***	-13.5***	-6.7***	-12.0***
health care	-11.0**	-7.3	-17.5***	-14.0***	-12.4***
Social Security		-22.0***	-10.8***	-10.4***	-14.4***
environment	-7.8+	-17.1***	-20.6***	-25.8***	-17.8***
poverty	-9.4	-36.0***	-15.2***	-11.7***	-18.1***
adjusted R-squared:					
in full model	.46	.48	.52	.58	
in model without issue indicator terms	.32	.05	.08	.14	
N:					
all cases	190	873	1,491	3,547	6,101
cases with issues of interest	136	669	1,176	3,003	4,984

Estimates are derived from the coefficients on the issue indicator terms in Equation 3.1. Models incorporate all controls included in the equation.

Cells are left blank where lack of adequate data precludes estimation.

Estimates significantly different from zero at +$p<.10$; *$p<.05$; **$p<.01$; ***$p<.001$ (two-tailed tests, robust standard errors).

correlated with aspects of the contemporaneous political environment, such as the public's ideological mood and national sentiment toward the two parties (Pope and Woon 2009). Because we are interested in how issue ownership fluctuates net of these kinds of forces, indicator variables are included in the regression for each year to capture temporal changes in the parties' relative standing.[10] Unlike previous work, the present dataset vastly expands the amount of data available by incorporating issue ownership questions about the parties' leaders, including those items asking Americans to rate the parties' presidential nominees and those in which respondents compare the incumbent president to members of the opposing party in Congress. In order to control for any approval or favorability that is leader specific, indicators are also included in the regression for these types of questions and then interacted with the year indicator variables.[11] An indicator variable is also included if the question included a third-party presidential candidate (such as John Anderson or Ralph Nader); this too is interacted with the year indicator variable. Finally, to correct for any systematic bias toward Democrats or Republicans that may be associated with different polling firms, indicator variables are included for each firm in the dataset.

While incorporating so many controls in the specification achieves the goal of reducing bias, this move also increases multicollinearity among the regressors and results in the loss of degrees of freedom. In a small dataset, this set of controls could thus severely reduce the statistical power of significance tests. This is why the issue ownership questions pertaining to issues not included in the analysis are kept in the dataset. By providing additional pieces of data used to estimate the controls, these questions allow for more efficient estimates of the quantities of interest.

Formally, the specification modeling responses to a survey question coded for the seventeen consensus issues i asked in year j by polling firm p is

---

[10] An alternate estimation strategy that controlled directly for macropartisanship and mood returned very similar results to those displayed here. See the online appendix for details.

[11] Because there is only one incumbent – and the parties can only have one nominee – at any given time, interacting these indicators with the year indicators has the same effect as including indicators for the incumbents and nominees themselves.

$$\left(\%REP - \%DEM\right)_{ijp} =$$

$$\sum_{i=1}^{17} \beta_i issue_i$$

$$+ \sum_j \delta_j year_j + \phi_1 nominee + \phi_2 pres\_cong + \phi_3 thirdparty$$

$$+ \varphi_{1j}\left(year_j \times nominee\right) + \varphi_{2j}\left(year_j \times pres\_cong\right)$$

$$+ \varphi_{3j}\left(year_j \times thirdparty\right) + \sum_p \lambda_p firm_p + \varepsilon, \qquad (3.1)$$

where $issue_i$, $year_j$, and $firm_p$ are indicator variables for each of the issues, years, and polling firms in the dataset, and *nominee, pres_cong,* and *thirdparty* are indicator variables for whether the questions pertain to presidential nominees or the president vis-à-vis Congress, and if a third-party candidate is included in the question. The estimates of interest are thus $\hat{\beta}_1$ through $\hat{\beta}_{17}$, which are the advantages (in percentage points) assigned to the Republican Party by Americans on the seventeen different consensus issues under analysis, net of any contemporaneous general sentiment toward the parties or their leaders. Negative values of the estimates correspond to a Democratic advantage.

Ownership of Consensus Issues, 1970 through 2011

Table 3.2 presents decade-by-decade estimates from the 1970s, 1980s, 1990s, and 2000–2011. Estimates were generated by simply limiting the questions analyzed in Equation 3.1 to the specified temporal interval. Because the number of issue ownership questions appearing in surveys increased rapidly throughout this period, a regression pooling all of the data would overemphasize reputations from the 1990s and 2000s at the expense of earlier observations. Thus to provide estimates of the two parties' issue ownership advantages over the entire four-decade interval, the final column presents the arithmetic mean of the decade-by-decade estimates. The issues are ordered by the Republican Party's strongest issue over the four decades (domestic security) to the Democrats' strongest issue (poverty).

The estimates show that long-term issue ownership advantages are substantial. The four-decade averages exceed ten points in absolute value for eight of the seventeen issues: domestic security and military issues for the Republicans; poverty, the environment, Social Security, health care, jobs, and education for the Democrats. Furthermore, despite the incorporation of all of the controls described above, a tremendous amount of the variation in responses is explained by the issue-specific indicators. In the 1980s, 1990s and 2000s, the percentage of variation in Americans' responses to issue-ownership questions explained by the model jumps by some forty percentage points after the indicators are included (as indicated by a comparison of the models' R-squared statistics).[12] This provides strong evidence that Americans make big, meaningful distinctions among the parties on their handling of these issues.

Issue ownership is not only substantial; it is largely consistent over time. This can be clearly seen in Figure 3.4, in which only the statistically significant issue ownership advantages are plotted by decade. Ownership remained in the hands of the same party over the entire forty-year period on no fewer than eleven issues (the eight listed above, plus the Republican-owned issues of crime, immigration, and taxes). Of the seven issues remaining, there are only two – the economy and foreign affairs – where we can say with a high degree of confidence that ownership changed hands, in that there are decades with statistically significant estimates that switch signs. As discussed later in this chapter, these are exactly the two issues that Petrocik identified as "performance issues" – issues so closely tied with the incumbent's performance that any ownership of these issues is expected to be short-term.

The estimates thus comport with a commonsense understanding of American politics. In fact, they seem so familiar it is worth taking a moment to step back and explicitly identify the themes that underlie the two parties' issue reputations. By design, all of the issues listed in Table 3.2 are linked with goals that are widely shared by Americans. When voters associate these goals with particular parties, Republican advantages consist of issues having to do with a smaller government (taxes) focused on public order (crime, immigration) and protecting

---

[12] When R-squared statistics are calculated on regressions run without an intercept term, they are no longer measures of total variance explained. The R-squared statistics in Table 3.2 are therefore those associated with the same regressions when intercept terms are included.

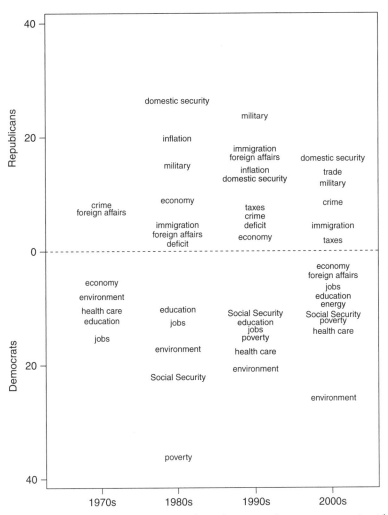

FIGURE 3.4. Significant issue-ownership advantages (in percentage points) by decade, 1970–2011.
Source: Estimates in Table 3.2.

Americans at home and abroad (domestic security, military). We might summarize these as a government whose functions are largely limited to providing what are truly *public goods* – the nonrivalrous, nonexcludable goods whose provision in the absence of government is most clearly threatened by free riding and other collective action problems. By contrast, Democratic strengths are found in government provision of rival and excludable *private goods* and resources (education, health care, and Social Security) and government intervention to correct for market externalities and failures (environment, jobs, and poverty). In sum, these estimates conform to our intuitions about what it means to be a "liberal" party or a "conservative" party while providing additional insight about Americans' perceptions of the Democrats and Republicans.

ISSUE OWNERSHIP AND ELECTIONS

The claim that parties whose owned issues are salient in presidential campaigns are more likely to win elections (as shown by Budge and Farlie and Petrocik and his colleagues) is central to the literature on issue ownership. Here I employ the estimates generated above to extend previous findings on aggregate election results though the 2012 U.S. presidential election. These analyses confirm the validity of the estimation strategy employed in Equation 3.1. In addition, they are the first to show that the relationship between issue ownership and election returns is not rendered spurious by other important variables known to affect election results.

Following Petrocik, Benoit, and Hansen (2003), I constructed an issue-salience dataset by calculating the proportion of Americans mentioning each issue as the nation's most important problem in surveys conducted after the conclusion of the fall campaign.[13] (These are the data used to construct Figure 2.1 in the previous chapter.) For each election, I calculated an "issue salience score" as the percentage of Americans naming a Republican-owned issue as the most important problem minus the percentage naming a Democratic issue (as classified by the four-decade averages in the final column of Table 3.2). As the economy and foreign policy changed hands during this period, they were not considered as being "owned" by either party.[14] In the top

---

[13] Like Petrocik, Benoit, and Hansen (2003) I use "most important problem" data collected in the post-election surveys by the American National Election Studies from 1960 through 2000, the final year this question appeared on the ANES. Data for the 2004, 2008, and 2012 elections therefore come from surveys administered by Gallup in mid-November of those years. I note that "most important problem" questions are not ideal indicators of issue salience (Wlezien 2005; Jennings and Wlezien 2011), but the questions analyzed here are the best consistent measures of salience available over time.

[14] This is therefore similar to the approach of Petrocik and his colleagues (1996, 2003), who count mentions of economic and foreign policy issues as "performance issues" not owned by either party.

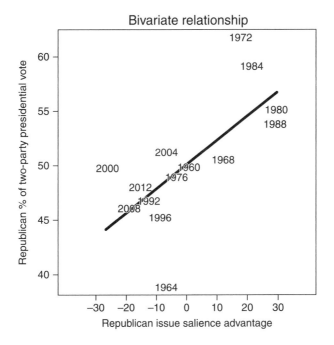

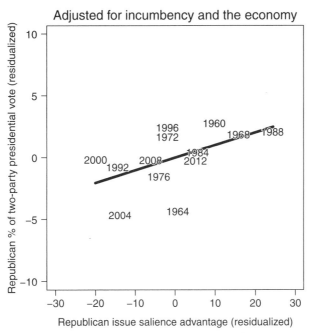

FIGURE 3.5. Issue salience, issue ownership, and vote share in U.S. presidential elections, 1960–2012.

Source: Estimates in Table 3.3.

h in Figure 3.5, these annual scores are plotted on the horizontal and the Republican share of the two-party presidential vote on the vertical axis. On average, Republicans enjoyed the slightest of issue salience advantages in these fourteen elections (.84 percentage points) that was subject to a fair amount of variation (the standard deviation of the issue advantage score was 18.0).

Figure 3.5 confirms the validity of the over-time estimates of issue ownership by replicating previous work showing that there is a strong, significant relationship between the extent to which a party's issues are salient and its performance in U.S. presidential elections since 1960. This is quantified by the bivariate regression displayed in Table 3.3, Model I, which indicates that a ten-percentage point advantage in the share of the population naming a party's owned issues as the nation's most important problem translates into an estimated gain of 2.2 percentage points in the presidential vote. To put this estimate in context, in 2000 George W. Bush faced a twenty-six–point disadvantage in the share of Americans naming Democratic-owned issues (particularly education, health care and Social Security) as the nation's most important problem compared to those naming Republican issues. By contrast, four years later the Democrats' advantage shrank to just seven points in the 2004 election, thanks in part to a large increase in the percentage of Americans ranking the Republican issue of domestic security as the nation's most important problem. According to Model I, a gain of this size in the Republican Party's issue salience advantage (an increase of nineteen percentage points, equivalent to a shift of about a one standard deviation) is estimated to be associated with a swing of 4.2 percentage points in the vote toward the Republican presidential candidate – a substantial shift that clearly is capable of affecting the outcome of an election.

However, this analysis ignores two influential factors shaping aggregate U.S. election outcomes identified by political scientists: the state of the national economy and the number of terms the incumbent party has held the presidency. Economic growth is associated with success for the incumbent party at the ballot box, but it becomes increasingly difficult for a party to maintain control of the presidency once it has held the office for two consecutive terms

TABLE 3.3. *Issue salience, economic conditions, and incumbency in presidential elections, 1960–2012*

	DV: Republican Candidate Share of Two-Party Vote			
	I	II	III	IV (1980 election omitted)
Republican issue salience advantage	.22** (.06)		.07 (.05)	.10+ (.05)
Republican incumbent		13.35* (5.28)	13.18* (4.96)	7.34 (5.00)
Change in GDP, Q4 to Q2 of election year (percentage points)		−2.54*** (.50)	−2.02* (.79)	−4.40+ (2.04)
Republican incumbent x change in GDP		4.69*** (.71)	3.71** (1.06)	5.87* (1.94)
Number of consecutive terms Republican has held presidency		−5.12** (1.35)	−4.76** (1.41)	−4.59* (1.37)
Intercept	50.18*** (1.19)	44.67*** (1.91)	44.61*** (1.97)	50.37*** (3.18)
N	14	14	14	13
R^2	.47	.84	.87	.88
Adjusted R^2	.42	.77	.79	.80
SEE	4.4	2.8	2.7	2.7
p–value of coefficient on issue salience advantage term	.005		.25	.06

OLS. Estimates significantly different from zero at $+p<.10$; $*p<.05$; $**p<.01$; $***p<.001$ (two-tailed tests, robust standard errors).

or more.[15] We see this in Table 3.3, Model II, which predicts the Republican candidate's share of the presidential vote with the change in the nation's Gross Domestic Product (GDP) from the fourth quarter of the year prior to the election to the second quarter of the election year (as suggested by Vavreck 2009: 36) and the number of consecutive terms the Republican Party has held the presidency.[16] The economic growth variable is interacted with an indicator term for the party of the incumbent president. As shown by the model's R-squared statistic, these variables account for 84 percent of the variation in vote share in presidential elections over the past fifty years.[17] Because economic growth in the year before a presidential election is causally prior to issue salience during a campaign, we should be concerned that it might confound any relationship we see between issue salience and election results. This threat would be particularly worrisome to the extent that the party benefitting from the state of the economy (the incumbent's party in good times or the challenger's party in bad times) were somehow able to more effectively raise the salience of its owned issues than its opponent.

To address this concern, issue salience, incumbency and economic conditions are all incorporated as predictors in Models III and IV. Controlling for these factors in Model III diminishes the association between issue salience and vote share. But post-regression diagnostics indicate that one election – 1980 – is a highly influential point that by itself is responsible for creating an artificial appearance of a strong relationship between economic conditions and issue salience.[18] Removing this election from the dataset (as is done in Model IV) yields an estimate of the association

---

[15] A comprehensive list of works in this field would be impossible to list here; early contributions include Kramer (1971) and Tufte (1978). For a discussion of notable recent research, see Lynn Vavreck's *The Message Matters* (2009: 26–40). For an in-depth examination of exactly how and when the economy affects vote intention and election results, see Robert S. Erikson and Christopher Wlezien's *The Timeline of Presidential Elections* (2012).

[16] If the incumbent is a Democrat, this variable takes on negative values for the number of consecutive terms the presidency has been held by Democrats.

[17] The choice of measure of the state of the economy is not of much consequence here. Scholars have used a range of alternate economic measures, all of which are highly correlated and have similarly large impacts on election results (see, e.g., Erikson and Wlezien 2012).

[18] This observation had a Cook's D statistic of 3.4; all other observations had D statistics of .35 or less. A rule of thumb is that any case with a D statistic greater than $4/(n\text{-}k\text{-}1)$ (which equals .5 in Model III) may be a highly influential outlier (Fox 2008: 255).

between issue salience and election results that remains substantial and statistically significant. In this model, economics, incumbency and issues explain nearly 90 percent of the variation in vote share in these thirteen elections. The strong relationship between issue salience and aggregate election results accounting for economic conditions and incumbency is displayed in the bottom graph in Figure 3.5, which plots residualized vote share in the thirteen elections against the residualized values of the issue salience measure. A ten-point shift in a party's issue-salience advantage is associated with a one-point increase in its presidential vote share after controlling for the economy and incumbency.

Thus as predicted by issue-ownership theory, there is a substantial relationship between presidential election results and the extent to which Americans name Democratic- or Republican-owned issues as critical problems facing the nation. To be clear, these analyses by no means prove that the latter are actually caused by the former. It cannot be ruled out that the "most important problem" data reflect the public's greater absorption of the winning candidate's message – and thus issue salience is the by-product of his victory rather than a contributory cause of it. Furthermore, given that the issue-salience data come from surveys fielded in the weeks just after the presidential election, they may also be affected by the national news coverage telling voters that the winning party's issues were what the election "was all about."

Regardless of the direction of causality, these data confirm that issue ownership is a meaningful concept – and that the estimation strategy introduced here is a valid way to measure it – as we seek to understand the national politics of the United States. Long-term associations between parties and consensus issues exist in the public's mind; these associations are correlated with which party wins a presidential election; this correlation is not confounded by the influence of national economic conditions or incumbency on election results.

THE MEANING OF ISSUE OWNERSHIP: A THEORETICAL QUESTION IN NEED OF AN EMPIRICAL ANSWER

Decades after scholars' initial work documenting the associations Americans make between parties and issues, the phenomenon of issue ownership continues to play a large role in scholarship on the nature of political campaigns and their effects on elections. With estimates derived from a comprehensive dataset incorporating literally every publicly available relevant survey question, this chapter has demonstrated that Americans' assessments of which party can better "handle" particular issues have been remarkably stable. The analyses here confirm that in the aggregate, survey responses to these questions are meaningfully related to substantively important political phenomena.

However, this chapter also highlights the drawbacks of the approach – taken implicitly and explicitly by scholars – of essentially conflating the definition of issue ownership with its measure. This conceptual vagueness leaves us with little guidance about how to interpret an issue ownership advantage, about what it means that candidates are more likely to win elections when their parties' owned issues are salient, and about the ultimate implications of these phenomena for governing and public policy. The models discussed in this chapter begin to shine some theoretical light on these questions. Using nothing more than the basic assumptions of the issue ownership literature, they show that a party's ownership of a consensus issue could derive from any or all of three kinds of advantages. We are unable to determine a priori if the parties own issues because they are closer to voters on the policies they offer these issues, if instead they are perceived as delivering superior performance on achieving the consensus goal associated with these issues, or finally if the parties prioritize the issue with government dollars and other scarce resources.

Thus questions about the meaning of issue ownership cannot be settled via logic. Satisfactory answers to these questions will instead require empirical investigation into whether we observe relationships between issue ownership and the policies, performance, and priorities of the Democratic and Republican parties over time. These empirical investigations begin in the following chapter.

4

Ruling Out the Policy and Performance Hypotheses

We have seen that a consensus exists in the United States across the ideological spectrum that Washington should address a broad set of national goals with spending and government action. In the previous chapter, we saw that over the past four decades, Americans have consistently associated most of these goals with one party or another. Here I begin to investigate why these associations persist so strongly over time. Political scientists have ascribed the sources of the parties' issue ownership to any or all of three explanations, hypothesizing that parties own issues because the public prefers their policies, their performance, or their priorities to those of the other party. In this chapter, I rule out the first two explanations, showing that the policy and performance hypotheses are profoundly unable to explain why parties own issues.

The chapter begins with a short discussion of why the questions that motivate this book require a focus on issue ownership at the aggregate, rather than the individual, level of analysis. Turning to the policy hypothesis, I show that policy preferences – as measured by four decades of survey items on which Americans have placed the parties and themselves on issue-specific scales – are remarkably unrelated to issue ownership. Americans do not particularly favor Democratic policies on Democratic-owned issues such as health care or jobs, nor do they favor Republican policies on the military or crime. The chapter then examines the performance hypothesis by comparing over-time issue ownership data with objective indicators of national conditions – such as crime, air quality, taxes, and health outcomes. This analysis shows that the parties' ownership of most issues is completely unrelated to whether conditions on that issue actually improve when they hold power in Washington. Remarkably, Americans' stated beliefs that one party is better able to "handle" a particular issue than the other have little to do with whether conditions actually improve on the issue when the trusted party holds power.

ISSUE OWNERSHIP AS AN AGGREGATE PHENOMENON

The analyses in this book are designed to yield insights about issue ownership at the aggregate level rather than the individual level. This is because issue ownership is most relevant to our understanding of American national politics and policy making as an aggregate-level phenomenon. After all, we conceive of parties owning specific issues among electorates rather than among individual voters. It is a party's aggregate net advantage on "handling" particular issues that is associated with election results and presumably the basis of a candidate's decision to emphasize particular issues in a campaign for office.

By contrast, examinations of the influences on issue ownership among individuals, although providing their own insights, can be misinterpreted and thus lead to incorrect conclusions about the factors affecting issue ownership in the American polity as a whole. As an illustration of the drawbacks of an individual-level analysis, consider data from the 1994 American National Election Studies, which included issue-ownership questions about which party would do a better job "dealing with the crime problem" and "making health care more affordable." The ANES also asked respondents about their policy preferences on these issues. On crime, Americans were asked whether they favored or opposed the crime bill spearheaded by President Clinton and passed by the Democratic-controlled Congress in 1994. Among other things, this law provided grants to states and localities to hire police officers and build prisons, expanded the list of crimes to which the federal death penalty applied, and established a ban on semiautomatic assault weapons (Congressional Quarterly 1997a). On health care, the ANES asked respondents to place themselves and the two parties on a scale indicating preferences over how Americans should obtain health insurance. The scale ran from support for a government-run health insurance plan on one end of the scale to support for privately provided plans on the other. Respondents were also asked to indicate where they thought the Democratic and Republican parties were located on this scale. Although this item did not specifically mention Clinton's failed attempt at health care reform, it was doubtlessly on many respondents' minds as they answered the question. Just weeks before the 1994 congressional elections, at a widely publicized news conference held by Senate Majority Leader George Mitchell, a key Clinton ally, health reform was declared effectively dead (Congressional Quarterly 1997b).

Thus on both of these issues, the 1994 ANES provides a rare opportunity to examine issue ownership at the individual level: is a voter more likely to say that a party will do a better job on a certain issue if she perceives herself as agreeing more with the party's policies on that issue? As shown in Table 4.1, the answer is unambiguously yes. The two panels are simple cross-tabulations of Americans' responses on the issue ownership and policy questions. As shown in the top panel, those opposing Clinton's crime bill were more likely to say they thought the Republican Party would do a better job than the Democrats at fighting crime. The bottom panel indicates that those with health insurance policy preferences closer to Democrats than the Republicans were more likely to say they thought the Democrats would do a better job making health care more affordable. These substantial relationships are highly statistically significant.

Nevertheless, it would be incorrect to use the evidence in Table 4.1 to draw the conclusion that the parties own their respective issues because of Americans' policy preferences on these issues. Year in and year out, more Americans say they trust the Republicans more than the Democrats to handle the issue of crime. This was certainly true in 1994: as shown in the final column of the top panel of Table 4.1, Republicans enjoyed a twenty-point lead at the time on which party would do a better job fighting crime. But the final row of the table indicates that the Republicans' ownership of this issue was *in spite of* – not because of – their opposition to the Democrats' popular

TABLE 4.1. *Issue ownership and policy preferences:*
individual-level relationships
Cell entries are total percentages.

a. Crime

Crime: Issue ownership	Crime: policy preferences		
	Favor Clinton crime bill	Oppose Clinton crime bill	Total
Democrats better job	35.1	4.6	39.7
Republicans better job	34.6	25.7	60.3
Total	69.7	30.3	100.0

Pearson's F (corrected for survey design): 66.99; $p < .001$

$N = 761$.

b. Health care

Health care: Issue ownership	Health care: policy preferences		
	Closer to Dems on health insurance plan	Closer to Reps on health insurance plan	Total
Democrats better job	43.3	18.9	62.2
Republicans better job	4.8	33.0	37.8
Total	48.1	51.9	100.0

Pearson's F (corrected for survey design): 194.99; $p < .001$

$N = 754$.

Source: American National Election Studies, 1994

Question wording:

CRIME

Issue ownership: Which party do you think would do a better job … dealing with the crime problem?

Policy preferences: As you may know this summer Congress passed President Clinton's crime bill. Do you favor or oppose this law?

HEALTH CARE

Issue ownership: Which party do you think would do a better job … making health care more affordable?

Policy preferences: There is much concern about the rapid rise in medical and hospital costs. Some people feel there should be a government insurance plan which would cover all medical expenses for everyone. Others feel that all medical expenses should be paid by individuals, and through private insurance plans like Blue Cross or other company paid plans. Where would you place yourself on this scale, or haven't you thought much about this? Where would you place … the Democratic Party? … the Republican Party?

crime bill, which was favored by nearly seven in ten Americans. A similar pattern arises in opinion on health care, where the Democrats' decades-long ownership of this issue persisted in 1994: the last column of the bottom panel of Table 4.1 shows that Americans thought the party could do a better job of making health care affordable by a nearly 2-to-1 margin. But again issue ownership was at odds with policy preferences: the final row of the table shows that slightly more Americans actually agreed with the Republicans on health insurance policy than the Democrats. (The fact that Democrats continued to own health care by such a substantial margin after the pummeling the party received over its failed health care reform plan in 1994 is another testament to the stability of issue ownership in American politics.) These tables once again show how it is possible that many Americans can find themselves disagreeing with the policies of the parties that own issues: 35 percent of Americans named the Republicans as the party better able to handle the issue of crime while simultaneously approving of the Democrats' crime policy; 19 percent said the Democrats were the party better able to handle health care while at the same time locating themselves closer to the Republican Party on health care policy.

Thus on an issue-by-issue basis, policy preferences and issue ownership in this example are negatively correlated at the aggregate level despite the fact that they are positively correlated at the individual level. The instinct to focus attention on the latter finding may be strong for those who are rightfully concerned about avoiding the ecological fallacy of making inferences from aggregates to individuals in other contexts. But the questions motivating this book lead us to be much more interested in reaching conclusions about aggregates than about individuals. Consider again Figure 3.1, the diagram in the previous chapter illustrating the concept of issue ownership as an advantage on policy. As shown in the figure, this conceptualization requires that the typical voter have policy preferences closer to parties on the issues they own. The findings in Table 4.1 indicate that just the opposite was true regarding two high-stakes policy debates that took place in 1994. The typical voter was closer to the Democrats on crime policy and to the Republicans on health policy, even as the American electorate continued to endorse the parties' long-standing reputations on handling these two issues. The issues of health care and crime in 1994 thus provide no evidence that parties own issues due to popular policies.

Focusing on the relationships between issue ownership and the parties' policies, performance, and priorities at the aggregate level is a superior approach to analyses conducted at the individual level in two other important respects. First, the aggregate approach avoids the contamination that would be likely to occur if these relationships were assessed using individual responses to questions fielded in the same surveys. An individual's response to a survey question such as "which party do you think can better handle [issue X]" might influence his or her responses to subsequent questions in the same survey, such as "which party's policies do you prefer on [issue X]?" This could lead to relationships among survey responses that are merely artifacts of question-order effects (Erikson and Tedin 2011: 41–42; see also Therriault 2012). Second, an aggregate-level strategy is necessary if we are ultimately interested in the parties' actual policies, performance, or priorities, rather than how these are perceived by voters. These perceptions are interesting in their own right, but they do not tell us how the parties actually go about establishing their ownership over issues. The relevant actions that the parties undertake that influence their issue reputations occur at the aggregate level; they do not vary by individual. Thus as much as possible in the analyses that follow, I employ aggregate-level data and avoid using individual-level measures of voters' perceptions.

ISSUE OWNERSHIP AND PARTY POLICIES

To test the hypothesis that issue ownership is due to policy preferences, I now expand the analysis to incorporate a broad range of issues over time. Questions similar to the 1994 items on health care and crime that ask Americans to locate themselves and the parties on policy scales have appeared regularly on the ANES for various issues over the past four decades. Unfortunately, issue ownership questions themselves appear on the ANES infrequently. They do not always cover the same issues as the policy preference questions, making the kind of within-survey comparisons shown in Table 4.1 infeasible under most circumstances. Fortunately, we have another source of data at hand: the decade-by-decade estimates of issue ownership generated in the previous chapter. To the extent that aggregate policy preferences explain aggregate issue ownership, the aggregate policy preferences in the ANES items should be correlated with the estimates of the parties' ownership across issues.

Survey items on which respondents placed themselves and the parties on policy scales regarding consensus issues have appeared on the ANES fifty-six times since 1970. In years where party placements were not available, I supplemented these data with another ten survey items on which voters placed themselves and the parties' presidential candidates.[1] The dataset includes policy placements data on eight consensus issues: crime, the environment, foreign affairs, health care, inflation, jobs, the military, and taxes. It should be noted that because they are based upon voters' perceptions of the parties' and candidates' positions on issues, these measures make for a less conservative test of whether a relationship exists between issue ownership and policy preferences than is ideal. It has been well documented that voters often take cues from parties and candidates when determining their preferences on different policies, with rank-and-file Democrats and Republicans shifting their views toward their parties' positions as they learn what these positions are (see, e.g., Bullock 2011, Lenz 2009, Zaller 1992). The ANES items are even more vulnerable to this process, as voters are presented with no factual information about the parties' and candidates' actual stances and thus many respondents may simply project their own policy views onto the party they trust to handle a given issue. The placement scales bias the analysis in favor of a finding that the typical voter perceives himself as closer on policy to parties that own issues.

Illustrative over-time trends and question wording for the policy placement scales on two issues – foreign affairs and jobs – are found in Figure 4.1 and its accompanying text. As shown in the figure, in neither case have Americans agreed consistently over the past forty years on policy with the party that owns the issue. If anything, the relationship is the opposite. Republicans are generally perceived as offering more popular policies on the Democratic-owned issue of jobs. Since the 1980s, Americans have agreed more with the Democrats on

---

[1] Results similar to those reported here are yielded by a dataset restricted to the party placements items. See this chapter's appendix for question wording.

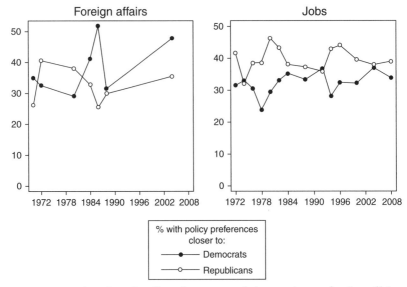

FIGURE 4.1. Americans' policy placements of the parties on foreign affairs and jobs, 1970–2008.
Source: American National Election Studies.
Question wording: See this chapter's appendix.

the chief policy controversies regarding the Republican-owned issue of foreign affairs. These include relations with Russia, intervention in Central America, and use of diplomacy instead of military force to protect U.S. interests abroad.

A systematic analysis across issues and time confirms that there is absolutely no evidence for the hypothesis that aggregate policy preferences explain aggregate issue ownership. The simplest way to see this is the scatterplot in the top panel of Figure 4.2. On the *x*-axis is plotted the average net policy advantage on each issue for the Republican Party (that is, the percentage of Americans perceiving themselves closer to the Republicans minus the percentage closer to the Democrats). On the *y*-axis is plotted the net Republican issue ownership advantage over the past four decades as estimated in Table 3.2. The figure includes a best-fit regression line, which is sloped in a slightly negative direction that is not statistically significant.[2] Thus

[2] The slope of this line is -.13 (p = .87); the *R*-squared statistic from the bivariate regression is .01.

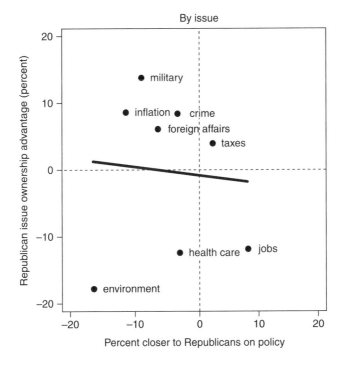

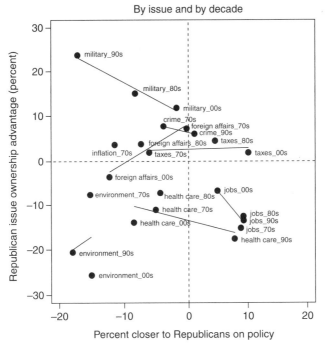

FIGURE 4.2. Policy placements and issue ownership, 1970–2008.
Sources: see text.

there is no relationship between how close Americans feel to the parties on their policies and the extent to which they think parties will do a better job handling these issues. In fact, as shown by the number of points falling into each quadrant of the scatterplot, Americans on average are more likely to disagree than agree with the policies of issue-owning parties.

A reasonable concern about this simple analysis is that it does not account for any change in issue ownership or policy placements over time. To address this concern, decade-by-decade means of the policy placement data are plotted against the decade-by-decade issue ownership data from the previous chapter in the bottom panel of Figure 4.2. Best-fit regression lines are traced for the seven issues on which there are multiple observations over time. These lines run in all different directions, and on only two of the issues (the environment and foreign affairs) do lines slope in the sharply upward fashion we would expect if parties improved their issue ownership advantages by moving closer to voters on policy. This lack of a relationship is confirmed by a mixed-effects model (not shown here) in which the effects of the policy placement items on issue ownership are permitted to vary at random by issue and intercepts are assumed to vary at random by issue and decade. The estimated effect of policy placements on issue ownership remains negative and statistically insignificant.[3]

Thus absolutely no evidence is found for a relationship between aggregate policy preferences and aggregate issue ownership. Given that the data analyzed here make for a test that actually favors the finding of such a relationship, we can quite confidently reject the policy hypothesis.

Issue Ownership and a Non-Consensus Issue: Abortion

As discussed in Chapter 2, we have strong theoretical reasons to expect the distinction between policies and priorities to be much less meaningful for non-consensus issues, and thus for the concept of issue ownership to be less analytically relevant for our understanding of

---

[3] The coefficient on policy preferences in the estimated model is -.12 (p= .68).

the politics of these issues. This is because non-consensus issues feature sharp disagreement on desired end states, and thus it is less likely that Americans who disagree with a party's policies on a non-consensus issue will nevertheless believe that the party can better "handle" that issue.

Perhaps no issue exemplifies these characteristics better than the issue of abortion, where there is deep division among Americans over the end state of the extent to which abortion should be legally available. For a number of reasons, the issue also provides a rare opportunity to explore the relationship between policies and ownership in depth. Following an "issue evolution" in the 1970s and 1980s, the parties' policy positions on abortion – as reflected in congressional roll-call votes, surveys of party activists, and planks in party platforms – have remained stable over the past few decades. The Republican Party has favored increased restrictions on abortion while the Democratic Party has been opposed to limiting abortion's availability (Adams 1997, Carmines and Woods 2002, Karol 2009).

Over-time survey data are particularly rich with regard to issue ownership and Americans' policy preferences on abortion. One of several survey houses that has fielded consistently worded survey questions on abortion over the years is the CBS News/*New York Times* poll, which asks respondents the question "Which comes closest to your view? (1) Abortion should be generally available to those who want it; or (2) Abortion should be available but under stricter limits than it is now; or (3) Abortion should not be permitted." The poll included this question fifty-five times in surveys it conducted from 1989 through 2009 (Bowman and Rugg 2012: 9–10). These data are displayed in the upper region of the graph in Figure 4.3, which plots the share of Americans saying abortion should be generally available minus the share saying it should not be permitted. As shown by the smoothed trend line, Americans became gradually more opposed to abortion over this period, with the gap between those with pro-choice and pro-life views diminishing from twenty-five percentage points in the early 1990s to fifteen points by 2009.

Over the same period, a total of thirty questions appeared on national surveys in which Americans were asked questions about which party is better able to "handle" or "deal with" the issue of

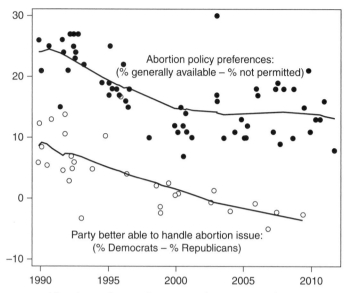

FIGURE 4.3. Abortion policy preferences and issue ownership, 1989–2009.
Sources: see text.

abortion.[4] These questions thus met the criteria necessary to fall into
the comprehensive dataset of issue ownership survey questions. As
discussed in the previous chapter, they were included in the analyses used to generate over-time estimates of the parties' ownership of
consensus issues in order to improve the precision of these estimates.
I now use these questions to generate estimates of Americans' assessments of which party is better able to handle the abortion issue. To
remove the noise introduced by contemporaneous sentiment toward
the two parties and their leaders as well as any bias associated with
particular survey houses, I used a modified version of the approach
taken to estimate issue ownership in Chapter 3. I first reestimated
Equation 3.1 without any of the issue-specific indicators. I then used
the resulting estimated model to generate predicted values for each

[4] The difficulty of differentiating issue ownership from policy preferences on a
non-consensus issue such as abortion is illustrated by the fact that many survey questions on abortion that met the criteria for inclusion in the issue-ownership dataset
were actually about policy preferences. Instead of asking respondents to name the
party better able to handle the issue of abortion, these questions asked which party
does a better job at "representing your views" or "having the correct position" on
abortion. Questions such as these were excluded from the analyses presented here.

of the survey questions in the issue-ownership dataset. The predicted values associated with the thirty issue-ownership questions on abortion are thus snapshot estimates of the parties' relative ownership of this issue cleaned of noise and bias. These data are plotted in the lower region of the graph in Figure 4.3 as the percentage of Americans naming the Democrats as better able to handle the issue of abortion minus the percentage naming the Republicans. The points trace a steady decline in the Democrats' advantage on this issue, which shrank from ten percentage points in the early 1990s to a slight deficit by 2009.

A glance at Figure 4.3 reveals that the two series are strongly correlated. This is confirmed by the first model in Table 4.2, in which issue ownership is regressed on policy preferences.[5] This bivariate regression finds a very strong relationship between the two trends: a one-percentage point increase in policy preferences in the pro-life direction is accompanied by a shift away from the Democrats of .67 percentage points. Time series such as these tend to be highly autocorrelated in that their past values can be strong predictors of present values. These two series also appear to be trended, in that they are both decreasing steadily over time. If not properly accounted for, autocorrelation and trending can lead to biased estimates and incorrect standard errors. I therefore follow standard econometric practice and estimate the relationship with a general autoregressive distributed lag (ADL) model. Estimates from this model, which also includes a time trend, are shown in the second column of Table 4.2. The significance tests associated with several coefficients in this model justify restricting the effects of many of these lags to zero (De Boef and Keele 2008), which yields the model shown in the table's third column. The final model in the table controls for a potentially confounding variable that is also trending in time and could conceivably be correlated with both abortion policy preferences and issue ownership: abortions as a percentage of all pregnancies ending in either live birth or abortion. This statistic, called the abortion ratio, has been calculated through 2008 by researchers affiliated with the Alan Guttmacher Institute (Jones and Kooistra 2011).[6] After rising sharply

[5] These analyses are conducted with a dataset constructed with the annual means of the data shown in Figure 4.3. In years where surveys on abortion issue ownership or policy preferences were not conducted, I rely on linear interpolation to supply missing values.

[6] Although the Guttmacher Institute is an avowedly pro-choice organization, it is nevertheless a reliable and objective source of data on abortion, cited frequently by news media and in U.S. government publications.

TABLE 4.2. *Abortion policy preferences and issue ownership, 1989–2009*

	DV: party better able to handle abortion at time t (% naming Democrats - % naming Republicans)			
	OLS	ADL	ADL	ADL
Abortion policy preferences$_t$	.67***	−.19		
	(.14)	(.24)		
Abortion policy preferences$_{t-1}$		−.10		
		(.29)		
Abortion policy preferences$_{t-2}$		.59+	.43*	.34+
		(.29)	(.20)	(.16)
Abortion issue ownership$_{t-1}$		.12		
		(.30)		
Abortion issue ownership$_{t-2}$		−.46		
		(.41)		
Abortion issue ownership$_{t-3}$		−.34+	−.37+	−.39**
		(.18)	(.19)	(.12)
year$_t$		−1.00**	−.72**	
		(.30)	(.22)	
% of pregnancies ending in abortion$_t$				−6.23*
				(2.28)
% of pregnancies ending in abortion$_{t-1}$				1.72
				(1.05)
% of pregnancies ending in abortion$_{t-2}$				6.64*
				(2.59)
N	21	18	18	17
Adjusted R-squared	.31	.57	.54	.79
p-value of Ljung-Box Q test for serial correlation of residuals	.29	.92	.52	.39

Sources: see text.

Estimates significantly different from zero at +p<.10; *p<.05; **p<.01; ***p<.001 (two-tailed tests, robust standard errors). All estimates include an intercept (not shown).

in the years following the Supreme Court's 1973 *Roe v. Wade* ruling, the abortion ratio began declining steadily in the early 1980s. (The percentage of pregnancies ending in abortion fell from a high of 30.1 percent in 1981 to 22.4 percent in 2008.) As shown in the final column of Table 4.2, the abortion ratio and its lags are significantly associated with abortion policy preferences; their inclusion reduces the effect of the time trend to statistical insignificance and thus the trend is not included in this final model.

Across all of the specifications with controls, the estimated effect of policy preferences on issue ownership remains significant and substantial. A shift of national preferences in the pro-life direction of one percentage point is estimated to presage a shift in issue ownership accorded to the Republicans two years later ranging between .34 and .59 percentage points. As mentioned earlier, over the two-decade span, abortion policy preferences and issue ownership both moved in a conservative (or Republican) direction by about ten percentage points. These estimates indicate that the ten-point shift in policy preferences may be responsible for as much as half of the change in issue ownership over this period.

In contrast to the consensus issues examined in Figure 4.2, ownership on the issue of abortion over the past two decades appears to have moved closely in tandem with Americans' policy preferences vis-à-vis the policies of the two parties. The analysis here is meant to be illustrative rather than definitive: unfortunately, data on which parties are better able to handle other non-consensus issues (such as gay rights or school prayer) are sparse. But the findings here strongly corroborate my contention that issue ownership on non-consensus issues is driven by policy preferences, that there is not much distinction between these two phenomena for these kinds of issues – and thus that issue ownership is not a particularly helpful way to understand the politics of non-consensus issues.

ISSUE OWNERSHIP AND PARTY PERFORMANCE

Having ruled out policy preferences as a substantive cause of issue ownership on consensus issues, I now turn to what could arguably be considered the literal meaning of the survey questions used to measure the reputations: is one party or another indeed better able to "handle" or "deal with" particular issues? This section examines this question head-on by exploring whether the parties' performance on these issues – as measured by change in objective indicators of national conditions on consensus issues such as taxes, crime, education, and the environment when the parties control the presidency – corresponds with their reputations.

Until now, explorations of the relationship between party control of government and performance have largely been limited to one policy domain: the economy. Pioneered by the work of Douglas Hibbs (1977, 1987), this research has generally found unemployment to be higher, and inflation to be lower, when a Republican is in the White House (Alesina 1988, Alesina and Sachs 1988, Beck 1982, Chappell and Keech 1988). The findings correspond to a characterization of Democratic administrations pursuing more expansionary policies than Republicans. More controversial research has found that economic growth decreases and economic inequality grows more rapidly when a Republican holds the presidency (Alesina and Rosenthal 1995, Bartels 2008; Hibbs and Dennis 1988; but see Campbell 2011 and Kenworthy 2010). Here I adopt a similar approach to see if relationships hold between party control of the presidency and measures of progress on other important consensus goals.

Measuring National Conditions

To score the parties on their ability to improve national conditions, we need objective measures of performance on a range of issues. Arriving at these measures requires overcoming three hurdles. First, a measure must be closely enough aligned with a particular consensus goal that we would expect audiences of most political stripes to agree in which direction the measure should change to achieve progress on the goal. Second, an indicator must actually measure what it claims to measure: in the parlance of measurement theory, it must have "construct validity." In many cases, the validity of a particular measure is not in question: for example, most would agree that the nation's murder and violent crime rates are good measures of the extent to which lawlessness is being controlled. But the validity of other measures is much more in contention, including test scores as a measure of student skills and support from allies abroad as a measure of the strength of U.S. foreign policy. The approach taken here is to err on the side of including too many measures – rather than too few – in the analysis, and to let readers determine for themselves whether these measures are valid indicators of performance with regard to shared goals. The final criterion is that the measure must be clearly about results, not effort. As explained at the beginning of this book, the parties' efforts at achieving consensus goals fall under the category of priorities. In this analysis, we are by contrast concerned with results: the extent to which national conditions are actually improving or getting worse.

Table 4.3 lists eighteen identified measures along with their sources keyed to the consensus issues discussed in the previous chapter. The table also explicitly specifies the consensus goal associated with each issue as the direction on which most Americans agree a change in the measure signifies progress toward the goal. Figure 4.4 displays trends in these measures from 1975 through 2010, an interval covering four Republican and three Democratic presidencies and the widest span of time for which data are available on nearly all of the indicators. Brief discussions and justifications for each of the measures follow.

The economy. Of all of the measures incorporated in this analysis, the economic indicators used here are the most straightforward and universally accepted as measures of national goals. There is widespread agreement that economic growth should be robust, with inflation and unemployment kept low. The measures used here are standard. Economic growth is measured in percent change in GDP, inflation with percent change in the consumer price index, and unemployment with the unemployment rate. Trends in these measures are shown in Figure 4.4.a which indicates that unemployment and growth have moved in largely opposite directions since the 1970s. By contrast, inflation was a serious problem in the early part of this period but has essentially remained flat since the early 1990s.

Government finances. These measures reflect the general consensus that – all things being equal – government deficits and federal taxes should be kept as low as possible. A standard measure of the deficit is its size relative to that of the national economy. With regard to taxes, a measure of aggregate taxation (such as taxes as a percentage of GDP or government spending) is more a measure of effort than results. A superior indicator is one that captures the effect of tax policy on the typical

TABLE 4.3. *Consensus issues, goals, and measures of national conditions*
Except where noted, data are available from 1975 through 2010.

Issue	Consensus Goal	Measure (source)
The economy		
Economy	*Increase* overall economic activity	Percent change in GDP (Bureau of Economic Analysis 2011)
Inflation	*Reduce* inflation rate	Change in Consumer Price Index (CPI-U) (Bureau of Labor Statistics 2011a)
Jobs	*Reduce* unemployment	Unemployment rate (Bureau of Labor Statistics 2011b)
Government finances		
Deficit	*Reduce* deficits, run surpluses	Surpluses or deficits as percent of GDP (White House Office of Management and Budget 2012a)
Taxes	*Reduce* taxes paid by typical American	Average Federal Tax Rate for Family of Four with Median Income (Tax Policy Center 2011)
Social welfare		
Education	*Increase* students' skills	Percent of 13-year-olds "able to search for specific information, interrelate ideas, and make generalizations about literature, science, and social studies materials" on the NAEP long-term trend assessment test (U.S. Department of Education 2010a). Data available through 2008.
	Increase proportion of Americans with college degree	Percentage of persons age 25 and over with college degree (U.S. Department of Education 2010b)

TABLE 4.3. *Consensus issues, goals, and measures of national conditions (continued)*

Issue	Consensus Goal	Measure (source)
Social welfare (continued)		
Health care	*Reduce* proportion of Americans without health insurance	Percent of Americans not covered by private or government health insurance (Cohen et al 2009; DeNavas-Walt, Proctor and Smith 2011)
	Improve Americans' health	Percent of Americans reporting their health as "excellent" or "good," adjusted for age (General Social Survey 2010)
Poverty	*Reduce* poverty	Poverty rate (DeNavas-Walt, Proctor, and Smith 2011)
Public order		
Crime	*Reduce* murder	Murders per 100,000 population (Federal Bureau of Investigation 2011)
	Reduce violent crime	Violent crimes per 1,000 population (Federal Bureau of Investigation 2011)
Immigration	*Reduce* unauthorized immigration to the U.S.	Millions of unauthorized immigrants living in the U.S. (Kandel 2011; U.S. Immigration and Naturalization Service, n.d.; Pew Hispanic Center 2011). Data available beginning 1986.

TABLE 4.3. *Consensus issues, goals, and measures of national conditions (continued)*

Issue	Consensus Goal	Measure (source)
Environment and energy		
Environment	*Reduce* air pollution	Carbon monoxide emissions (thousand short tons) (U.S. Environmental Protection Agency 2011a). Data available through 2009.
	Reduce emissions linked with global warming	U.S. greenhouse gas emissions and sinks (Tg CO2 Eq.) (U.S. Environmental Protection Agency 2011b). Data available 1990–2008.
Energy	*Lower* energy costs	Energy prices (dollars per million BTU), all sources (U.S. Energy Information Administration 2011).
Foreign affairs and trade		
Foreign affairs	*Increase* worldwide support for U.S. foreign policy goals	Affinity scores between U.S. and other U.N. member states in General Assembly votes (Gartzke 2010). Data available through 2008.
Trade	*Increase* exports of goods and services	Total U.S. exports of goods (balance of payment basis) and services as percent of GDP (U.S. Census Bureau Foreign Trade Division 2012).

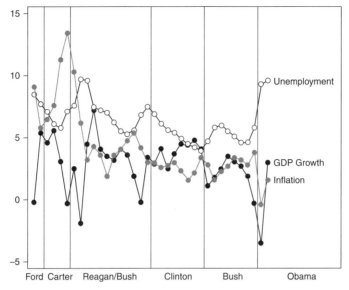

a. The Economy

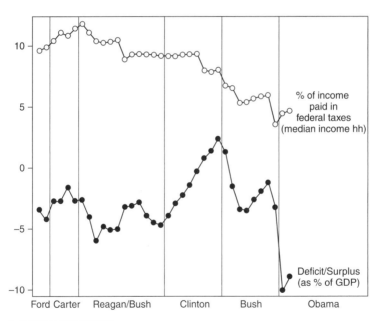

b. Government Finances

FIGURE 4.4. Trends in national conditions, 1975–2010.
Sources: See Table 4.3.

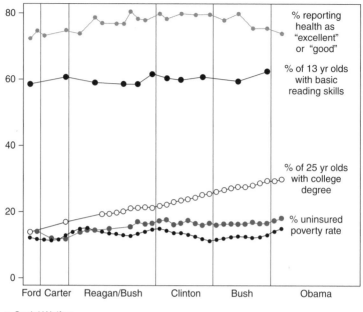

c. Social Welfare

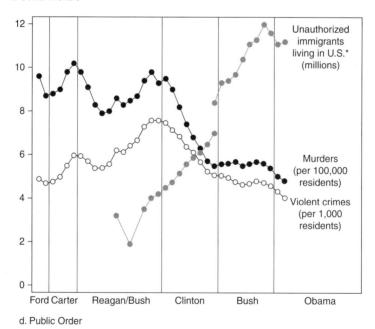

d. Public Order

FIGURE 4.4. Trends in national conditions, 1975–2010 (*continued*)
*Two estimates of unauthorized immigration trends are shown.

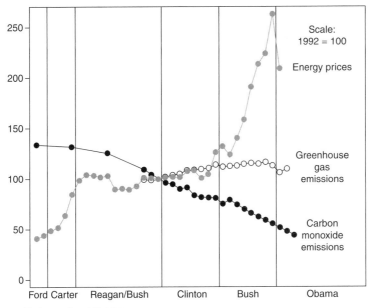

e. Enviroment and Energy

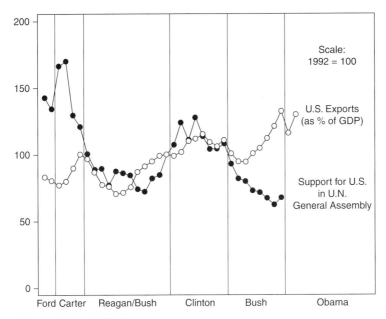

f. Foreign Affairs and Trade

FIGURE 4.4. Trends in national conditions, 1975–2010 (*continued*)

American. Fortunately, such a measure exists: the average federal tax rate for a family of four at the median of the income distribution calculated by the Tax Policy Center, which is jointly run by the Urban Institute and the Brookings Institution. This measure, which incorporates rebates, credits, and deductions, is designed to reflect the actual federal tax bill faced by the household at the median of the income distribution. As such, it is the best possible over-time measure of federal income taxes paid by the typical U.S. family. Figure 4.4.b shows how trends in government finances have moved over time. The share of income paid in federal income taxes by the typical family generally declined between 1975 and 2010, with notable drops occurring during the Reagan, Clinton, and George W. Bush administrations. The deficit fluctuated in a relatively narrow range between 1975 and 1992, shrunk to zero during the Clinton administration, and then grew dramatically thereafter.

Social welfare. Although social welfare issues can be among the most contentious in U.S. politics, there is relatively broad consensus on the goals measured by the five indicators analyzed in this domain. Few Americans would disagree with the objectives of increasing students' skills, raising educational attainment, reducing the share of the population without health insurance, improving the public's health, and reducing poverty. For three out of these five goals, the measures – the percent of Americans with college degrees, the percent uninsured, and the percent under the poverty line – are straightforward. Two other measures are more problematic, but still worthy of analysis. The debate over test scores as measures of students' true abilities is well trodden (e.g., Dee and Jacob 2011; Jacob 2005; Neal and Schanzenbach 2010; Winters, Trivitt, and Greene 2008). But the scores analyzed here – derived from tests administered by the National Assessment of Educational Progress (NAEP) – comprise the only over-time assessment of pupils' abilities on specific subjects that is administered to nationally representative samples of students. The NAEP test booklet stays nearly the same every year, allowing for over-time comparison that is more accurate than any available. The scores examined here are for reading skills, as it is the subject with the longest-running time series, stretching back to 1971. The group whose scores are analyzed is thirteen-year olds, chosen because they are old enough to have had some exposure to schooling, but young enough that their aggregate test scores are relatively unaffected by dropout rates (the NAEP is administered only to those actually in school). The final measure is calculated from data from the General Social Survey, which since 1972 has been asking its nationally representative sample of U.S. adults the question, "Would you say your own health, in general, is excellent, good, fair, or poor?" The measure is the percentage of Americans reporting their health as "excellent" or "good," regression-adjusted for the respondents' ages. Of course, self-reports – whether with regard to income, health, or other status – are notoriously unreliable. But because the question has been asked in the same way by the same survey outfit, any over-time change in the aggregate responses to this measure is meaningful.

Compared to many of the other measures discussed here, four of these trends (shown in Figure 4.4.c) were remarkably steady between 1975 and 2010. Over this thirty-five–year period, the share of students reading at a basic level varied over a range of only four percentage points (from fifty-nine to sixty-three). Ranges for the poverty rate, the ranks of the uninsured, and self-reported health (four, six, and eight percentage points, respectively) were similarly narrow. The exception is the share of Americans with a college degree, which rose steadily over the entire time period.

Public order. The goals examined in this domain – all of which have to do with maintaining public order and reducing lawlessness – are widely shared among those on the Left and the Right. Across the political spectrum, Americans want low rates of violent crime and homicide, and (even among those who welcome immigrants) they want to reduce the rate of unauthorized immigration. The three measures used here are straightforward. Murder and violent crime rates are those issued in the Federal Bureau of Investigation's Uniform Crime Reports. Estimates of the number of unauthorized immigrants living in the United States are provided by the nonpartisan Pew Hispanic Center, which has published estimates going back to the year 2000; an earlier time series beginning in the mid-1980s was generated by the U.S. Immigration and Naturalization Service (which has since been renamed and is now part of the Department of Homeland Security). Figure 4.4.d indicates that the two leading indicators of crime dropped precipitously after reaching historic highs in the late 1970s (the murder rate) and late 1980s (the violent crime rate). At the same time, the number of unauthorized immigrants living in the United States rose by an estimated 600 percent between the Reagan and George W. Bush administrations before tapering off in recent years.

The environment and energy. Two objective measures of national conditions on the environment are available as reliable time series from the U.S. Environmental Protection Agency: carbon monoxide emissions (estimates are provided from 1970 onward) and greenhouse gas emissions (available from 1990 onward). As shown in Figure 4.4.e (which scales these measures to their values in 1992 for comparison purposes), carbon monoxide emissions have declined dramatically since 1975. By contrast, greenhouse gas emissions have moved in the opposite direction, and recent declines are most likely due to the fact that the country was in recession (greenhouse gas emissions and U.S. GDP over the period were strongly correlated at .88). With regard to energy, although there is a strong disagreement about where U.S. energy should come from, there is a general consensus that – all things being equal – energy should be as inexpensive as possible. To capture the total cost of energy over time, I use annual energy prices for consumer energy from all sources (in dollars per billion British Thermal Units, or BTUs) as reported by the U.S. Energy Information Administration. (Here "consumer energy" includes residential, commercial, transportation and industrial use.) As shown in Figure 4.4.e, energy prices climbed steadily until the 1980s, remained relatively stable until the late 1990s, and have spiked notably since then.

Foreign affairs and trade. Although objective indicators of performance on foreign affairs are difficult to come by, one that can be measured in a straightforward fashion is the extent to which United Nations member states agree with the United States in votes held in the UN General Assembly. Votes taken in this body are often thought to be merely symbolic, but that fact arguably strengthens this indicator as a measure of America's standing in the world – that is, as a measure of its ability to persuade other nations to take similar public stances on global issues (Gartzke 2006). As shown in Figure 4.4.f, this measure (scaled to its value in 1992) was highest during the first half of Carter's presidency but then dropped dramatically, climbing again only after George H.W. Bush succeeded Reagan. It began to fall again in the middle of the Clinton presidency and reached an all-time low in 2007. With regard to trade, national conditions are often measured in terms of the trade deficit, defined as imports of goods and services as a share of exports. However, as discussed in Chapter 3, a rising trade deficit may make domestic manufacturers worse off while making domestic consumers better off. An indicator that sidesteps this conflict is simply to measure exports, increases in which make many Americans better off while making very few worse off. Figure 4.4.f displays trends in exports measured as their share of the size of the nation's economy. By this indicator, exports rose (albeit with some significant fluctuation) between 1975 and 2010.

Barriers to Accountability

The performance hypothesis predicts that there should be a relationship between how these indicators change under Republican and Democratic presidents and which parties own which issues. Before testing this hypothesis with these data, let us first observe that there are two obstacles standing in the way of the public's assigning proper credit and blame to the parties for these national conditions. The first is widespread ignorance about the direction of many of these trends – or for that matter, their existence in the first place. Although these data are arguably the best measures possible of national conditions on issues that are central to the quality of life in the United States, most of them nevertheless receive very little attention in news coverage of politics and public affairs. Thus it is unlikely that many Americans (or for that matter, political scientists!) could correctly state that over the past four decades test scores have been essentially flat, air quality has dramatically improved, federal tax rates have fallen, and energy prices have climbed markedly.

But Americans are often unaware of important changes on less obscure indicators. For example, despite the fact that murder and violent crime have fallen in a steady fashion since the early 1990s, Americans have been consistently more likely to agree than disagree that "there is more crime in the U.S. than there was a year ago" in Gallup surveys administered over this period. (See the top panel of Table 4.4.) For example, in November 2010, as crime rates had fallen over the previous year to lows not seen since the 1950s, two-thirds of Americans nevertheless mistakenly believed that there was more crime in the United States than a year beforehand. Even on a highly salient topic such as the economy, Americans can hold inaccurate views to a

TABLE 4.4. *Perceptions of national conditions and actual conditions*
a. Crime, 1989–2010 (selected years)

Year	% saying that compared to a year ago, crime is …		Actual change in violent crime rate from previous year (incidents per 100,000 population)	Are perceptions correct?
	… increasing	… decreasing		
1989	84	5	26.3	x
1992	89	3	−0.5	
1996	71	15	−47.9	
2000	47	41	−16.5	
2004	53	28	−12.6	
2008	67	15	−13.2	
2009	74	15	−26.7	
2010	66	17	−28.3	

Sources: Gallup News Service 2010; Federal Bureau of Investigation 2011.

Question wording: Is there more crime in the U.S. than there was a year ago, or less?

b. The Economy, 1992–2010 (selected years)

Year	Mean annual % saying that economy is getting…		Actual change in GDP growth from previowus year (percentage points)	Are perceptions correct?
	… better	… worse		
1992	14.2	34.3	3.6	
1994	24.0	23.2	1.2	x
1996	17.9	24.8	1.2	
1998	25.0	20.0	−0.1	
2000	30.0	15.0	−0.7	
2002	19.7	31.7	0.7	
2004	27.8	28.0	1.0	
2006	16.0	39.1	−0.4	x
2008	4.6	66.6	−2.2	x
2009	24.1	31.1	−3.2	x
2010	27.4	25.8	6.5	x

Sources: New York Times/CBS News Poll 2012; Bureau of Economic Analysis 2011.

Question wording: Do you think the economy is getting better, getting worse, or staying about the same?

remarkable extent. In surveys administered by the *New York Times* and CBS News from 1992 through 2010, poll respondents were asked if they thought the economy was "getting better, getting worse, or staying about the same?" Comparing annual mean survey responses to changes in GDP growth by year reveals that Americans' aggregate perceptions were incorrect nearly 40 percent of the time during this period.[7] (A selection of these data is shown in the bottom panel of Table 4.4.)

We would be less concerned about this lack of knowledge if the trends tended to move together, as the public could then use its knowledge of the most salient indicators to accurately infer the direction of movement in other national conditions. But this is not the case: a second barrier to accountability is that only a handful of national conditions tend to change in coordinated ways. This is shown by a factor analysis of year-to-year changes in each of the sixteen indicators for which data are available from 1975 onward, the results of which are displayed in Table 4.5.[8] Four indicators – murder, violent crime, poverty, and economic growth – all loaded to a substantial degree on a common first factor (each was correlated with the underlying factor at an absolute value of .6 or greater). Not surprisingly, increases in GDP growth were accompanied by declines in poverty and crime. Change in the size of the nation's deficit, the unemployment rate, and the inflation rate were also found to move together, loading on a second factor with the signs predicted by the Phillips Curve: as unemployment goes up, inflation tends to decline. The national deficit tends to climb with unemployment and fall with inflation, likely due to the government's attempts to counter joblessness with expansionary policy and to reduce inflation with contractionary policy. However, no other factor has any explanatory value, meaning that none of the other measures move together to a meaningful degree. In other words, progress on important consensus goals such as increasing educational attainment, reducing taxes, improving the United States' standing in the world, keeping energy prices low, and reducing the share of Americans without

---

[7] Aggregate perceptions reflected actual economic conditions in eleven out of the eighteen years for which survey data are available between 1992 and 2010.

[8] In this analysis and those that follow, missing data in the time series were imputed via linear interpolation.

TABLE 4.5. *Relationships among trends*
in national conditions, 1975–2008

	Factor loadings			
	1	2	3	4
Murder	**.775**	.316	−.144	.333
Violent crime	**.753**	.184	−.324	.409
Poverty	**.620**	−.596	.130	.002
GDP	**−.620**	−.148	−.322	.036
Surplus/deficit	−.287	**.762**	−.162	−.143
Inflation	.298	**.741**	.339	.073
Unemployment	.541	**−.740**	.200	−.076
Exports	.427	.559	.148	−.130
College attainment	−.246	.030	**.704**	.358
Uninsured	.097	−.403	−.313	.050
Taxes	.053	.172	−.391	.368
Reading scores	.383	.163	−.099	−.374
Carbon monoxide emissions	−.205	−.147	.147	.518
Energy prices	.402	.080	.304	−.324
Self-reported wellbeing	−.417	.071	.222	.192
Support for U.S. at U.N.	−.093	.051	−.208	−.136

Exploratory factor analysis. Only the first four factors are shown; eigenvalues for these factors were 3.2, 2.8, 1.4, and 1.2 respectively. No other factor had an eigenvalue greater than one. Factor loadings of absolute value greater than .6 are shown in bold. Because of lack of data availability for the entire time period, the factor analysis does not include indicators for greenhouse gas emissions or unauthorized immigration.

Sources: See Table 4.3.

health insurance occurs largely independently of other fundamental indicators. Thus Americans cannot use national economic conditions as an accurate heuristic for their evaluations of progress on these other important issues.

Taken together, these observations suggest that our expectations should be low regarding the extent to which Americans translate progress and setbacks on consensus goals into evaluations of the political parties. Americans are unlikely to be aware of all but the most salient trends – and can perceive even these indicators inaccurately. And even as the most carefully watched trends (such as economic growth, crime or jobless rates) get better or worse, other important national conditions may be moving in an entirely opposite direction. As much as Americans say education, taxes, health care, and crime are important national problems, conditions are poor for their understanding of national progress on these consensus issues – and thus their ability to reward or punish the parties for their performance on them.

Do the Parties Earn Their Reputations for Handling Issues?

I now turn to two related questions. To what extent do Americans experience meaningful changes in national conditions depending on whether the Democrats or the Republicans are in power? And do these changes correspond with the parties' long-term ownership of these issues?

National conditions and control of the presidency. A simple way to look for relationships between national conditions and the party in power is to examine how annual change in each of the indicators differs under Democratic and Republican presidents. This has been the basic approach of the research on the link between partisan control and economic conditions since Douglas Hibbs's work in the 1970s. Table 4.6 explores this question using all data available from 1975 to the present. As is standard in analyses such as these, presidencies are lagged by one year to account for the fact that policies rarely have immediate effects on national conditions. For both substantive and methodological reasons, changes – rather than levels – of these measures are the variables of interest. Change is more likely to reflect the actual impact of any presidential policy initiatives, rather than erroneously assigning blame or credit for conditions inherited from previous years.

The table first lists the average annual differences in change in each indicator under Republican presidents and Democratic presidents during the 1975–2010 period. For example, the second row of Table 4.6 tells us that the inflation rate declined substantially more under Republicans than Democrats during this time span: the difference in average change was more than a full percentage point. To take another example, the second-to-last row of the table indicates that on average, Democrats have presided over budgets that have moved away from deficit toward surplus by over 1 percent of GDP compared to Republicans.

TABLE 4.6. *Control of the presidency and change in national conditions, 1975–2010*

| | | change under Republican presidents – change under Democratic presidents | | | | | |
| | | Annual change (difference in means) | | | Long-run change (multiplier estimated with error correction models) | | |
		estimate	se	p-value	estimate	se	p-value
Improved more under G.O.P.	Taxes (Effective rate paid by median household)	-.08	(.24)	.74	-.82	(.22)	<.01
	Inflation (% change in CPI)	-1.08	(.59)	.08	-1.80	(.96)	.06
	Carbon monoxide emissions (thousand short tons)	-570.00	(1036.42)	.59	-24500.00	(29312.58)	.40
Improved more under Democrats	GDP (% change)	-.16	(.91)	.86	-.14	(.59)	.81
	Energy prices (dollars per million BTU)	-.21	(.44)	.63	.43	(1.41)	.76
	Unemployment (%)	.34	(.38)	.38	.40	(.63)	.52
	Self-reported health status (% "excellent"/ "good")	.10	(.48)	.83	-.89	(1.10)	.42
	College attainment (% of 25-year-olds with degree)	-.11	(.08)	.16	-3.98	(4.80)	.41
	Greenhouse gas emissions (Tg CO$_2$ Eq.)	-112.33	(64.41)	.10	36.02	(41.60)	.39
	Poverty (% below poverty line)	.19	(.21)	.37	1.16	(1.11)	.30

TABLE 4.6. *Control of the presidency and change in national conditions, 1975–2010 (continued)*

	change under Republican presidents – change under Democratic presidents					
	Annual change (difference in means)			Long-run change (multiplier estimated with error correction models)		
	estimate	se	p-value	estimate	se	p-value
Uninsured (%)	.31	(.23)	.18	1.03	(.70)	.14
Reading scores (% of 13-year-olds w/ basic skills)	.17	(.19)	.39	-.57	(.33)	.08
Violent crimes (per 100,000 population)	.16	(.10)	.12	.71	(.35)	.04
Murders (per 100,000 population)	.16	(.15)	.32	.83	(.35)	.02
Improved more under Democrats Unauthorized immigrants living in U.S. (millions)	-.18	(.19)	.34	.49	(.19)	.01
Exports of goods and services (as % of GDP)	-.21	(.23)	.37	-.87	(.34)	.01
Budget surplus or deficit (as % of GDP)	-1.14	(.55)	.05	-4.96	(1.73)	<.01
Support for U.S. at U.N. (-1 to 1 scale)	.05	(.03)	.17	-.58	(.18)	<.01

For details on estimation procedure, see text and this chapter's appendix. Significance tests are two-tailed.

As a measure of performance, however, a difference in means test with time-series data is likely to be biased by autocorrelation and time trends. The final columns of the table therefore display the differences in change in national conditions under Republicans and Democrats estimated using error correction models (ECMs). These models account for dynamics by incorporating up to four annual lags of the measures as well as lags of party control of the presidency, with the number of lags chosen according to which resulting model explains the data in the most efficient fashion.[9] The models also include a quadratic time trend. Formally, the estimated model of change in an indicator Y in year t incorporating a total of L lags is written as follows:

$$\Delta Y_t = \alpha_0 + \sum_{l=1}^{L} \alpha_l Y_{t-l} + \sum_{l=1}^{L} \beta_l REP\_PRES_{t-l} + \delta_1 YEAR_t + \delta_2 YEAR_t^2 + \upsilon_t$$

(4.1)

For our purposes, the key estimate of interest from the ECM is known as the "long-run multiplier," calculated as the ratio $-\sum_{l=1}^{L} \beta_l \Big/ \sum_{l=1}^{L} \alpha_l$. It is the change in national conditions associated with Republican control of the presidency (compared to Democratic control) distributed over all future time periods. These long-run estimates, their standard errors, and the p-values associated with significance tests are shown in the table. The p-values are used to rank the national conditions from those which we are most confident improve under Republicans to those we are most confident improve under Democrats. Given that conditions are measured on so many different scales across issues, this is the best way to make comparisons across issues. Although researchers are often rightly advised to avoid making too much of significance tests and associated p-values, in this context the p-values themselves are meaningful quantities of interest. Quite literally, they are the relative degree of confidence Americans should have that there are true

---

[9] These models are more precisely called "dead-start" error correction models (De Boef and Keele 2008), as it assumed that change in control of the presidency has no immediate effect on national conditions and thus the models do not incorporate a term for the contemporaneous change in party control. The number of lags was chosen according to Akaike's Information Criterion (AIC). For each of the eighteen models, Ljung-Box tests did not detect serial correlation in the residuals. The full models may be found in this chapter's appendix.

differences in change in national conditions under Democratic and Republican presidents.

Here we see that the long-run change in many of these conditions is strongly associated with party control of the presidency. Using a significance threshold of .10, Americans can be confident that taxes and inflation became significantly lower under Republican presidents between 1975 and 2010. Under Democratic presidents, significant improvement occurred in the support for the United States at the United Nations, the national deficit, exports of goods and services, the number of unauthorized immigrants, crime, and reading scores. In many cases, the long-run impact associated with presidential control is not only significant but substantial. Compared to Democratic presidents, the legacy of Republican presidents is a reduction in taxes by nearly a percentage point and a decline in the inflation rate of nearly two percentage points. The long-run reduction in budget deficits associated with Democratic control is nearly 5 percent of GDP more than under Republicans; likewise, exports rise by nearly a full percentage point more of GDP.

A careful reader will note that the descriptions of these results scrupulously avoid invoking the language of causality. On their own, the data here do not provide definitive evidence that Democratic presidents actually caused deficits to shrink – or that Republican presidents' policies caused inflation to decline. This is because there are almost certainly unobserved factors that are correlated with both national conditions and which party successfully wins the presidency, and these factors undoubtedly have long-term impacts on future national conditions. One need not look very far for these factors: the analysis of presidential election returns in Chapter 3 shows the extent to which issue salience (which is almost certainly correlated with national conditions) affects whether a Democrat or Republican is elected president. Thus we cannot rule out the possibility that these factors may be confounds that render observed relationships spurious – or, just as damaging, may be acting as suppressors that cloak the true effects of policies on national conditions. (To be clear, the same concerns threaten the inferences that generations of scholars have made about partisan control and national economic conditions.) Rather, the point of the analysis is to explore whether Americans have experienced real differences in these conditions under Democratic and Republican presidencies – and whether these differences explain the long-term reputations of the parties as described in Chapter 3.

National conditions and issue ownership. We can think of the two sets of results displayed in Table 4.6 as corresponding to the inferences about party control of the presidency drawn by two different kinds of observers trying to make sense of the parties' performance on improving national conditions. As noted above, the estimates derived from differences in annual means do not account for dynamic factors that can confound the relationship between party control and national conditions. But given the lack of knowledge about national trends discussed earlier, these estimates would appear to represent the upper limit of what a typical American voter might know about the parties' relative records on these issues. The second set of estimates represents our best set of "educated guesses" about the long-term impact of Republican versus Democratic control of the presidency on national conditions. Many more sophisticated estimates are of course possible: for example, controls for exogenous shocks to the national economy might improve our estimates of change in national conditions such as poverty or energy prices. But absent the sort of issue-by-issue judgment calls that such more complex models would require, the estimates displayed in Table 4.6 provide measures of the relationship between party control and national conditions that are comparable across issues. To the extent that Americans are taking dynamics into account in their assessments of the effect of Republican and Democratic presidencies on the achievement of consensus goals, their evaluations should reflect the rankings shown in the table.[10]

A glance at Table 4.6 should immediately give us some pause about whether Americans use change in national conditions under Republican and Democratic presidents to assign ownership to the parties on different issues. With the exception of taxation and inflation for the Republicans, and reading test scores for the Democrats, none of the national conditions that are significantly associated with

---

[10] An even more difficult task for the typical voter would be to take partisan control of Congress into account as well when forming these assessments. As shown in this book's online appendix, they do not. Estimates that also incorporate congressional control produce the same finding as that presented here: no relationship is found among improvement in national conditions, party control of government, and issue ownership.

party control (according to the long-run estimates) are aligned with the long-run issue ownership estimates derived in the previous chapter. In fact, crime rates, unauthorized immigration, the deficit, support for the United States at the United Nations, and exports all improved significantly more under Democratic presidents than Republicans between 1975 and 2010 despite being conditions associated with Republican-owned issues.

The bivariate scatterplots in Figure 4.5 confirm these observations. They plot the *p*-values associated with the differences associated with party control in annual change (in the top graph) and long-run change (in the bottom graph) in national conditions against the parties' long-run ownership of the associated issues as estimated in Chapter 3. To the extent that Americans use these measures to determine which party is better able to handle particular issues, we would expect the points on the scatterplot to lie on the diagonal extending from the bottom left quadrant to the upper right quadrant of these graphs. This is true in neither case: as indicated by the best-fit regression lines traced on the graphs, there is no relationship whatsoever between these two variables.[11] An even more straightforward way to assess this question is simply to examine whether Americans "correctly" assign ownership to the party under which conditions improve more. In the graphs in Figure 4.5, correct classifications are plotted with dark circles; incorrect classifications are plotted with hollow circles. By this criterion, Americans correctly assign issue ownership based upon performance 44 percent of the time with regard to annual change in national conditions and 55 percent of the time with regard to long-run change – accuracy rates that are no better than guesses that would be yielded by merely flipping a coin.[12]

---

[11] The *R*-squared statistics associated with the bivariate regression lines in these plots are both less than .01. The regression coefficient on annual change in conditions is .59 with a robust standard error of 3.8; the coefficient on long-run change is -.13 with a robust standard error of 4.1.

[12] Not shown here is another way to examine this relationship, which is to assume that issue ownership reflects the public's collective memory of past party performance. However, regressions of issue ownership between 2000 and 2011 on the parties' performance over the entire four-decade period in fact yielded even weaker results than those discussed here. In these estimates, poor performance was slightly and insignificantly associated with issue ownership.

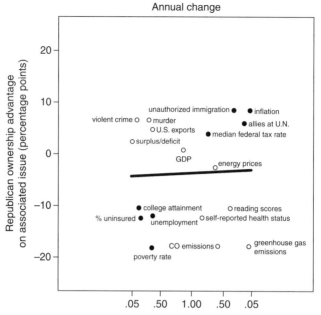

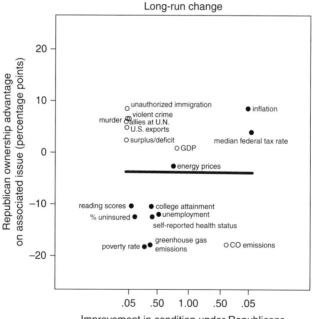

FIGURE 4.5. Change in national conditions, party control, and issue ownership. *Correct classifications: dark circles; incorrect classifications: hollow circles*

Conclusion: The Lack of a Relationship between Party Performance and Issue Ownership

By developing a comprehensive inventory of trends in important national conditions, estimating how they change with the party in control of the presidency, and examining the relationship between estimated change and issue ownership, these analyses definitively reject the premise that ownership is derived from the parties' relative performance on issues. Despite the fact that the environment is owned by the Democrats, air quality and greenhouse gas emissions improve no more under Democratic presidents than Republicans. The Republicans own the issue of crime, but violent crimes and murders have actually decreased significantly more under Democrats. Democrats own the issue of jobs, but the level of unemployment appears to be unaffected by party control of the presidency. Americans think the Republicans are better able to handle trade issues, but exports actually grow more under Democrats. Readers may not all agree that every one of these measures is an equally valid indicator of national conditions, and I duly refrain from interpreting these relationships as causal. Nevertheless the degree to which issue ownership, party control of the presidency, and real change in objective metrics of national progress are unrelated is nothing short of astounding.

Why do Americans consistently say one party is better than the other at dealing with particular national problems that fail to improve when that party controls the executive branch? In addition to the barriers to accountability discussed above, an explanation more generous to the American public mind is that in many issue domains, the real consequences of the parties' policies – whether they be No Child Left Behind's effect on student skills, the Clean Air Act's effect on air quality, or the Affordable Care Act's effect on the share of Americans without health insurance – may take years to unfold. These legacies are so long in the making that they will go undetected in analyses that look merely for relationships between party control and national conditions. Although this interpretation credits American voters with more foresight than is probably warranted, there is certainly some truth to the claim that the mixture of tools at a president's disposal – including legislation, executive orders and executive branch initiatives – allows for less immediate control over national conditions on some policy domains than others. In this sense, the relatively quick effect of Democratic and Republican fiscal policies on economic conditions identified by Hibbs and his intellectual descendants may be the exception rather than the rule. However, although this explanation helps us understand why Americans assign issue ownership to parties even when they do not noticeably make national conditions better, it does not tell us why the public ignores obvious, rapid improvements. During the period 1975 through 2010, three issues fell into this category: crime, the deficit, and trade – issues all owned by Republicans, but which both sets of performance analyses indicate improved significantly more under Democratic presidents. If issue ownership were driven solely by performance and Americans were updating their beliefs accordingly, these issues would currently stand on the Democratic side of the ledger.

This entire discussion raises a much more fundamental point. For the moment, let us grant the contention that the effects of policies take years to unfold, making it unlikely that change in national conditions occurs quickly enough for proper credit or blame to be assigned to the party that was responsible for the change when it held power. How, then, are voters expected to hold the parties accountable in an accurate way? Voters might attempt to do so by relying on the parties' sustained *efforts* to address consensus goals – rather than any immediate *results* – as noisy indicators of their actual performance on achieving these goals. Whether this is an accurate way to go about determining ultimate responsibility for the country's progress is, of course, debatable. After all, such an approach would boil down to making the assumption that, on average, lawmaking and national spending on issues such as crime, health care, education, and unauthorized immigration lead to improvements in national conditions on these issues.

This is of course an assumption that would be contested by many policy experts. It is also a way of thinking about the causes and effects of policy making for which we would be surprised to find many adherents in the United States. Our nation's political culture is particularly skeptical of government's ability to solve problems – a skepticism so eloquently captured by Ronald Reagan's declaration in his first inaugural address that "government is not the solution to our problem;

government is the problem." But as the next chapter shows overwhelmingly and decisively, this is exactly the approach that the American electorate appears to use when faced with the task of determining which party is better able to handle a particular issue. Americans assign issue ownership to the party that cares more about the issue, makes more laws about the issue, and spends more federal dollars on the issue – in short, the party that is more committed to using government to solve problems on the issue.

Appendix to Chapter 4

Question Wording for ANES Questions Used in Evaluations
of Policy Hypothesis

(Data Used to Construct Figures 4.1 and 4.2)

In the table below are the wordings for questions used by the ANES to
place respondents on policy scales. Each of these stems was followed
with a series of questions asking respondents to place themselves and
the parties or the parties' presidential candidates on the scales. In some
cases, branching format questions were used instead of actual scales.
Question wording comes directly from the codebooks associated with
each ANES Time Series Study (available at electionstudies.org).

In this book's online appendix is a list of all the ANES variable
numbers for the questions used in the analyses. The variable numbers
listed refer to the self-placement survey item; items for the parties and
candidates may typically be found in the ANES codebooks directly
following the self-placement items.

ISSUE	QUESTION WORDING FOR STEM (years asked) (*indicates that placements were of presidential candidates instead of parties)
Crime	There is much discussion about the best way to deal with the problem of urban unrest and rioting. Some say it is more important to use all available force to maintain law and order – no matter what results. Others say it is more important to correct the problems of poverty and unemployment that give rise to the disturbances. (1970, 1972, 1974, 1976)
	Some people are pretty upset about rioting and disturbances on college campuses and in high schools. Some feel sympathetic with the students and faculty who take part in these disturbances. Others think the schools should use police and the national guard to prevent or stop disturbances. And others fall somewhere between these extremes ... (1970, 1972)
	Some people are primarily concerned with doing everything possible to protect the legal rights of those accused of committing crimes. Others feel that it is more important to stop criminal activity even at the risk of reducing the rights of the accused ... (1970, 1972, 1976, 1978)
	Some people say that the best way to reduce crime is to address the social problems that cause crime, like bad schools, poverty and joblessness ... other people say the best way to reduce crime is to make sure that criminals are caught, convicted and punished ... (1996*)
Environment	There are many sources of air and water pollution; one of them is private industry. Some say the government should force private industry to stop its polluting. Others believe industries should be left alone to handle these matters in their own way ... (1970)
	Some people think we need much tougher government regulations on business in order to protect the environment...others think that current regulations to protect the environment are already too much of a burden on business ... (1996, 1998, 2000*)
	Next, we'd like to ask whether you favor, oppose, or neither favor nor oppose a series of ways that the federal government might try to reduce future global warming. Power plants put gases into the air that could cause global warming. Do you favor, oppose, or neither favor nor oppose the federal government lowering the amount of these gases that power plants are allowed to put into the air? [Do you favor that a great deal, moderately, or a little?/Do you oppose that a great deal, moderately, or a little?] (2008*)

(continued)

(continued)

ISSUE	QUESTION WORDING FOR STEM (years asked) (*indicates that placements were of presidential candidates instead of parties)
Foreign affairs	There is much talk about "hawks" and "doves" in connection with Vietnam, and considerable disagreement as to what action the United States should take in Vietnam. Some people think we should do everything necessary to win a complete military victory, no matter what results. Some people think we should withdraw completely from Vietnam right now, no matter what results … (1970, 1972)
	Some people feel it is important for us to try very hard to get along with Russia. Others feel it is a big mistake to try too hard to get along with Russia … (1980, 1984, 1988)
	Some people think that the United States should become much more involved in the internal affairs of Central American countries. Others believe that the U.S. should become much less involved in this area … (1984, 1986)
	Some people believe the United States should solve international problems by using diplomacy and other forms of international pressure and use military force only if absolutely necessary … others believe diplomacy and pressure often fail and the U.S. must be ready to use military force … (2004)
Health care	There is much concern about the rapid rise in medical and hospital costs. Some people feel there should be a government insurance plan which would cover all medical and hospital expenses for everyone … others feel that all medical expenses should be paid by individuals through private insurance plans like Blue Cross or other company paid plans … (1970, 1972, 1976, 1978, 1988, 1994, 1996*, 2008*)
	Do you favor, oppose, or neither favor nor oppose the U.S. government paying for all necessary medical care for all Americans? [Do you favor that a great deal, moderately, or a little? / Do you oppose that a great deal, moderately, or a little?] (2008*)
Inflation	There is a great deal of talk these days about rising prices and the cost of living in general. Some feel that the government must do everything possible to combat the problem of inflation immediately or it will get worse. Others say that the problem of inflation is temporary and that no government action is necessary … (1970, 1972)
Jobs	Some people feel that the government in Washington should see to it that every person has a job and a good standard of living. Others think the government should just let each person get ahead on his own … (1972, 1974, 1976, 1978, 1980, 1982, 1984*, 1988, 1992, 1994, 1996*, 2000, 2004, 2008*)

(continued)

ISSUE	QUESTION WORDING FOR STEM (years asked) (*indicates that placements were of presidential candidates instead of parties)
Military	Some people believe that we should spend much less money for defense ... others feel that defense spending should be greatly increased ... (1980, 1982, 1984, 1986, 1988, 1990, 1992, 1996, 2008, 2004, 2008*)
Taxes	As you know, in our tax system people who earn a lot of money already have to pay higher rates of income tax than those who earn less. Some people think that those with high incomes should pay even more of their income into taxes than they do now. Others think that the rates shouldn't be different at all—that everyone should pay the same portion of their income, no matter how much they make...(1972, 1976)
	Some political leaders think federal income taxes should be cut by 30% over the next three years. Other political leaders think this would be a bad policy for the government to follow. Do you have an opinion on this matter, or haven't you thought much about this?...Which of these statements best describes what you would like to see happen over the next three years? Over the next three years, federal income taxes:
	1. Should not be cut
	2. Should be cut by 10%
	3. Should be cut by 20%
	4. Should be cut by 30%
	5. Should be cut by more than 30% (1980)
	As you may recall, [Congress passed/President Bush signed] a big tax cut last year. Did you favor or oppose the tax cut, or is this something you haven't thought about? Did you [favor/oppose] the tax cut strongly or not strongly? (2002)
	There has been a lot of talk recently about doing away with the tax on large inheritances, the so-called "[estate/ death] tax". Do you favor or oppose doing away with the [estate/death tax]? Do you [favor/oppose] doing away with the [estate/death] tax strongly or not strongly?...Which would you say is closer to the [Democratic Party's/ Republican Party's] position – that they favor or oppose doing away with the [estate/death] tax? (2002)

Control of the presidency and change in national conditions, 1975–2010
(Full models generating estimates of long-run change in Table 4.6)

DEPENDENT VARIABLE (annual change)	INDEPENDENT VARIABLES												p-value of Ljung–Box test
	Lags of Democratic presidency				Lags of levels of DV				year	year²	intercept	N	
	1	2	3	4	1	2	3	4					
Reading scores	.23	.03			.26	-.71**	.10	.37*	-5.01	.00	4993.66	34	.89
Self-reported well-being	.49	-.45	-.75	1.11+	-.77***	-.14			48.84*	-.01*	-48612.66*	35	.51
CO₂ emissions	-478.69	235.38	2729.53*		-.47+	.44	-.07		-13719.61	3.32	1418367.05	37	.79
Energy prices	-.11	.35			-.25				-16.91*	.00*	16754.86*	35	.99
Exports	.92**		-.35	-.18	-.50+	-.01	.06	-.41+	-2.68	.00	2570.07	36	.34
Change in GDP	2.65*	-2.50+			-.73**	-.34+			25.34+	-.01+	-25192.75+	36	.95
Greenhouse gas emissions	-31.80				-.88**				24184.50**	-6.04**	-2.42e+07**	20	.87
Inflation	.99+	.14	-.14	-.38*	-.31+	-.32*	-.09	-.10	-21.03	.01	21062.20	36	.78
Murder rate	.12	.02	-.14	.13	-.01	-.25	-.15	.53*	10.48**	-.00**	-10376.32*	36	.32
College attainment	-.01	.21+	.06	.13	-.29*	-.18			-5.5*	.00**	5494.58**	36	.81
Poverty	-.34	.33	.43*	-.65***	.55**	-.84***	.19	-.10	.12	-.00	-118.19	36	.88
Surplus/deficit	1.36***				-.27***				23.63+	-.01+	-23528.25+	36	.61
Tax rate paid by median family	.62*				-.75***				17.72*	-.00*	-17500.53*	36	.68
Unauthorized immigration	-.09	-.36	-.31	-.17	-.37	-.58	-.37	-.58	75.99**	-.02*	-75986.79**	20	.50
Unemployment rate	-.86+	.69			.02	-.43+			-13.19+	.00+	13161.93+	36	.99
Uninsured	-.35			-.18*	-.34*				7.60	-.00	-7613.39	36	.81
Support for U.S. at U.N.	.01	-.21***	.10+		-.07	.02	.18	.35	3.59*	-.00*	-3587.90*	34	.56
Violent crime	.07	.06	-.17+	-.20*	.06	-.17	-.28	.03	12.90**	-.00**	-12837.43**	36	.19

Error correction models. Estimates significantly different from zero at +p<.10; *p<.05; **p<.01; ***p<.001 (two-tailed tests, robust standard errors).

Lag length (out of a maximum of four possible lags) chosen by AIC.

5

Partisan Priorities

The Source of Issue Ownership

Thus far, our investigations of how Americans determine which party is better able to handle particular issues have come up short. The American electorate neither accords issue ownership to parties because it prefers their policies nor because the parties deliver superior performance. This chapter explores the final proposed explanation for issue ownership: the priorities hypothesis. It proceeds from the definition of prioritization introduced in Chapter 2: a party's commitment to devoting scarce time, resources, and political capital to address consensus goals. It analyzes the parties' priorities through the familiar triumvirate of considering the party as organization, the party in the electorate, and the party in government.

I find that the priorities of all three elements of the parties are strongly correlated with issue ownership. For the past four decades, party elites and party voters have consistently said that their parties' owned issues are more important problems than other issues, that they should be high governmental priorities, and that spending on these issues should be increased compared to other issues. These priorities are reflected by the party in government, as when they are in power in Washington, Democrats and Republicans spend more federal dollars and enact more major legislation on their parties' owned issues than other issues.

The chapter concludes by proposing a new definition of issue ownership that reflects this book's findings. The new definition remains true to the meaning of issue ownership as introduced by previous scholarship, but it brings needed clarity to our understanding of the concept that is empirically justified by the analyses found here.

PARTISAN PRIORITIES

To determine the priorities of America's two major political parties requires first deciding who counts as a "partisan." Happily, this decision was made by V. O. Key in his 1942 classic *Politics, Parties and Pressure Groups* and has been followed by generations of scholars of political parties thereafter. Key argued that a comprehensive understanding of parties can be reached by examining them through three different lenses: as the "regulars" who populate party organizations, as the rank-and-file voters who identify with the party in the electorate, and as coalitions of party politicians in government. I take the same approach here. The "party as organization" is considered with surveys of delegates to the parties' national conventions and strong party identifiers who are deeply engaged in the political process. These data show that party elites have been polarized for the past forty years on which issues are the nation's most important problems along the lines of the issues the parties own. Republican activists consistently say that lawmakers should focus on problems such as national security, crime, and high taxes. By contrast, Democrats believe issues such as education, the environment, and health care should be the government's priority. Surveys of Democratic and Republican voters – the "party in the electorate" – show that rank-and-file partisans echo the same priorities as their leaders. Two analyses then find that these priorities are pursued in turn by the "party in government." First, major legislation is more likely to be enacted on Democratic- and Republican-owned issues to the extent that those parties are in control in Washington. Second, the parties direct government dollars toward programs and agencies devoted to the issues they own.

The Priorities of Party Elites

Measuring the sincere preferences of party elites presents a problem that arguably has not been addressed by previous work on issue ownership, which has focused on elites' public pronouncements. This approach includes analyses of the degree to which parties emphasize their owned issues in party platforms or manifestos (Budge and Farlie 1983), in news stories generated by presidential campaigns (Petrocik 1996), or in campaign television ads and speeches (Petrocik, Benoit, and Hansen 2003). In none of these cases can we be assured that these are purely sincere expressions of party priorities, as parties and candidates undoubtedly strategically calibrate their communications to appeal to the electorate. Fortunately, another source providing insights on the issue priorities of party elites exists that is much less likely to be biased by such strategic calculations: surveys of the elites themselves. Questions about issue priorities were asked in representative sample surveys of delegates attending the Republican and Democratic National Conventions in five of the six presidential elections between 1972 through 1992.[1] These surveys were confidential; furthermore, because they were academic studies, respondents knew that results would not be published until well after the end of the presidential campaigns and would be unlikely to garner much attention from news media. Thus there is much less cause for concern about these responses being insincere expressions of the true priorities of the party elites than there is for communications directed at the broader public.

Two questions appearing on different subsets of these surveys will serve as indicators of the relative issue priorities of partisan elites. In three of the surveys (1984, 1988, and 1992), delegates were asked their preferences on whether federal spending on a list of consensus goals should be increased, decreased, or kept the same – questions similar to the federal spending questions discussed in Chapter 2. In a different subset of three surveys (1972, 1980, and 1984), delegates were asked an open-ended question asking them to name the nation's most important problems.[2] Although this question should generally elicit answers that are good proxies for respondents' true priorities, it appears that this was not entirely the case for two issues – the economy and foreign affairs. Delegates from the out-party were more likely to name these issues as

---

[1] Sources for these data are Herrera and Miller (1995), Jackson, Bostis, and Baer (1988), Jackson and Brown (1988), Miller et al. (1976), and Miller and Jennings (1988, 1995).

[2] Rather than providing the verbatim responses themselves, the datasets include the issues mentioned as coded by the scholars conducting the surveys. In some cases, I re-coded these data to correspond with the list of issues developed in Chapter 3. Details of this re-coding process may be found in this book's online appendix. Delegates could name up to three national problems in 1972 and 1980 and up to four in 1984.

"problems" than those from the in-party, indicating that these issues are proxies of expression of allegiance or opposition to the party in control of the White House.[3] Therefore responses to the most important problem question naming either of these two issues are excluded from the analyses.[4]

To obtain estimates of the issue priorities of party elites in more recent years, I turn to the American National Election Studies cumulative datafile, which includes biennial surveys with representative samples of American adults. In the ANES, respondents indicate their federal spending preferences by answering a battery of issue-specific items similar to those appearing in the surveys of convention delegates. The surveys also ask respondents whether they participated in several different political activities during the most recent campaign. To identify respondents most likely to be members of party organizations, I restricted the dataset only to those who reported participating in all of three different activities in support of a candidate or party during the most recent campaign: attending a meeting or rally, working or volunteering for a campaign, and making a campaign donation. Among these respondents (representing just 1 percent of American adults), I further limited the analysis to those identifying as "strong" Democrats or Republicans. I assume that the resulting dataset consists primarily of party activists: it includes just 73 individuals out of the 11,642 Americans interviewed by the ANES between 1994 and 2008. It provides as much insight as possible into the views of those involved in the party organizations as can be derived from surveys with nationally representative samples of Americans.

Estimates of the relative priorities of party elites derived from these measures are displayed in Figure 5.1. The top graph displays issues arrayed by the difference (in percentage points) in the share of Republican delegates naming them as the nation's most important problem minus the share of Democrats doing so. To facilitate the

---

[3] Over the three surveys, delegates from the party not in control of the White House were on average six percentage points more likely to name these two issues as national problems compared to delegates from the party controlling the presidency.

[4] As noted in Chapter 3, the economy and foreign affairs are categorized by Petrocik and colleagues as "performance issues" and excluded from their analyses of the relationship between issue salience and election results (Petrocik 1996; Petrocik, Benoit, and Hansen 2003).

display of information, only issues on which there were statistically significant differences in prioritization (at $p < .05$) by the two parties' delegates of three percentage points or more are shown. The bottom graph displays the relative spending priorities of the two parties' convention delegates in 1984, 1988, and 1992 and the priorities of all party activists surveyed by the ANES between 1994 and 2008. It plots issues by the net percentage of Republicans favoring a spending increase (that is, those supporting an increase minus those favoring a cut) minus the net support for a spending increase similarly calculated among Democrats.[5] The issues displayed on this graph are only those on which there were statistically significant spending preferences between the parties.

The graphs in Figure 5.1 show that the relative priorities of party elites are substantial and consistent across the entire four-decade span. In the results from the 1970s and 1980s shown in Figure 5.1.a, the deficit, inflation, and the military appear repeatedly as issues mentioned significantly more often as national problems by Republican elites than Democrats; the opposite is true for the jobs issue. Figure 5.1.b shows that from 1984 through 2008, net support for spending on crime and the military by Republican elites outstripped these issues' support among Democrats multiple times. By contrast, elite Democratic support for spending on the environment, the homeless, schools, and Social Security was repeatedly significantly higher than that of Republicans. (The differences were so stark among party activists in the ANES that statistically significantly different priorities on four issues were found among them despite their very small sample.)

A reader cracking open this book to Figure 5.1 could be forgiven for assuming that these were graphs of issue ownership: the issue priorities of party elites and the issues owned by the two parties are uncannily similar. A comparison of these graphs with the four-decade estimates of issue ownership from Chapter 3 (as displayed in the final column of Table 3.2) leads to an absolutely striking conclusion. *Every* issue significantly prioritized by Republican elites at one point or another between 1972 and 2008 was owned by the Republican Party over the

---

[5] The theoretical range of this differences-in-differences estimate is thus 200 percent (if all Republicans favored a spending increase and all Democrats favored cuts) to -200 percent (if vice versa).

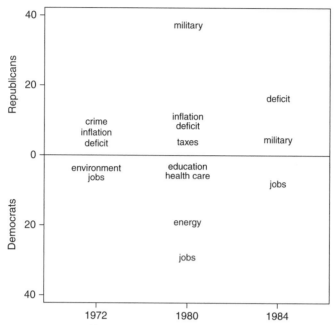

a. Most important problems named by convention delegates
   percentage difference in those naming issue as problem

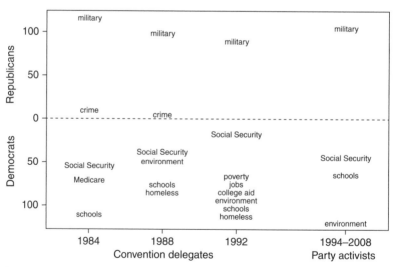

b. Federal spending priorities among convention delegates and party activists
   percentage difference in net support for spending increase

FIGURE 5.1. The Priorities of partisan elites.
Sources: see text.

same four-decade period. Likewise, *every* issue significantly prioritized by Democratic elites was owned by the Democratic Party.[6]

In the next section of this chapter, the relationship between party priorities and issue ownership will be analyzed in more detail. For the moment, however, let us note how remarkable this finding is. It is derived from survey questions that on their face would seem to be about different concepts: spending and concern for national problems on the one hand, and which party can better handle issues on the other. These questions are put in different surveys to very different populations: those at the most elite levels of participation in party activities and nationally representative samples of Americans. Nevertheless, they reach the same conclusion. The issues that Democratic and Republican elites sincerely care about and on which they wish to spend government funds are the same issues that the public says the two parties own.

The Priorities of Partisans in the Electorate

Having shown the strong relationship between issue ownership and the issue priorities of party activists, I now turn to the party in the electorate. Here I document the issue priorities among rank-and-file Democratic and Republican party identifiers. Previous work on attitude formation leads us to strongly expect that the concerns of ordinary partisans will mirror those of party elites. Scholars have shown that exposure to elite partisan cues leads many party identifiers to change their attitudes about policies – even on issues such as abortion and gay rights that are presumed to be associated with long-standing moral principles (Bailey, Sigelman, and Wilcox 2003; Layman and Carsey 2002; Layman et al 2010; Zaller 1992). As we shall see, a similarly strong relationship will be found between the issue priorities of party elites and everyday partisans in the electorate.

To assess the relative prioritization of the parties in the electorate, I revisit the survey questions first discussed in Chapter 2. There I analyzed Americans' responses to questions on the nation's priorities for the president and Congress (collected by Pew) and their responses

---

[6] To draw this conclusion, I make the uncontroversial pairings of support for Medicare spending with the issue of health care, homelessness with the issue of poverty, and college aid with the issue of education.

to questions about national spending on consensus goals (from the General Social Survey) to demonstrate widespread support for government action and spending on a series of consensus goals even in 2010 and 2011, an era believed to be defined by a strong desire for limited government. Fortunately, these surveys extend into the past: Pew has been asking questions about the nation's priorities since 1994; the GSS has included questions about national spending on its surveys since 1972.

Figure 5.2 displays the over-time priorities of Democratic and Republican voters in a similar fashion to those of party elites: the percentage difference in prioritization of different consensus goals of American voters identifying with the two parties.[7] In Figure 5.2.a, issues are arrayed by the percentage of Republicans naming the issue as a "top priority" for the president and Congress minus the share of Democrats.[8] Republicans were consistently more likely to name domestic security, immigration, the military, and (in five out of the six years) taxes as top priorities; Democrats were significantly more likely to name education, energy, the environment, health care, jobs, and poverty as top priorities in nearly every survey. National spending priorities, shown in Figure 5.2.b, follow suit. Most of the issues displayed here fall below the line, reflecting the fact that the battery of spending items on the GSS is heavily tipped toward Democratic priorities. Nevertheless, the relative support for spending on these issues among partisans is very similar to the patterns already seen.

Thus the priorities among rank-and-file Democrats and Republicans in the electorate are strikingly similar to the priorities of party elites – and therefore the issues owned by the two parties. Party elites and their voters are in agreement about the kinds of problems that should be the government's focus and the kinds of consensus goals toward which federal dollars should be directed. Who affects whom (party elites influencing party rank-and-file or vice versa) is an interesting

---

[7] In the Pew surveys, voters are defined as registered voters who reported voting in the most recent national elections (in surveys administered in 1997, 2002, 2005, and 2011) or those who said they were likely to vote in upcoming national elections (surveys in 1994 and 2008). In the GSS samples, voters are defined as those reporting voting in the most recent presidential elections. As is done throughout this book, those who "lean" toward one party or another are included as partisans.

[8] In some years, multiple items were asked about the same issue and were averaged.

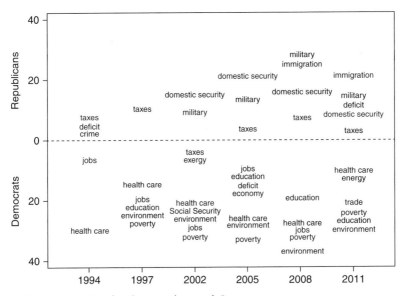

a. Voters' priorities for the President and Congress, 1994–2011
   percentage difference in those naming goal as a top priority
   Source: Pew Research Center.

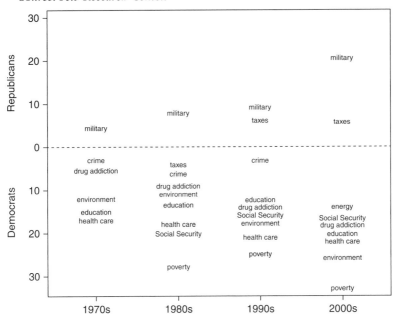

b. Voters' national spending priorities, 1972–2010
   percentage difference in net support for spending increase
   Source: General social survey cumulative file.

FIGURE 5.2. The priorities of partisans in the electorate.

question, but not one that needs to be explored here. For the purposes of understanding where issue ownership comes from, the decisive finding is that ordinary voters who identify as Republicans or Democrats overwhelmingly share the priorities of their parties' leaders. These voters can thus be legitimately considered as supporters for government action and federal spending on these priorities when their favored party gains power in Washington.

The Priorities of Parties in Government

A final pair of analyses explores whether the priorities of partisan elites and voters are reflected in the actions taken by Democrats and Republicans in enacting federal laws and allocating the budget. Where the previous chapter's investigations into the parties' relative performance focused on results, these analyses have to do instead with the parties' *efforts* to focus government action and spending on specific issues. Both analyses reveal a substantial and unambiguous relationship between the issue priorities of the Democrats and Republicans when they control the government and the issues that the parties own.

Major federal legislation. David Mayhew compiled a well-regarded inventory of major laws enacted by Congress for his classic study *Divided We Govern* (1991). In his book, Mayhew shows that divided control of government – long believed to be associated with "gridlock" that impedes Washington from addressing important national problems – has little effect on whether important laws are enacted in any particular legislative session. To reach this conclusion, Mayhew required an objective way to identify the universe of laws considered "important." His list relies both on contemporaneous accounts by news media and other sources of the importance of enacted legislation as well as on the retrospective judgments of policy experts on those laws for which enough time had elapsed since enactment to make these judgments possible. As of this writing, Mayhew has updated this list through 2008; it now includes a total of 370 laws enacted since 1947 (Mayhew 2012). The advantage of using the *Divided We Govern* dataset for this study is not just that Mayhew's list is widely respected by political scientists and has been used in scores of subsequent articles and books on policy making in Washington. It is also that Mayhew's dataset was developed for a completely different purpose than the one here, providing assurance that the selection of laws for analysis has nothing to do with issue ownership.

To prepare the *Divided We Govern* dataset for analysis, I used Mayhew's brief description of each piece of enacted legislation to code the laws by issue. Up to three codes could be assigned per law. For example, a law passed in 1973 that Mayhew describes as providing aid for development of health maintenance organizations is coded, quite obviously, under the issue of "health care." One of the final major laws in the dataset is the United States–India Nuclear Cooperation Approval and Nonproliferation Enhancement Act of 2008, for which Mayhew's synopsis is "Nuclear trade agreement with India. Gives India access to U.S. civilian nuclear technology." This law was thus coded as both "military" and "foreign affairs." A full list of all laws and their issue codes may be found in this chapter's appendix.

For comparability to previous analyses in this book, I limit the dataset to laws passed between the first session of Congress to be convened entirely in the 1970s (the 92nd session, which began in early 1971) through the final session in Mayhew's dataset (the 110th session, ending in 2008). A very simple way to explore whether parties are more likely to enact important legislation on their owned issues is to compare the average number of such laws passed on each issue under sessions of united Democratic control (that is, where Democrats control the presidency and both chambers of Congress), united Republican control, and divided party control of the government. These figures are displayed in the first four columns of Table 5.1. Here we see that over the past four decades, unified governments under Republican control enacted a greater number of important laws than Democrats on Republican-owned issues such as domestic security, the military, and immigration. The opposite was true for important laws on Democratic issues such as poverty, education, and the environment.

Although this approach is straightforward, it ignores what happens under divided government and thus leaves valuable data on the table about how differential control of Congress and the presidency affects lawmaking. This information can be taken into account with a more sophisticated multiple regression approach in which the unit of analysis is issue-session. The number of laws enacted per issue per session is "count data," in that it takes on possible values of zero and the positive integers. Thus I use a count regression model in which the number

TABLE 5.1. *Control of Government and Enactment of Important Laws, 1971–2008*

Issue	Mean number of laws enacted per congressional session by partisan control of government				Mean difference in number of laws under Republican control compared to Democratic control	
	Unified Republican control	Divided control	Unified Democratic control	Actual	Actual	Estimates that account for differential effects of control of Congress, presidency
Domestic security	1.33	.79	.00	1.33	1.97+	
Military	1.00	.93	.33	.67	.65	
Foreign affairs	1.33	1.07	.67	.66	.55	
Immigration	.33	.21	.00	.33	.35	
Economy	1.00	1.07	1.00	.00	.24	
Jobs	.00	.43	.00	.00	.14	
Taxes	1.00	1.21	1.67	-.67	-.16	
Deficit	.00	.43	.33	-.33	-.19	
Social Security	.00	.29	.33	-.33	-.26	
Trade	.67	.36	1.00	-.33	-.28	
Crime	.00	.36	.67	-.67	-.35	
Energy	.67	.50	1.00	-.33	-.49	
Health care	.33	.86	.67	-.34	-.59	
Poverty	.33	1.50	1.00	-.67	-1.04	
Education	.00	.64	1.33	-1.33	-1.26+	
Environment	.67	1.14	2.33	-1.66	-2.05**	

Estimates in final column of table are average predictive differences estimated from a Poisson model. See text and this chapter's appendix for additional details.

Estimates significantly different from zero at +$p<.10$; *$p<.05$; **$p<.01$; ***$p<.001$ (two-tailed tests, robust standard errors clustered on congressional session).

of important laws Y_{ij} enacted in congressional session i on issue j is modeled as a random variable that follows the Poisson distribution.[9] The parameter of interest in this distribution is the mean μ_{ij}, and it is assumed to be a function of the issue in question, which party controls the presidency and Congress, and their interaction as follows:

$$\mu_{ij} = \exp[\alpha + \alpha^p pres\_control_i + \alpha^c congress\_control_i$$

$$+ \sum_{j=1}^{J=16} \beta_j issue_j + \beta_j^{\,p}(pres\_control_i \times issue_j)$$

$$+ \beta_j^{\,c}(congress\_control_i \times issue_j)] + \varepsilon_{ij} \qquad (5.1)$$

In this model, *pres_control_i* is scored 1 if a Republican holds the presidency during session i and -1 for a Democratic president; similarly *congress_control_i* is scored 1 if both the House and Senate are under Republican control, -1 if both are under Democratic control, and zero if one party controls each chamber. The variables *issue_1 ... issue_16* are indicator terms assigned to each of the consensus issues analyzed in this book (except for inflation, the only issue on which no laws in the Mayhew dataset were enacted after 1970).

The model was used to generate estimates of the number of important laws per session expected for each issue under unified Republican and Democratic control of the government. The final column of Table 5.1 displays issues sorted by the estimated difference in the number of laws per session on each issue expected under Republican control minus the number expected under Democratic control. These estimates confirm the earlier, simpler tally: important legislation on Republican-owned issues is more likely to become law when Republicans control the presidency and Congress; the opposite is true for Democratic-owned issues. A horizontal line is drawn in the table separating issues on which major legislation is enacted more under Republicans than Democrats. Statistically significant differences in lawmaking between the two parties exist on only a few issues. But the enactments of important laws are strongly correlated with the parties' long-term ownership of

[9] This distribution has the probability mass function $\Pr\left[Y_{ij} = y\right] = \dfrac{e^{-\mu_{ij}}\mu_{ij}^{\,y}}{y!}$. A test for overdispersion failed to reject the null that these data are distributed Poisson ($p = .15$). Additional details about these estimates may be found in this chapter's appendix.

the issues. Above the line are three issues on which the Republican Party enjoyed an unambiguous issue-ownership advantage during the period in which these laws were enacted: domestic security, the military, and immigration. Below the line are five issues the Democrats owned significantly over the same period: Social Security, health care, poverty, education, and the environment. In some cases, the differences in effects of party control are significant and substantial. If the patterns established over the past four decades sustain themselves, we can be confident in the expectation that unified Democratic control should yield two additional important laws on the environment to be passed per congressional session – and one law on education – compared to unified Republican control. The opposite is true for major legislation on domestic security, which has been enacted significantly more frequently under Republican than Democratic control.

Allocation of federal expenditures. Previous work leads to relatively strong expectations about the relationship between the party that controls the government and spending on specific issues, which has been explored by an extensive literature on what has come to be known as the "mandate model" of elections. The general approach of this line of research is to examine allocations of national budgets across representative democracies to determine if the issues emphasized in a party's platform (known in most other parts of the world by the rather more grand term "party manifesto") are apportioned a greater share of the budget when the party gains power. Ian Budge and Richard I. Hofferbert have argued this is true in the United States, although subsequent work found the relationship to be less substantial and significant than originally thought (Budge and Hofferbert 1990; King et al 1993; Thome 1999). Additional research has found relationships between the election of left-wing parties and the size of government and the amount of social welfare expenditure (Blais, Blake, and Dion 1993; Bräuninger 2005). Country-specific analyses have found evidence of this relationship in Great Britain (Hofferbert and Budge 1992) but less so in Canada (Pétry 1995).

A related line of work with a long lineage in political science has found a strong relationship between partisanship and policies in the American states (examples include Berry et al 1998; Erikson, Wright, and McIver 1993; Klingman and Lammers 1984; and Sharkansky and Hofferbert 1969). Some of this research has examined spending on specific issues and programs (Garand 1985; Garand and Hendrick

1991; Peterson 1995). The most extensive recent work in this area has been conducted by William G. Jacoby and Saundra K. Schneider, who use a scaling model to place state expenditures on a range of issues on a single-dimensional continuum (Jacoby and Schneider 2001, 2009). Republican-owned issues (including corrections and law enforcement) generally fall on one side of the resulting scale, Democratic-owned issues (including health care and education) on the other. States with more liberal, Democratic voters are more likely to have budgets that emphasize Democratic issues, and vice versa (Jacoby and Schneider 2009: 19).

Nevertheless, no systematic analysis has ever directly explored the relationship between issue ownership and federal spending in the United States. I do so here with over-time data on federal outlays compiled by the White House Office of Management and Budget 2012a: Table 3.2). The OMB classifies expenditures by government function, many of which can be assigned in a straightforward manner to the issue categories analyzed throughout this book (as shown in Table 5.2). Determining federal spending on two additional important issues requires using different data made available by the OMB. Domestic security spending is not assigned a separate function code, but outlays for the Department of Homeland Security are calculated by the OMB along with those for all other cabinet-level agencies. Furthermore, the OMB has revisited budgets prior to the department's establishment in 2002 and generated annual historical estimates of federal dollars spent on domestic security spending (White House Office of Management and Budget 2012a: Table 4.1). Thus I use actual and estimated DHS spending as a measure of federal spending on domestic security. The issue of taxes also requires special consideration because it is not a spending category per se and thus does not appear in the OMB's tables of federal outlays. However, the OMB does compile records of federal tax receipts – including income, corporate, payroll, estate, excise and gift taxes. As is done throughout this book, I consider cuts in taxation as "spending" on the issue of taxes and thus decreases and increases in the annual sum of all of federal taxes serve as indicators of, respectively, increases and decreases in spending on taxes.[10] All told, relevant spending data can be identified for twelve of the consensus issues analyzed in this book.

---

[10] These are calculated from White House Office of Management and Budget 2012a (Tables 2.1 and 2.5).

TABLE 5.2. *Categorization of government spending functions by issue*

Issue	OMB Function Codes, except where noted
Crime	751 Federal law enforcement activities
	753 Federal correctional activities
	754 Criminal justice assistance
Domestic security	Department of Homeland Security
	(actual spending or imputed by OMB from historical budget data)
Education	501 Elementary, secondary, and vocational education
	502 Higher education
	503 Research and general education aids
	702 Veterans' education, training, and rehabilitation
Energy	272 Energy conservation
	274 Emergency energy preparedness
	276 Energy information, policy, and regulation
Environment	304 Pollution control and abatement
Foreign affairs	151 International development and humanitarian assistance
	152 International security assistance
	153 Conduct of foreign affairs
	154 Foreign information and exchange activities
Health care	551 Health care services
	552 Health research and training
	554 Consumer and occupational health and safety
	571 Medicare
	703 Hospital and medical care for veterans
Jobs	504 Training and employment
	505 Other labor services
Military	051 Department of Defense-Military
	053 Atomic energy defense activities
	054 Defense-related activities
Poverty	451 Community development
	452 Area and regional development
	506 Social services
	603 Unemployment compensation
	604 Housing assistance
	605 Food and nutrition assistance
	609 Other income security
	701 Income security for veterans
Social Security	651 Social security
Taxes	all taxes collected by the federal government (includes income, corporate, estate, excise and gift taxes)

In contrast to other analyses in this chapter, the analyses here begin in the 1980s – specifically, federal fiscal year 1982. This fiscal year started on October 1, 1981, making it the first in which Republican Ronald Reagan presided over the federal budget. Analyses of federal spending (not shown here) beginning in the 1970s reveal a relationship between issue ownership and spending that is a much more faint rendition of the strong patterns that I will proceed to demonstrate have been in place since the beginning of Reagan's presidency. There are a number of possible reasons for this, all of which have to do with a lack of sharp polarization in the 1970s on budget issues that later become flashpoints of partisan conflict in the 1980s. The Vietnam War likely constrained the amount of discretion available in developing military budgets, and it left little taste for defense spending among members of either party in its immediate aftermath. (Military spending as a percentage of the federal budget fell from 42 percent in 1970 to 23 percent in 1980; levels of military spending during this period are correlated with an annual time counter at -.93). The anti-tax revolt that would ultimately manifest itself as an item of faith among Republicans did not begin in earnest until 1978 with the passage of California's Proposition 13. As shown earlier in this chapter, environmentalism ranked high on the list of Democratic concerns in the 1970s, but nevertheless the decade began with the creation of the Environmental Protection Agency via an executive order issued by Republican Richard Nixon in 1970 – which was followed by substantial increases in federal expenditures on the environment. Factors such as these dampened distinctions between the two parties in the 1970s on allocations of government spending that would come into full relief in the 1980s, and thus the analysis begins there.

The measure of interest is annual spending on each issue as a percentage of all federal expenditures for that year. Using shares of federal expenditures instead of actual dollars better captures the fiscal trade-offs made among different issues. As in the performance analyses discussed in the previous chapter, analyzing change in spending – rather than levels of spending – is more likely to capture the effect of decisions made by elected officials net of any secular trends in spending patterns. The estimation strategy applied in the analysis of government expenditure is similar to that used to examine the parties' relative performance in Chapter 4. I again use error correction models

(ECMs) to estimate the long-run impact of control of the presidency and Congress on spending patterns. The specifications of the ECMs are similar to those employed in the tests of the performance hypothesis. They account for dynamics by incorporating up to four annual lags of the dependent variable and party control of the presidency as well as a quadratic time trend.[11] These estimates thus address the concerns researchers have expressed regarding dynamics in the analysis of party control and federal budgets (King et al 1993; Thome 1999). Formally, the estimated model of change in spending on issue Y in year t incorporating a total of L lags is written as follows:

$$\Delta Y_t = \alpha_0 + \sum_{l=1}^{L} \alpha_l Y_{t-l} + \sum_{l=1}^{L} \beta_l REP\_PRES_{t-l}$$

$$+ \sum_{l=1}^{L} \delta_l REP\_CONG_{t-l} + \phi_1 YEAR_t + \phi_2 YEAR_t^2 + \upsilon_t \qquad (5.2)$$

As before, the estimate of interest is the long-run multiplier, here calculated as the ratio $-\sum_{l=1}^{L}\beta_l + \delta_l \Big/ \sum_{l=1}^{L}\alpha_l$, which is the change in spending on an issue associated with unified Republican control of the government (that is, control of both the presidency and Congress) compared to unified Democratic control distributed over all future time periods. (See the discussion in Chapter 4 for more details about the ECM estimation method.)

Estimates from the ECMs are displayed in Table 5.3. The issues are sorted based on the p-values on the long-run multiplier estimates from the ECM. Thus at the top of the table are the issues on which we are most confident there is a relative long-term spending increase under Republican control of the government (taxes, foreign affairs, and the military). At the bottom of the table are the issues on which by contrast we are most confident that net long-run federal spending increases are associated with Democratic control (energy, jobs, and poverty). A comparison of the four-decade averages of issue ownership estimated in Chapter 3 (shown in Table 3.2) with these estimates finds another strong relationship between issue ownership and this measure

---

[11] Lag length chosen via AIC. Ljung-Box tests did not detect serial correlation in the residuals. The full models may be found in this chapter's appendix.

TABLE 5.3. *Control of government and federal spending, 1982–2010*

		Difference in long-run change in spending, unified Republican control – unified Democratic control (estimated with error correction models)		
		estimate	se	p-value
spending increased more under Republicans	Taxes*	12.31	(3.47)	<.01
	Foreign affairs	.25	(.08)	<.01
	Military	5.94	(2.81)	.03
	Domestic security	.58	(.30)	.05
	Education	.25	(.30)	.41
	Crime	.04	(.08)	.60
	Health care	.16	(.57)	.78
spending increased more under Democrats	Social Security	−.47	(.70)	.50
	Environment	−.04	(.03)	.24
	Poverty	−6.91	(3.93)	.08
	Jobs	−.04	(.02)	.04
	Energy	−.18	(.08)	.03

*For the purposes of comparison with other issues in this table, decreases in taxes are considered "increases in spending" on taxes.

of partisan priorities. In fact, by this criterion, issue ownership "misclassifies" only two issues – education and health care, which are owned by the Democrats, but on which spending increased more under Republican control of the government than under Democrats. All told, the conclusion to be drawn from this test is straightforward: a party's control of the government is accompanied by a net increase in federal spending on the issues it owns.

PARTISAN PRIORITIES AND ISSUE OWNERSHIP

By now, the evidence for the priorities hypothesis of issue ownership is overwhelmingly clear: a party owns an issue to the extent that its members – whether they be party activists, party voters, or party ele~ officials in government – believe that the consensus go⁻¹ with the issue should be prioritized with governmeı eral spending. A precise summary of the strong relat party priorities and issue ownership is found in Table 5.4, in which all six measures of priorities are used in a series of bivariate regressions to predict long-run issue ownership as estimated in Chapter 3. For measures of priorities on which there are multiple annual indicators, a simple average of these is used as the predictor. Each of these relationships is highly statistically significant, and the total percentage of variation in long-term ownership explained by these measures of party priorities is substantial, ranging from 35 to 86 percent. In Figure 5.3, each of the six measures of party priorities is plotted against issue ownership. Here it can be seen that the results are not being driven by particular issues and are generally robust to outliers.[12] As in our evaluations of the policy and performance hypotheses, we can also consider the extent to which issues that are classified "correctly" – that is, where the party that prioritizes the issue more also owns the issue. In the graphs, correctly classified issues are plotted with dark circles; those classified incorrectly are plotted with hollow circles. Each of the six analyses classifies issues at rates much better than chance; the worst-performing analysis has a correct classification rate of 73 percent. To be clear, party priorities do not perfectly explain issue ownership on every issue in every era. A careful examination of Figure 5.3 reveals two issues – crime and trade – that are frequently (if narrowly) misclassified by the party priorities criterion, in that Democrats generally appear to care more and do more about these two issues yet they are owned by the Republican Party.

Taken separately, any of these plots would make a good case that issue ownership is being driven by partisan priorities. Considered together – and in contrast to the tests of the policy and performance hypotheses in the previous chapter – they deliver overwhelming evidence that parties own issues because they prioritize them with their beliefs and actions. Quite simply, parties own issues because they make them priorities.

---

[12] One exception is the analysis of national spending priorities among party elites in Figure 5.3.b, where the significant relationship found here is dependent on two issues considered outliers (crime and the military). However, a glance at the other graphs suggests that had surveys of elites included more spending priorities that appealed to Republicans, those issues would also have been plotted in the upper-right quadrant of the graph, and thus crime and the military would have had much less influence on the calculation of the slope of the regression line.

TABLE 5.4. *Partisan priorities and issue ownership*

	DV: Republican Issue Ownership Advantage (Percentage Points)					
Priorities of Party Elites						
Most Important Problem (average % naming problem among convention delegates, 1972–1984)	.99** (.24)					
National Spending Priorities (net average % support for spending among convention delegates and party activists, 1984–2008)		.16*** (.02)				
Priorities of Party Voters						
Top Priorities for President and Congress (average % naming issue as priority among party identifiers in electorate, 1994–2011)			.64*** (.08)			
National Spending Priorities (net average % support for spending among party identifiers in electorate, 1972–2008)				.92*** (.10)		
Priorities of Parties in Government						
Important Laws (difference in number of laws enacted per session per issue under party control, 1970–2008)					9.39*** (1.29)	
Federal Spending (p-value of difference in long-run spending associated with party control, 1982–2010)						10.95** (2.71)
Intercept	−2.46 (2.61)	−1.74 (2.24)	1.43 (1.56)	4.38* (1.47)	−.02 (1.86)	−15.46** (3.73)
R-squared	.35	.78	.80	.86	.59	.58
SEE	9.7	5.9	5.2	4.6	7.3	8.2
number of issues correctly classified	12	7	11	8	12	10
number of issues in analysis	14	8	15	9	16	12

OLS. Estimates significantly different from zero at +p<.10; *p<.05; **p<.01; ***p<.001 (two-tailed tests, robust standard errors).

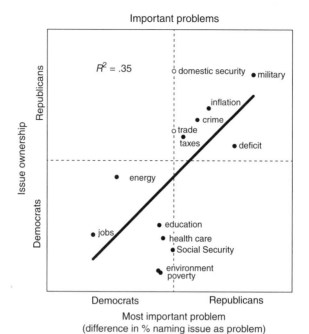

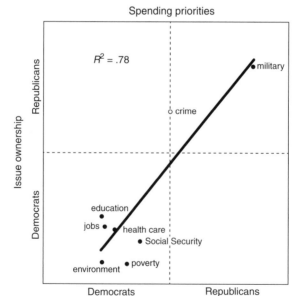

a. Priorities of party elites and issue ownership

FIGURE 5.3. Partisan priorities and issue ownership.

Correct classifications: dark circles; incorrect classifications: hollow circles.

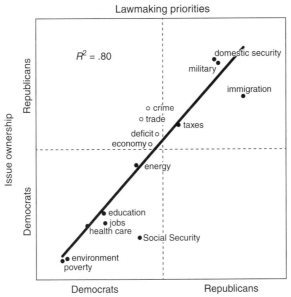

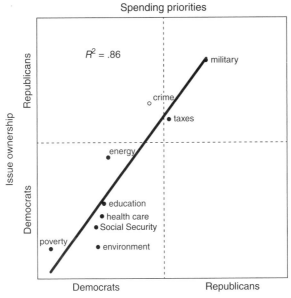

b. Priorities of party voters and issue ownership

FIGURE 5.3. Partisan priorities and issue ownership (*continued*)

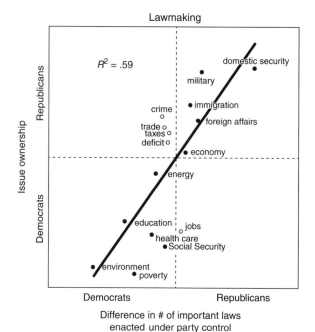

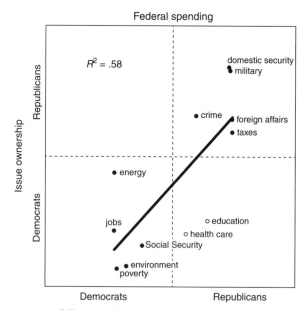

c. Priorities of the parties in government and issue ownership

FIGURE 5.3. Partisan priorities and issue ownership (*continued*)

Why "Issue Trespassing" Fails to Yield Lasting Change in Issue Ownership

As seen in Figures 5.1 and 5.2, partisan priorities are relatively steady over time. Because priorities are anchored in the core concerns of the constituencies that make up the Democratic and Republican party coalitions, we would expect it to be difficult for priorities to shift without a change in the coalitions themselves. The fact that the parties' priorities are resistant to change thus helps explain why issue ownership is steady over time, and it provides insight on an additional phenomenon that has intrigued scholars of issue ownership. This is the concept of "issue trespassing," a term used to describe one party's attempt to neutralize an issue owned by the other party – usually by attempting to advance significant legislation on the trespassed issue. Here I show that although such initiatives can lead to the temporary loss of a party's ownership advantage, it is unlikely that long-term ownership of an issue can permanently change hands absent a seismic shift in the commitments of the parties' elites, voters, and elected officials to specific issues.

The difficulty of bringing about an enduring transformation in issue ownership can be seen in three recent, highly salient attempts by presidents to "trespass" onto issues owned by the opposing party: Bill Clinton's efforts in the mid-1990s to blunt the Republicans' ownership of the crime issue, and George W. Bush's initiatives on the Democratic-owned issues of education (in his first term as president) and Social Security (in his second term). All of these cases buttress the claim that a party's priorities are what lead Americans to associate issues with the two parties. A party's unusual prioritization of an issue outside its usual purview with a major policy proposal can catalyze an immediate shift in ownership on that issue. But without a sustained shift in partisan priorities, issue ownership subsequently reverts to its long-term values. To explore these dynamics, I again generate snapshot estimates of issue ownership (as done in the previous chapter's investigation of Americans' assessments of the parties' ability to handle the abortion issue). I again use a modified version of the approach taken to estimate issue ownership in Chapter 3. After running an estimation of Equation 3.1 without any of the issue-specific indicators, I use predicted values from the model associated with issue ownership questions on crime, education, and Social Security as estimates of the parties' relative ownership of these issues at specific points in time. To avoid clouding the analysis with issue-specific associations with Presidents Clinton and Bush themselves, I limit the analysis to only issue ownership questions asking explicitly about the parties. Figure 5.4 displays the over-time dynamics in ownership of each of the three issues. Each point represents a separate survey question; trends are traced over time.

Bill Clinton and crime. Bill Clinton made crime – an issue used by Republicans to pillory Democrats in elections since the Nixon era – a centerpiece of his primary and general election campaigns for the presidency. In August 1993, he launched a campaign for his omnibus crime bill with a Rose Garden press conference accompanied by Democratic leaders from the House and Senate. By the following September, Congress had passed – and Clinton had signed the law – a $30-billion piece of legislation assessed as "an unprecedented federal venture into crime-fighting" by the nonpartisan *Congressional Quarterly Almanac* (Congressional Quarterly 1995). Figure 5.4.a shows how the Republican Party's advantage on crime – ranging between 8 to 12 points from the 1970s into the early 1990s – plummeted dramatically as Clinton lobbied for the legislation, working hand in hand with allies Representative Jack Brooks (D-TX) and Senator Joe Biden (D-DE), chairs of their respective chambers' Judiciary Committees. The nadir of the Republicans' advantage on this issue occurred around April 21, 1994, when the House of Representatives passed Clinton's bill in a bipartisan vote. As discussed in the previous chapter, the bill was popular (see Table 4.1) and crime rates were already beginning to fall (see Figure 4.4.d). Nevertheless, the share of Americans saying Republicans could better handle the crime issue quickly rebounded, reaching its equilibrium level in just one year's time. Why might this be the case? As mentioned earlier, the issue of crime presents a less-than-perfect example of the concordance between party priorities and issue ownership, as several measures suggest that Democrats put slightly higher priority on the crime issue than Republicans. However, crime still ranks relatively low on the list of Democratic priorities, and – as is clear from a glance at the priorities of party elites and party voters in Figures 5.1 and 5.2 – this did not change with the Clinton crime bill. Before 1994, to the extent that Democrats cared about crime, it

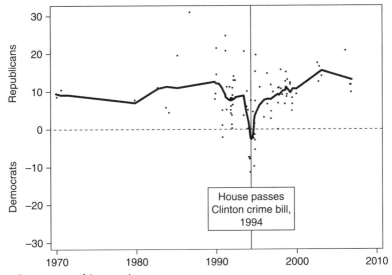

a. Issue ownership on crime

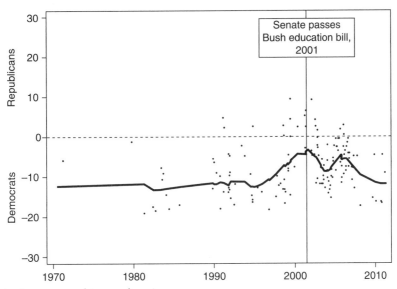

b. Issue ownership on education

FIGURE 5.4. Party initiatives and issue ownership, 1970–2010.

Sources: see text.

excludes questions about "protecting" Social Security or making it "financially sound"

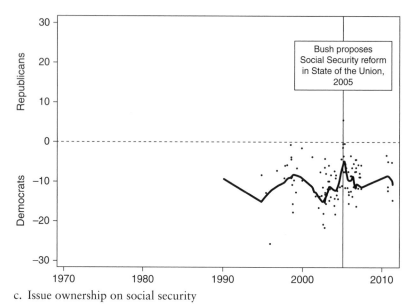

c. Issue ownership on social security

FIGURE 5.4. Party initiatives and issue ownership, 1970–2010 (*continued*)

was consistently less than their concern over other traditional party issues such as education, the environment, or health care. This did not change after 1994, and ownership of the crime issue quickly reverted back to the Republicans.

George W. Bush and education. A very similar story can be told about Republican George W. Bush's efforts to counteract the Democrats' long-term ownership of the education issue. Improvement of Texas public schools through a focus on accountability and testing was a signature aspect of Bush's single term as the state's governor. His presidential campaign touted the state's declining dropout rates and rising indicators of student achievement as the "Texas miracle." Shortly after his election, Bush nominated Rodney Paige – who had become well-known for his innovations as the superintendent of Houston's public schools – as his Secretary of Education. Just three days after his inauguration, Bush sent to Congress a bill that would largely survive intact as the No Child Left Behind Act (NCLB), which he signed into law a little less than one year later. Many aspects of the bill were highly popular: for example, a *Newsweek* poll in February 2001 about Bush's plan to "require regular student testing ... and reward schools that show improved test scores with increased federal funding" found Americans approving of these ideas by 73 percent to 22 percent (PSRA/*Newsweek* Poll 2001). The margin of support was even larger in a survey conducted by the *Los Angeles Times* one month later, standing at 80 percent to 15 percent (*Los Angeles Times* Poll 2001).

Establishing education standards via a law such as NCLB was a key component of the plan of Bush's most prominent political adviser, Karl Rove, to fundamentally realign American politics in the Republican Party's favor. Rove managed both of Bush's presidential election campaigns and served as deputy White House chief of staff for policy in the administration's second term. In Rove's vision, education reform joined other Bush initiatives – such as directing government antipoverty funds toward religious organizations, moving Medicare and Social Security toward more privatized models, and achieving immigration reform – as undermining traditional Democratic Party strengths on these issues and thus reducing its support from these issues' constituencies (Green 2007). By the summer of 2001, as Bush's education proposal was being approved by both chambers of Congress in overwhelmingly bipartisan votes, it appeared that this plan was beginning to bear fruit. The parties were approaching parity on the education issue, which had been owned by the Democratic Party by more than ten percentage points over the previous three decades (see Figure 5.4.b).

But this shift was short-lived: issue ownership immediately began slipping back toward the Democrats. This slide appears to have been briefly interrupted during the 2004 election (perhaps because the Bush campaign's credit-claiming for NCLB made the law salient again for a short time), but by the end of Bush's presidency the Democrats' advantage was right where it started. The reason for this is again the lack of a sustained change in the parties' priorities. As shown in Figure 5.2, Bush's efforts on education represented merely a temporary shift of his party's focus on an issue that had long been considered relatively less important by Republican elites and voters than other issues. This remained true after the passage of NCLB.

George W. Bush and Social Security. The issue of Social Security provides a final illustration of the strong relationship between party priorities and issue ownership and the difficulty of achieving permanent change in the associations voters make between issues and parties. As a cornerstone of President Franklin D. Roosevelt's New Deal that is widely credited with wiping out poverty among America's senior citizen population, Social Security is a popular government program that has long been strongly associated with the Democratic Party. However, the ratio of active workers to retirees is declining, and there are projected to be fewer and fewer contributors to the Social Security system for each American drawing benefits from it. Concern has thus grown about whether the system is financially sustainable without fundamental changes (see, e.g., Arnold 1998). During his 2000 campaign, Bush was the first Republican in a generation to call for fundamental changes to the Social Security program, proposing to allow younger Americans to effectively opt out of the system by directing their payroll tax payments into personal retirement accounts. Part of Bush's justification for his plan was that the higher returns generated from private accounts invested in the stock market could help resolve the Social Security system's long-term financial problems.

The plan remained mostly in the background until after Bush's reelection in November 2004, when the administration signaled it would make changes to the Social Security system a top domestic priority in its second term – with Karl Rove leading the campaign to get the plan approved by Congress. The proposal was the highlight of Bush's State of the Union address in February 2005, during which he billed the plan as part of his vision for an "ownership society" in which Americans would become more self-reliant and less dependent on government support. In contrast to Bush's successful first-term initiatives on education, Medicare, and taxes, however, opposition from a united front of Democratic lawmakers as well as interest groups such as the powerful seniors lobby AARP quickly took the wind out of the proposal's sails. Polls indicated that support for Bush's proposal was lukewarm, at best. A *Newsweek* survey fielded at the same time as Bush's State of the Union speech found the public evenly split on the "best way to run Social Security," with 40 percent supporting the status quo of "tax[ing] one generation to pay for the retirement of another" while 39 percent preferred Bush's proposal to "direct workers' money into the stock market in an effort to generate a higher rate of return on retirement savings" (Princeton Survey Research Associates International/Newsweek Poll, 2005). Later that month, a Marist College survey found that by 52 to 40 percent Americans thought "allowing private investments for Social Security" was a "bad idea" rather than a "good idea" (Marist College Institute for Public Opinion Poll 2005). In the end, the forces of opposition were too strong: Congress adjourned at the end of 2005 without taking any action on Social Security, and the Bush plan never resurfaced in any serious fashion.

What is remarkable about the trajectory of issue ownership on Social Security over this time period is that it appears that Bush was able to achieve a temporary shift in ownership on this issue simply by talking about it. Despite the fact that Bush's proposal was never particularly popular, Bush's State of the Union address reduced the Democrats' issue ownership advantage on Social Security to its lowest point ever (Figure 5.4.c).[13] As Bush's proposal died a slow death in Congress, ownership of the Social Security issue returned to the safe Democratic territory where it had resided for the previous two decades. Bush's initiative did not presage a shift in his party's priorities toward the issue of Social Security. Issue ownership thus essentially stayed put.

The examples of crime, education, and Social Security provide additional evidence that the reason long-term issue ownership so rarely changes hands between the two parties has to do with the parties' fundamental priorities. Highly salient efforts by Democrats and Republicans to tackle each other's owned issues are unusual. They usually originate in the executive branch, as presidents relying upon the approval of a national electorate have much stronger incentives to neutralize the opposing party's owned issues than legislators representing more homogeneous constituencies. In return, the public can reward these unusual initiatives by rapidly reassessing which party it trusts to handle these issues. This can be true regardless of whether an initiative is particularly popular. But even if the proposal succeeds in becoming law, it is no guarantee of the kind of permanent transformation in the political landscape hoped for by a strategist such as Karl Rove. Absent a sustained shift in a party's priorities at all levels of its membership, the public is unlikely to change the deeply ingrained associations it has been making between issues and parties for the past four decades.

---

[13] For maximum comparability over time, this graph excludes issue-ownership questions asking about which party will do a better job "keeping the Social Security system financially sound" (a question wording that tends to favor the Republicans) and which party will do a better job "protecting the Social Security system" (which favors the Democrats).

DEFINITION OF ISSUE OWNERSHIP

ogether, the analyses presented in this and the previous chapter ͵ ᵥ.... ᵤₑ way toward clearer ways for scholars to discuss and analyze the impact of issue ownership on American politics. The unambiguous rejection of the policy and performance hypotheses and the convincing evidence found in support of the priorities hypothesis recast some long-held assumptions about the associations voters make between parties and issues while affirming others. These findings suggest that the proposal of a conceptually distinct, empirically justified definition of issue ownership is in order:

Issue ownership describes the long-term positive associations between political parties and particular consensus issues in the public's mind – associations created and reinforced by the parties' commitments to prioritizing these issues with government spending and lawmaking.

By locating issue ownership in the parties' priorities, this definition echoes Petrocik's stipulation that issue ownership is "produced by a history of attention, initiative and innovation" that a party devotes toward an issue (Petrocik 1996: 826). But this new definition reflects this book's findings by (1) emphasizing the long-term nature of issue ownership; (2) limiting the concept's domain to consensus issues; (3) limiting its causes to the parties' priorities; and (4) explicitly stating the ways in which the public becomes aware of these priorities. It also discards any mention of the notion of "handling" an issue – and thus avoids the vexing ambiguity of a term lending itself to the multiple interpretations that have muddied scholars' attempts to understand issue ownership.

This definition – and the findings that justify it – should bring needed clarity to the ways political scientists and other observers of our nation's politics talk about the associations voters make between parties and issues. For example, it is a mistake to stipulate that Americans believe Democrats can better handle the health care issue because they prefer the Democrats' health care policies or because national conditions with regard to health improve under Democratic control: neither of these things is true. Rather, when Americans say that Democrats are better able to handle health care, they are recognizing that Democrats – in their words and their deeds – prioritize this particular issue over others. On television and the Internet, they see Democratic elites saying health care is a problem and that federal funds should be channeled toward solving it. They hear their Democratic coworkers and friends say the same things over the watercooler or at the coffee shop. And when Democrats are in the White House and control Congress, Americans see major legislation enacted – and government dollars spent – on health care. The same can be said for the Republican Party and its ownership of the interrelated issues of domestic security, foreign affairs, and the military. Americans don't necessarily like the Republicans' policies on these issues, and there is no evidence that the party's performance on these issues is any better than the Democrats'. But for four decades, Republican Party activists and voters have consistently said these issues should take precedence over other concerns – and when the Republican Party rises to power in Washington, they usually do.

Appendix to Chapter 5

**List Compiled by David Mayhew of Important Laws Enacted
1971–2008, with Coding for Consensus Issues**

Where a law did not address a consensus issue analyzed in this book,
no code is indicated for that law. These laws comprise the omitted category in the Poisson regression used to estimate legislative
productivity.

KEY TO CODE ABBREVIATIONS:

DOMSEC: domestic security

ECON: economy

EDUC: education

ENV: environment

FORAFF: foreign affairs

HEALTH: health care

IMM: immigration

MIL: military

POV: poverty

SOCSEC: Social Security

Congress	Code 1	Code 2	Code 3	Law
92	SOCSEC			Social Security increase.
92	TAXES	ECON		Tax reduction for economic stimulus purposes.
92	HEALTH			National Cancer Act.
92	JOBS			Emergency Employment Act.
92				18-year-old voting age as constitutional amendment.
92				Federal Election Campaign Act.
92	ENV			Water Pollution Control Act.
92				State and Local Fiscal Assistance Act.
92	SOCSEC			Social Security increase.
92				Equal rights amendment to the constitution (ERA).
92	ENV			Pesticide Control Act.
92	MIL	FORAFF		ABM treaty ratified.
92	HEALTH			Consumer Product Safety Act.
92				Equal Employment Opportunity Act.
92	POV			Supplementary Security Income (SSI) program approved.
92	EDUC	POV		Higher Education Act. Created Pell grants program.
93	MIL			War Powers Act.
93				Federal Aid Highway Act.
93				Agriculture and Consumer Protection Act.
93	JOBS	EDUC		Comprehensive Employment and Training Act (CETA).
93	SOCSEC			Social Security increase.
93				District of Columbia Home Rule.
93	ENERGY			Trans-Alaskan pipeline authorized.
93	FORAFF			Foreign Assistance Act.
93				Regional Rail Reorganization Act.
93	HEALTH			Aid for development of Health Maintenance Organizations (HMOs).

(continued)

(continued)

Congress	Code 1	Code 2	Code 3	Law
93	ENERGY			Emergency Petroleum Allocation Act.
93	TRADE	FORAFF		Trade Act.
93				Employee Retirement Income Security Act (ERISA).
93				Federal Election Campaign Act.
93	POV			Minimum wage increase.
93				Congressional Budget and Impoundment Control Act.
93				Freedom of Information Act Amendments.
93	ENERGY			Nuclear Regulatory Commission (NRC) and Energy Research & Development Administration (ERDA) created.
93				Magnuson-Moss product warranty act.
93	HEALTH			National Health Planning and Resources Development Act.
93				National Mass Transportation Assistance Act.
93	POV			Housing and Community Development Act.
93	ENERGY	ENV		Energy Policy and Conservation Act.
94				Voting Rights Act extension.
94				New York City bailout.
94	ECON			Repeal of domestic fair-trade laws.
94	TAXES	ECON		Tax Reduction Act to fight economic recession.
94				Securities Act Amendments.
94	POV	JOBS		Unemployment compensation overhaul.
94				Copyright law revision.
94	ENV	HEALTH		Toxic Substances Control Act.
94	TAXES			Tax Reform Act.
94				Railroad Vitalization and Regulatory Reform Act.
94	ENV			National Forest Management Act (NFMA).

160

Congress	Code 1	Code 2	Code 3	Law
94	ENV			Federal Land Policy and Management Act (FLPMA).
94	ENV	HEALTH		Resource Conservation and Recovery Act.
95	SOCSEC	TAXES		Social Security tax increase.
95	TAXES	ECON		Tax cut and stimulus package.
95	POV			Minimum wage hike.
95	ENV			Surface Mining Control and Reclamation Act.
95	POV			Food and Agriculture Act. Expanded food stamp program.
95	ENV			Clean Water Act.
95	ENV			Clean Air Act Amendments.
95	TAXES			Tax revision.
95	ENERGY	ENV		Comprehensive energy package with conservation provisions.
95	MIL	FORAFF		Panama Canal treaties ratified.
95				Civil Service Reform Act.
95				Airline deregulation.
96	ECON			Chrysler Corporation bailout.
96	FORAFF	TRADE		Foreign trade act extension.
96	EDUC			Department of Education established.
96	ECON			Depository Institutions and Monetary Control Act.
96				Trucking deregulation.
96				Staggers Rail Act.
96	TAXES	ENERGY		Windfall profits tax on oil.
96	ENERGY			Synthetic fuels program.
96	ENV			Alaska lands preservation.
96	ENV	HEALTH		Toxic waste Superfund.
97	TAXES	ECON		Economic Recovery Tax Act.
97	POV	HEALTH		Omnibus Budget Reconciliation Act (OBRA). Domestic spending cuts.

(continued)

(continued)

Congress	Code 1	Code 2	Code 3	Law
97				Agriculture and Food Act.
97	TAXES			Transportation Assistance Act. Raised the gasoline tax.
97	TAXES	POV		Tax Equity and Fiscal Responsibility Act.
97				Voting Rights Act extension.
97	ENERGY			Nuclear Waste Repository Act.
97	ECON			Garn-St. Germain Depository Institutions Act.
97	EDUC	JOBS		Job Training Partnership Act.
98				Martin Luther King's birthday declared a legal holiday.
98	SOCSEC	TAXES		Social Security Act Amendments. Included tax increases and benefit cuts.
98	JOBS	ECON		Anti-recession jobs measure.
98	CRIME			Anti-crime package.
98	DEFICIT	TAXES		Deficit reduction measure.
98	TRADE			Trade and Tariff Act.
98				Cable Communications Policy Act.
99	DEFICIT			Gramm-Rudman-Hollings anti-deficit act.
99				Food Security Act.
99	TAXES			Tax Reform Act.
99	IMM	CRIME		Immigration Reform and Control Act.
99	FORAFF			South Africa sanctions.
99	CRIME			Anti-narcotics measure.
99	ENV	TAXES		Cleanup of toxic waste dumps. Includes new taxes.
99				Omnibus water projects act.
99	MIL			Goldwater-Nichols Reorganization Act (Defense Department).
100	ENV			Water Quality Act.
100				Surface Transportation Act.
100	DEFICIT	TAXES		Deficit reduction measure. Includes tax increases.

Congress	Code 1	Code 2	Code 3	Law
100	POV			Housing and Community Development Act.
100	POV			McKinney Homeless Assistance Act.
100	HEALTH			Catastrophic health insurance for the aged.
100	POV	JOBS		Family Support Act.
100	TRADE			Omnibus foreign trade measure.
100	CRIME			Anti-drug-abuse act.
100				Grove City civil rights measure.
100	MIL	FORAFF		Intermediate-Range Nuclear-Force (INF) treaty ratified.
100				Japanese–American reparations.
101	POV			Minimum wage hike.
101	ECON			Savings-and-loan bailout.
101	DEFICIT	TAXES		Deficit reduction package. Includes tax hikes.
101				Americans with Disabilities Act.
101	ENV			Clean Air Act.
101	EDUC	POV		Child care package.
101	IMM			Immigration Act.
101	POV			National Affordable Housing Act.
101				Agriculture act.
101	MIL	FORAFF		Persian Gulf Resolution.
102				Surface transportation act (ISTEA).
102				Civil Rights Act.
102	ENERGY	ENV		Omnibus energy act. Includes conservation measures.
102	MIL	FORAFF		Strategic Arms Reduction Treaty ratified.
102	FORAFF			Economic aid package for ex-Soviet republics.
102				Cable TV regulation.

(continued)

(continued)

Congress	Code 1	Code 2	Code 3	Law
102	ENV			California water policy.
103	DEFICIT	TAXES	POV	Omnibus Deficit Reduction Act. Includes tax increase and increase in Earned Income Tax Credit.
103	TRADE			North American Free Trade Agreement (NAFTA) approved.
103	HEALTH			Family and Medical Leave Act.
103				Motor Voter act.
103	EDUC			National Service act.
103	EDUC			Reform of college-student loan financing.
103	CRIME			Brady bill.
103	EDUC			National education goals.
103	CRIME			Omnibus crime act.
103	ENV			California desert protection.
103				Abortion clinic access.
103	TRADE			General Agreement on Tariffs and Trade (GATT) approved.
104				Curb on unfunded mandates.
104				Congressional Accountability Act.
104				Lobbying reform.
104	ECON			Curb on shareholder lawsuits.
104	POV			Welfare reform.
104				Telecommunications reform.
104				Agriculture deregulation.
104				Line-item veto.
104	DOMSEC			Anti-terrorism act.
104	DEFICIT			Spending cuts.
104	HEALTH			Health Insurance Portability and Accountability Act.

Congress	Code 1	Code 2	Code 3	Law
104	POV			Minimum wage hike.
104	ENV			Overhaul of pesticides regulation.
104	ENV			Overhaul of safe drinking water legislation.
104	IMM	CRIME		Immigration reform. Focus on unauthorized immigration.
105	DEFICIT	TAXES	HEALTH	Deal to balance the budget by 2002. Includes tax cuts and creation of Children's Health Insurance Program (CHIP).
105	MIL	FORAFF		Chemical Weapons Convention ratified.
105	HEALTH			Overhaul of Food and Drug Administration.
105	POV			Adoption of foster children.
105				Transportation construction act.
105	TAXES			Overhaul of Internal Revenue Service.
105	DEF	FORAFF		NATO expansion ratified.
105	POV			Reform of public housing.
105	EDUC			100,000 new school teachers.
106	ECON			Banking reform.
106				Y2K planning.
106	EDUC			Ed-flex program.
106	TRADE	FORAFF		Permanent Normal Trading Relations with China.
106	ENV			Florida Everglades restoration act.
106	POV			Community Renewal and New Markets Act.
107	TAXES			Bush tax cut.
107	DEF	DOMSEC	FORAFF	Use of Force Resolution.
107	DOMSEC			USA PATRIOT Act.
107	ECON	DOMSEC		Airline bailout in response to September 11 attacks.
107	DOMSEC			Airline security. Creates Transportation Security Administration (TSA).

(continued)

Congress	Code 1	Code 2	Code 3	Law
107	MIL	DOMSEC		Emergency spending for defense, domestic security, recovery of New York City.
107	EDUC			Education reform. To require annual student testing; provides new funds.
107	DEF	FORAFF		Iraq Resolution.
107	DOMSEC			New Homeland Security Department.
107				Campaign finance reform.
107				Agriculture subsidies.
107	ECON			Corporate Responsibility Act.
107	TRADE	FORAFF		Fast-track trade authority.
107				Election reform.
107	DOMSEC	ECON		Terrorism insurance.
107	DOMSEC			Commission created to investigate September 11 attacks.
108	HEALTH			Medicare reform.
108	TAXES			Tax cut.
108	FORAFF			AIDS funding focused on Africa and the Caribbean.
108				Partial Birth Abortion Ban Act.
108	MIL			Funding for military operations and reconstruction in Afghanistan and Iraq.
108	ENV			Healthy Forests law.
108	TAXES			Corporate tax overhaul.
108				Disaster relief (hurricane and drought relief).
108				Unborn Victims of Violence Act.
108	DOMSEC	MIL		Intelligence overhaul.
109	POV			Bankruptcy reform.
109	ECON	ECON		Class Action Fairness Act.
109				Transportation measure.

Congress	Code 1	Code 2	Code 3	Law
109	ENERGY	TAXES		Energy measure (includes tax breaks).
109	TRADE	FORAFF		Central American Free Trade Agreement.
109				Hurricane assistance after Katrina.
109	ECON			Pension reform.
109	DOMSEC			Military Commissions Act.
109	DOMSEC			Port security.
109	IMM	DOMSEC		700 miles of new fencing authorized for U.S.-Mexico border.
109	ENERGY	ENV		Gulf of Mexico opened to oil and gas drilling.
109	TRADE	FORAFF		Trade measures (Vietnam, Andean nations, sub-Saharan countries, and Haiti).
109				Postal Service reform.
109	FORAFF	MIL		India pact.
110	POV			Minimum wage hike.
110	DOMSEC			Implementation of recommendations of the 9/11 commission.
110				Ethics and lobbying reform.
110	EDUC	POV		Overhaul of college student aid programs.
110	ENERGY	ENV		Energy conservation.
110	POV	ECON		Housing relief program.
110	TAXES	ECON		Bailout of the financial sector (includes tax breaks).
110	ECON	TAXES		Economic stimulus package (includes tax incentives for business investment).
110				Agriculture subsidy bill.
110	DOMSEC			Domestic surveillance.
110	EDUC	MIL		New G.I. bill for veterans.
110	FORAFF	MIL		Nuclear trade agreement with India.
110	HEALTH	TAXES		Guarantee of mental illness insurance.

**Control of the Government and Enactment of Important Laws,
1971–2008**
(Full model generating estimates in final column of Table 5.1)

	DV: Mean number of laws enacted per session of Congress	
	coef	se
Topic of law		
Crime	.111	(.411)
Deficit	.147	(.334)
Domestic security	.134	(.467)
Economy	1.087***	(.211)
Education	.581+	(.351)
Energy	.331	(.423)
Environment	1.202***	(.184)
Foreign affairs	1.102***	(.309)
Health care	.781*	(.325)
Immigration	−.622	(.456)
Jobs	−7.172***	(.458)
Military	.779+	(.445)
Poverty	1.258***	(.250)
Social Security	−1.046	(.739)
Taxes	1.300***	(.321)
Trade	.484	(.330)
Control of presidency (Dem = 1; Rep = −1)	.028	(.134)
x crime	.273	(.456)
x deficit	.249	(.336)
x domestic security	−1.049*	(.436)
x economy	−.181	(.226)
x education	.368	(.290)
x energy	−.102	(.294)
x environment	.244	(.239)
x foreign affairs	−.201	(.268)
x health care	.083	(.229)
x immigration	−.271	(.412)
x jobs	−7.092***	(.301)
x military	−.387	(.409)
x poverty	.058	(.250)
x Social Security	−.245	(.543)
x taxes	−.062	(.298)
x trade	.199	(.322)
Control of Congress (Dem = 1; Rep = −1; divided = 0)	.250	(.183)
x crime	−.091	(.402)
x deficit	−.276	(.363)

	DV: Mean number of laws enacted per session of Congress	
	coef	se
x domestic security	−.924**	(.345)
x economy	−.221	(.271)
x education	.290	(.370)
x energy	.343	(.472)
x environment	.319	(.236)
x foreign affairs	−.352	(.247)
x health care	.043	(.323)
x immigration	−.885+	(.492)
x jobs	.512	(.456)
x military	−.333	(.318)
x poverty	.102	(.266)
x Social Security	.943	(.713)
x taxes	−.147	(.304)
x trade	−.213	(.359)
Intercept	−1.116***	(.163)
N	569	

Poisson regression. Omitted category: law not about any of these topics.

Estimates significantly different from zero at +*p*<.10; *p*<.05; **p*<.01; ***p*<.001 (two-tailed tests, robust standard errors clustered on congressional session).

Control of Government and Federal Spending, 1982–2010
(Full models generating estimates in Table 5.3)

	crime	education	energy	environment	foreign affairs	health care	jobs	military	poverty	domestic security	Social Security	taxes
DV: Change in Federal Outlays (as % of all spending)												
Lags of levels of DV:												
1	-.747***	-1.226***	-1.000**	-.460**	-.626*	-.309	-.741***	-.261**	-.676**	-.931***	-.443**	-.316
2	.067	1.014*	-.309		-.195	-.211	.116		.589			-.303*
3	-.258*	-1.537**	.239		-.414	.104	-.020		-.354*			
4	.143	.428	-.238			-1.177*	-.132					
5			-.055				.112					
6			-.223									
7			-.152									
Lags of control of presidency (Dem = 1; Rep = 0)												
1	-.089	-.381	.074	.019	-.021	.111	.007	-.853	.289	-.334*	.650***	4.903*
2	.070	-.174	-.000		-.116	.303	.001		-.785			-.554
3	-.125	.123	-.004		-.146	.691	.021		1.672***			
4	-.220**	-.017	.007			.596	.011					
5			.017				.015					
6			-.015									
7			-.008									
Lags of control of Congress (Dem = 1; Rep = 0; Divided= .5)												
1	-.086	-.865*	-.031	-.001	-.032	-1.380	.037	-.698	1.634**	-.208	-.443	-5.951**
2	.012	.948*	.015		-.132	-.712	-.004		-.489			-6.020
3	.081	-.724	-.041		.138	-.425	.036		.728			
4	-.115	.764	-.036			-.292	-.021					

5			−.021			.019					
6			−.018								
7			−.069								
year	2.421*	−15.408	−7.537*	−7.411***	−16.235	.900	−45.176***	−13.270	−3.991	12.043	213.030**
year²	−.001*	.004	.002*	.002***	.004	−.000	.011***	.003	.001	−.003	−.053**
p-value of Ljung-Box test	.60	.12	.15	.65	.52	.21	.93	.34	.80	.29	.58

Error correction models. Estimates significantly different from zero at +p<.10; *p<.05; **p<.01; ***p<.001 (two-tailed tests, robust standard errors).

Lag length (out of a maximum of four possible lags) chosen for each series by AIC, with the exception of spending on energy and jobs, which required seven and five lags respectively to remove autocorrelation. Estimates include an intercept term (not shown).

6

How Issue Ownership Distorts American Politics

The previous two chapters have shown that rather than being driven by popular policies or superior performance, issue ownership instead derives from the fact that the Democratic and Republican parties prioritize different sets of issues. Evidence for these priorities are found in partisans' beliefs and actions. In survey after survey, party elites and party voters say their parties' owned issues are the nation's most important problems and that they favor increased federal spending on them. When a party comes to power in Washington, its politicians convert these beliefs into action by devoting more major legislation and increased federal spending to the issues it owns.

If issue ownership's effects were limited to this, we might consider the phenomenon as having at worst benign and perhaps even positive implications for American politics and policy making. Political scientists have long held that voters benefit to the extent that the parties' stances are consistent and distinctive and thus party labels of candidates represent clear, easy-to-understand choices. The results from previous chapters show that issue ownership is a meaningful, accurate aspect of these labels. In this sense, issue ownership may help voters make choices aligned with their preferences – and in fact, this is precisely how scholars of issue ownership explain the finding that parties gain votes when their owned issues are more salient during national elections.

However, this chapter provides evidence of a more troubling phenomenon that counterbalances the polity's informational gains from issue ownership: it is also associated with a distortion in the relationship between what the public wants and what the government does. The very same forces that lead political parties to prioritize their owned issues also lead them to pay less attention to public opinion on these issues than others. The result is that parties often pursue policies on their owned issues that are more extreme than the public wants, and they can ignore shifts in the public's priorities as they doggedly push for spending on the issues they own.

This chapter investigates this claim about issue ownership with theory and evidence. My theory derives from a spatial model of elections that incorporates the now well-documented assumption that issue ownership is about party priorities rather than policies or performance. Because partisans (including party activists, affiliated interest groups, and the rank-and-file) care more about the issues their parties own, they are less tolerant of deviations from policy on these owned issues than on issues they consider less important. The model shows how issue ownership therefore pulls parties further away from the center on the issues they own than on the issues they do not. The rigidity associated with issue ownership also leads to lack of responsiveness to shifts in public opinion on policies and priorities.

Evidence for the association of issue ownership with lack of responsiveness is provided by two empirical analyses. First, I show that key roll-call votes of Democratic and Republican members of Congress are less responsive to constituency opinion on the issues their parties own than on the issues they do not own. Second, I show that the president and Congress are less responsive to shifts in the public's preferences for government spending on the issues their parties own than on the issues they do not. Both analyses demonstrate that the differences in how parties respond to public opinion on owned and non-owned issues are stark. In fact, they suggest that the parties' responsiveness on the issues they own is essentially zero.

Thus the story of issue ownership is really one of a trade-off. Owning parties can be relied upon to devote attention and funds to addressing goals on which there exists a broad natior ˙ ‑‑ᶜⁱˢ Voters appreciate this, which is why they consistently parties to handle the issues they own. But the devotion ε issue ownership comes with a price: a party's ideolog and rigidity on the issues it owns.

ISSUES AND REPRESENTATION

The notion that public policy should generally reflect public opinion is a core democratic principle. If with Robert Dahl (1971), we assume that a democracy is characterized by "the continuing responsiveness of the government to the preferences of its citizens, considered as political equals," we naturally seek to examine the nature and extent of that responsiveness. Do the decisions of elected officials correspond to the public's preferences? Do elected officials change their actions when these preferences change? Since the pioneering work of Warren Miller and Donald Stokes examining the influence of constituency opinion in Congress in the 1960s, empirical scholars of representation have found the answers to these questions to be – generically – "yes," across time, jurisdictions, and policies (Miller and Stokes 1963). A full discussion of these findings is beyond the scope of this book; for recent summaries see Burstein (2010), Druckman and Jacobs (2009), Shapiro (2011), and Wlezien and Soroka (2007).

Thus on balance, political science research has found that politicians are largely responsive to the preferences of citizens in America's two-party system. But this work has generally not explored in a satisfactory way how representation might vary from one political issue to another. Empirical analyses rarely compare the relationship between public opinion and public policy across issues. And we have very little theory providing guidance regarding how responsiveness might differ by issue. One exception is that there is relatively consistent evidence indicating that policy makers are more responsive to public opinion on more salient issues (Page and Shapiro 1983; Soroka and Wlezien 2010; Wlezien 2004). Salience also plays a role in another, quite long line of research exploring how the structure of policies and the organized interests supporting various policy outcomes should affect policy making (Schattschneider 1935; Lowi 1964) and in turn the effect of citizen preferences on policy (Arnold 1990; Wilson 1973). For example, R. Douglas Arnold argues that diffuse, unorganized interests can be victorious over concentrated, special interests when costs or benefits can be easily recognized by the public and thus made salient to voters.

A potential source of theory about how representation varies across issues is the spatial model of electoral competition, a term political scientists use to describe a family of formal analyses that make predictions about how the platforms – and thus the policies – adopted by candidates respond to citizens' preferences in a policy space. But generally, spatial models have provided few insights and guidance regarding how responsiveness of public policy to public opinion might differ by issue. Thus to the extent that government responds to public opinion to varying degrees on different issues, a consistent explanation for this phenomenon has yet to be developed by political scientists. In this chapter, I show how issue ownership – as a persistent, substantively important phenomenon that distinguishes parties on different issues – can provide some theoretical explanation for how government responds to the public's preferences across issues. I begin by incorporating issue ownership – that is, the fact that parties care to different degrees about different sets of issues – into the spatial model of elections.

A SPATIAL MODEL OF ISSUE OWNERSHIP

The point of departure for many spatial models is generally the model developed by Downs (1957), who showed that simple assumptions about two-party electoral competition yield the powerful prediction that candidate platforms should converge to the preferences of the voter located at the median of the distribution of all voters' preferences. The assumptions required to obtain this result are over the policy space (that it is one-dimensional), the electorate (that citizens have single-peaked preferences in the policy space and that all citizens vote for the candidate located closer to them in the space), and the candidates (that they are motivated solely by winning office). The simplicity of Downs's model and the intuitiveness of his assumptions have led to the enduring appeal his theory, which came to be known as the Median Voter Theorem.

Much of the work since Downs has focused on identifying how the spatial model might incorporate assumptions that are more realistic and thus yield predictions that comport more closely with what is observed in actual politics. Of these, two substantive changes to the basic spatial model are needed in order for it to yield insights regarding issue ownership. First, we must move to a policy space that consists of more than one issue in order to capture the trade-offs parties make among issues. Second, we must assume that candidates care about policies as well as winning office. Both of these assumptions have been explored in depth by previous work (for discussions see Duggan 2012, Mueller 2003, and Roemer 2001). To these assumptions, I now add a final, additional change justified by the findings of the previous chapters: parties and their candidates care about policies on different issues to different degrees.[1] Readers who are not interested in the technical details of the model may skip ahead to the section entitled "The Model: A Nontechnical Summary" for a plain-language summary of the theory.

Setup of the Model

Two parties, the Democrats (or D) and the Republicans (R), compete in an election. (The scenario modeled here may also be considered an election between candidates affiliated with these two parties; I use the terms "candidates" and "parties" interchangeably.) As before, I consider the case of a single, typical voter, V. Representing an entire electorate with a single voter is a dramatically simplifying assumption, and one not made lightly. This move is motivated by the fact that the mathematical challenges arising in multidimensional models with continuums of voters are legion. Without making additional assumptions, in many of these models equilibria can fail to exist; in others the predictions yielded are not particularly useful.[2] It is hoped that the insights yielded by this simpler model compensate for what it lacks in verisimilitude.

The parties compete for V's vote by proposing policies in a two-issue space. One issue is owned by the Democrats (for example, health care) and one by the Republicans (say, domestic security). In this model, a campaign for V's vote and subsequent election proceeds with D and R first simultaneously proposing policies and then V electing the party with the platform that yields a higher utility. If V is indifferent

---

[1] As discussed earlier in Chapter 3, this is a different approach than that taken by the two extant versions of the spatial model that incorporate the notion of issue ownership. Simon (2002) assumes that issue ownership is associated with having more popular policies; Krasa and Polborn (2010) assume that issue ownership is associated with performance, which in turns leads to prioritization.

[2] John E. Roemer has provided a particularly thorough and insightful discussion of these challenges (Roemer 2001).

between the two candidates' policy proposals, he flips a coin to determine which party to elect. The winning candidate then implements her policy platform.[3]

Preferences of parties. As justified by the previous chapters, the parties are policy-oriented: rather than being solely concerned with winning office, they also care about the policies enacted by the winner. The utility the two parties derive from any policy is specified in a standard fashion in that utility is declining in a policy's Euclidean distance from the party's ideal point. Thus

$$U_D(x,y) = -\alpha(x-d)^2 - (y-d)^2$$
$$U_R(x,y) = -(x-r)^2 - \alpha(y-r)^2 \tag{6.1}$$

are the utility functions for the Democrats and Republicans respectively, where x is the policy implemented by the election winner on the health care dimension and y is the policy implemented on the domestic security dimension. The quantities d and r represent the parties' ideal points, which for simplifying purposes in this model are assumed to be equidistant from the origin on both dimensions. That is, D's ideal points x_D and y_D are assumed to each be equal to d; similarly R's ideal points $x_R = y_R = r$; and $d = -r$. As shown in Figure 6.1, D's ideal point (now in two dimensions) lies in the lower-left quadrant of the policy space; R's ideal point in the upper-right quadrant. Finally, α is a measure of the relative priority the parties put on each issue. It is assumed that $\alpha > 1$, and that this parameter is rising to the extent that a party prioritizes one issue over the other. Again, for simplifying purposes, I assume that the Democrats prioritize health care over domestic security to the same degree as the Republicans prioritize domestic security over health care, and thus α is the same for both parties.

As shown in Figure 6.1, these utility functions specify a series of ellipses in the xy plane centered on the parties' ideal points. The ellipses are indifference contours: the points making up any ellipse are the set of all (x, y) policy pairs yielding an equal level of utility. The narrow, tall indifference contours around D's ideal point reflect the fact that because Democrats care more about health care than domestic security, they are willing to concede a fair amount regarding domestic security policy before budging much on health care policy. By contrast,

---

[3] Parties are referred to with feminine pronouns, the voter with masculine pronouns.

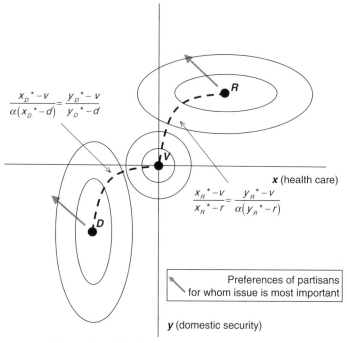

FIGURE 6.1. A Spatial model of issue ownership.

the wide, squat indifference contours around R's ideal point are drawn to reflect the fact that Republicans take just the opposite approach to the tradeoff: they care much more about domestic security than health care, and thus are much less concerned about the extent to which health care policy is distant from their ideal point than they are about domestic security policy.[4]

Preferences of the voter. I assume that the voter is located away from both parties by equal distances on both dimensions with ideal points $x_V = y_V = v$. Furthermore, I assume V cares equally about the two issues. (These two assumptions allow us to see the implications of the parties' priorities as clearly as possible, abstracted away from other potentially confounding factors.) Like D and R, V's utility is quadratic in the two dimensions and thus written as

---

[4] Note that these indifference contours are not electorally induced but rather represent the actual policy preferences of the parties and the weights they place on the two issues.

$$U_V(x,y) = -(x-v)^2 - (y-v)^2. \tag{6.2}$$

As shown in Figure 6.1, this utility function specifies a series of circular indifference contours centered on V's ideal point, which in the diagram is set at the origin with $v = 0$.

Uncertainty. In order for realistic equilibria to exist in spatial models with policy-oriented parties – that is, equilibria in which they adopt different platforms – it is generally the case that some uncertainty is required about how voters respond to changes in party platforms (for discussions see Mueller 2003: 249–255; Roemer 2001: 103–144). The incorporation of uncertainty also arguably adds verisimilitude to the model: as Dennis C. Mueller notes, it seems unrealistic that candidates would be perfectly informed about voters' ideal points (Mueller 2003: 251). Therefore I assume that rather than voting deterministically, V instead votes for a party with increasing probability as the party's platform offers him greater utility compared to the other party's platform. This is incorporated in the model by specifying that V has a preexisting bias, δ, toward D (or if δ is negative, toward R) that he takes into account along with the parties' platforms when determining his vote. Formally, V elects D if

$$U_V(x_D{}^*, y_D{}^*) + \delta > U_V(x_R{}^*, y_R{}^*),$$

where D and R's platforms are $(x_D{}^*, y_D{}^*)$ and $(x_R{}^*, y_R{}^*)$ respectively. Although the parties know the range over which the voter's partisan bias can potentially fall, they do not observe its precise value. Therefore from D and R's perspective, δ is a random variable and the probability π that R wins the election is written

$$\pi = \Pr\left[U_V(x_D{}^*, y_D{}^*) + \delta < U_V(x_R{}^*, y_R{}^*)\right].$$

D's chances of winning the election are therefore $1-\pi$. I assume δ is uniformly distributed with support on $[-1/2\beta, 1/2\beta]$ and density $\beta > 0$.[5] We thus rewrite

[5] As can be seen in Equation 6.3, β thus represents the extent to which the election result is affected by the parties' platforms. As β gets larger, the value of π depends more heavily on which party is located closer to V's ideal point. As β tends toward zero, D and R have more leeway in their positioning as the probability of either party's victory is simply ½ regardless of their platforms. I assume that β is high enough that parties cannot propose their ideal points in equilibrium.

$$\pi = \Pr\left[\delta < U_V\left(x_R{}^*, y_R{}^*\right) - U_V\left(x_D{}^*, y_D{}^*\right)\right]$$

$$= \beta\left[U_V\left(x_R{}^*, y_R{}^*\right) - U_V\left(x_D{}^*, y_D{}^*\right) + \frac{1}{2\beta}\right] \qquad (6.3)$$

$$= \frac{1}{2} + \beta\left[U_V\left(x_R{}^*, y_R{}^*\right) - U_V\left(x_D{}^*, y_D{}^*\right)\right].$$

Now the preferences of D and R can be specified with *expected* utility functions. These are functions of the utilities experienced by each party under both platforms, with the utilities multiplied by the probability of each party's victory. The expected utility functions for the Republicans and Democrats are therefore written as

$$E[U_R] = \pi U_R\left(x_R{}^*, y_R{}^*\right) + (1 - \pi)U_R\left(x_D{}^*, y_D{}^*\right)$$
$$E[U_D] = \pi U_D\left(x_R{}^*, y_R{}^*\right) + (1 - \pi)U_D\left(x_D{}^*, y_D{}^*\right).$$

Equilbria. The solution concept used to solve this game is Nash equilibrium in pure strategies. In this model, a Nash equilibrium is defined as a scenario where neither D nor R wishes to change her platform given the strategy of the other candidate.[6] Nash equilibria can be identified by optimizing each party's expected utility function. R's best response to D's platform $\left(x_D{}^*, y_D{}^*\right)$ satisfies the first-order conditions

$$\frac{\partial\pi}{\partial x_R{}^*}\psi_R + \pi\frac{\partial U_R}{\partial x_R{}^*} = 0 \quad \text{and} \quad \frac{\partial\pi}{\partial y_R{}^*}\psi_R + \pi\frac{\partial U_R}{\partial y_R{}^*} = 0$$

$$\text{and thus} \quad -\frac{\pi}{\psi_R} = \frac{\partial\pi / \partial x_R{}^*}{\partial U_R / \partial x_R{}^*} = \frac{\partial\pi / \partial y_R{}^*}{\partial U_R / \partial y_R{}^*},$$

where $\psi_R \equiv U_R\left(x_R{}^*, y_R{}^*\right) - U_R\left(x_D{}^*, y_D{}^*\right)$.[7] Using Equations 6.1, 6.2, and 6.3 to compute the needed partial derivatives and noting that D's maximization problem is symmetric to R's, we have

---

[6] I rule out as solutions any nonsensical cases where parties fail to locate between their own ideal points and that of the voter, and thus limit the focus to equilibria in which $d < x_D{}^* < v, d < y_D{}^* < v, v < x_R{}^* < r$, and $v < y_R{}^* < r$.

[7] It is the case (but not shown here) that the *second*-order conditions for a maximum are satisfied in that the matrices of each party's pair of second derivatives are negative definite when evaluated at the critical point identified by the first-order conditions. Technically, what is being identified here is a local equilibrium – that is, one that is immune to small deviations by the two candidates – rather than a global equilibrium, which would require that the two parties' expected utility functions be strictly concave. The platforms derived from the model and displayed in Table 6.1 are the only equilibria satisfying the rules $d < x_D{}^* < v, d < y_D{}^* < v, v < x_R{}^* < r$, and $v < y_R{}^* < r$ for the model parameterizations specified.

$$\frac{x_R{}^*-v}{x_R{}^*-r} = \frac{y_R{}^*-v}{\alpha\left(y_R{}^*-r\right)} \quad \text{and} \quad \frac{x_D{}^*-v}{\alpha\left(x_D{}^*-d\right)} = \frac{y_D{}^*-v}{y_D{}^*-d}. \tag{6.4}$$

These ratios specify that in equilibrium, the parties' platforms are located upon curves connecting the parties' ideal points with the voter's ideal point. As shown in Figure 6.1, these curves (drawn with dashes) bow toward the issue dimensions the two parties own: in equilibrium, the parties' platforms are closer to their ideal points on the issues they own than on the issues they do not. These curves become more bowed to the extent that α is large. As will be seen, the parties locate at points on these curves where they gain just as much expected utility by moving toward the center (and thus increasing their chances of winning) as they do by moving away from it (and proposing a policy they prefer).[8]

Implications for Representation

The model developed here yields clear expectations about the relationship between a party's ownership of an issue and the extent to which its policies reflect public opinion. These expectations can be phrased in terms of the phenomena in which empirical scholars of representation are most interested: congruence (or proximity) and responsiveness (Achen 1978). Congruence is the extent to which policy mirrors the preferences of an electorate's typical voter. Responsiveness is the extent to which policy changes with a shift in preferences – across, say, legislative districts or over time. Here I show that the implications of this model are unambiguous with regard to both congruence and responsiveness: to the extent that a party cares more about an issue, it establishes policies that are less representative of citizen preferences.

Congruence. In the model, congruence is measured by the distance between the policies proposed in equilibrium and the voter's ideal point on each dimension. In the case of R's policies, for example, these distances are $x_R{}^* - v$ and $y_R{}^* - v$. R cares more about issue y (domestic security) than issue x (health care) by a factor of $\alpha > 1$. A simple analysis demonstrates that R's policies are always more proximate to the voter's preferences on issue x than issue y, and that

---

[8] This point is specified by a slightly different manipulation of the first-order conditions (shown here for R; they are symmetric for D). It is where $\psi_R\left(\partial\pi / \partial x_R{}^*\right) = -\pi\left(\partial U_R / \partial x_R{}^*\right)$ and $\psi_R\left(\partial\pi / \partial y_R{}^*\right) = -\pi\left(\partial U_R / \partial y_R{}^*\right)$.

this difference in congruence increases to the extent that α is large. Define the difference in R's proximity on the two issues as h, with $h \equiv y_R^* - v - \left(x_R^* - v\right) = y_R^* - x_R^*$. It can be shown that h is always positive, and thus it is always the case that R's platform on the y-dimension (that is, on the issue it owns) is less proximate to the preferences of V than R's policy on the x-dimension. Furthermore, because it can also be shown that h is increasing in α, R becomes relatively less congruent on y as the party cares more about its owned issue, y. By symmetry, these results hold the same for D and the issue it owns, issue x.[9]

Responsiveness. The model also shows us why we should expect parties to be less responsive to public opinion to the extent that they care about issues and thus own them. This can be seen by conducting numerical simulations with the model that explore how the parties' positions change as the voter's preferences change.[10] The simulations are generated using the assumptions that D and R are located at opposite corners of the policy space with $d = $ -1 and $r = $ 1 and that $\beta = \frac{1}{4}$. Table 6.1 displays simulated platforms adopted in equilibrium as the voter's ideal point ranges from moderately liberal (at $v = $ -.5) to moderately conservative ($v = $ .5). These simulations are generated while varying α, the factor by which partisans care more about their party's owned issues relative to other issues, from 1 to 3.

The final columns of the table are estimates of the parties' responsiveness to voter preferences on issue y. (This is the issue owned by R; symmetric results hold for issue x and its owner, D.) The responsiveness estimates are calculated from the simulated data in the same way that they will be estimated from actual data later in this chapter: by running least-squares regressions of the parties' simulated platforms on the voter ideal points. Responsiveness is measured with the coefficients

---

[9] Rewrite R's first-order condition in Equation 6.4 and solve for h as follows:

$$\frac{x_R^* - v}{x_R^* - r} = \frac{x_R^* + h - v}{\alpha\left(x_R^* + h - r\right)} \quad \Rightarrow \quad h = \frac{(1-\alpha)\left(x_R^* - v\right)}{\dfrac{\alpha\left(x_R^* - v\right)}{x_R^* - r} - 1}. \quad \text{Because } v < x_R^* < r \text{ and } \alpha > 1,$$

the numerator and denominator of h are both negative, and so h is always positive. The ratio h is also increasing in α: $\dfrac{\partial h}{\partial \alpha} = \dfrac{-(r-v)\left(r - x_R^*\right)\left(v - x_R^*\right)}{\left(r - x_R^* - v\alpha + \alpha x_R^*\right)^2} > 0.$

[10] These simulations were generated using the Mathematica software program. Code and additional details about these simulations are available in this book's replication archive.

TABLE 6.1. *Simulated platforms
in the issue ownership spatial model*

extent of issue ownership (a)	voter ideal point (v)	D's platform		R's platform		Responsiveness on issue y		
		x (owned issue)	y	x	y (owned issue)	R (issue-owner)	D	Ratio
1	−.50	−.78	−.78	−.05	−.05	.84	.84	1.0
	−.25	−.60	−.60	.17	.17			
	.00	−.39	−.39	.39	.39			
	.25	−.17	−.17	.60	.60			
	.50	.05	.05	.78	.78			
2	−.50	−.83	−.74	−.17	.04	.79	.92	.86
	−.25	−.66	−.54	.07	.26			
	.00	−.47	−.31	.31	.47			
	.25	−.26	−.07	.54	.66			
	.50	−.04	.17	.74	.83			
3	−.50	−.85	−.72	−.21	.07	.78	.96	.81
	−.25	−.70	−.50	.01	.30			
	.00	−.51	−.26	.26	.51			
	.25	−.30	−.01	.50	.70			
	.50	−.07	.21	.72	.85			

estimated in these bivariate regressions, which can be interpreted as the change in a party's platform caused by a one-unit change in voter opinion. A coefficient of one indicates perfect responsiveness to voter preferences; responsiveness is declining to the extent that the coefficient is less than one.

The first rows of Table 6.1 display simulated party platforms in a baseline condition where both parties care about both issues to the same degree and there is no issue ownership (that is, when $a = 1$). Here the parties propose the same policies on both dimensions on opposite sides of the voter's ideal point, and thus both parties are equally responsive to the voter's preferences. Differences in the parties' responsiveness arise as a – and thus issue ownership – increases. When $a = 2$, partisans care about their party's owned issue twice as much as the other issue. The table shows that at this level of prioritization, the owning party becomes slightly less responsive on its owned issue than at the baseline. Furthermore, the other party becomes *more* responsive on this issue in order to compensate for the fact that it is in turn becoming less responsive on the issue it owns. The result is that the owning party is less responsive to public opinion on the issue it owns than the non-owning party. The final entries of the table show that an additional increase of α to 3 shifts the parties' responsiveness further in opposite directions, and the gap in responsiveness on the two issues increases accordingly.

The model presented here incorporates the findings of the previous chapters into the standard spatial model of elections by adding a single assumption: parties prioritize some issues to a greater degree than others. The conclusion to be drawn from the model is simple: we should expect parties to pay less attention to voter preferences on the issues they own than on the issues they do not.

The Model: A Nontechnical Summary

The assumptions behind my spatial model of issue ownership and the insights it yields are straightforward. When parties face off in electoral competition, they craft policy platforms with two competing goals in mind: winning office and establishing policies that are as desirable as possible to their partisans. The first goal leads parties to be responsive to the preferences of the typical voter, who wants moderate policies on most issues. The second goal means that parties must also heed the preferences of their members, who want liberal policies (if they are Democrats) or conservative policies (if they are Republicans). However, as we learned in the previous chapter, all issues are not created equal in the minds of partisans: they care about different issues to different degrees. Republicans – their elites, their elected officials, and their voters – prioritize the party's owned issues (such as domestic security and taxes) over others; Democrats care more about the issues they own (such as health care and the environment) than others. Thus partisans are more likely to demand ideological orthodoxy on the issues the party owns than on other issues, where they are more willing to abide moderation.

Parties therefore balance the goals of satisfying partisans and winning votes by taking extreme positions on the issues they own (which pleases party activists) while moving closer to the middle on the issues they do not own (which helps them compete for the support of moderate voters). This trade-off means that parties establish policies on the issues they own that are both less congruent with the preferences of the electorate and less responsive to shifts in voter preferences. In sum, the parties' policies are less representative of public opinion on issues they own than on issues they do not.

An Addendum: The Preferences of Partisans Who Care Most about Issues

To allow us to see the implications of issue ownership for representation as clearly as possible, until now I have assumed that the parties' ideal points are located equidistantly from the voter on both issue dimensions. But this assumption may lead to predictions that actually understate the distortionary impact of issue ownership on the opinion–policy relationship. This is because survey data suggest that on issues parties own, partisans who care most about these issues hold views that are far away from the center. Remarkably, the opposite tends to be true for issues parties do not own: partisans who care deeply about these issues tend to hold views that are actually *nearer* to the center. Thus parties that own issues not only have more partisans who think these issues are important, it is also the case that these partisans tend to hold views on these issues that are extremely ideological compared to those who care deeply about the issue in the other party. Therefore to the extent that those who care most about issues have the most say in determining a party's position on an issue, we should expect parties to be pulled even further away from the center on the issues they own than is predicted by the model.

Evidence for extreme partisan preferences on owned issues is found in survey data taken from the American National Election Studies conducted in 2008. On five consensus issues, the ANES asked its national sample of American adults questions about their policy preferences on a seven-point scale. Two of these were Republican-owned issues (the military and unauthorized immigration); the other three were Democratic issues (health care, jobs, and the environment). On each of these issues, survey participants were also asked, "How important is this issue to you personally?" Respondents indicated the personal importance of the issue using a scale ranging from "not important at all" to "extremely important."

In Figure 6.2, ANES respondents' policy preferences on the five issues are displayed graphically in a left–right fashion. Respondents' preferences are rescaled in terms of the preferences of the average

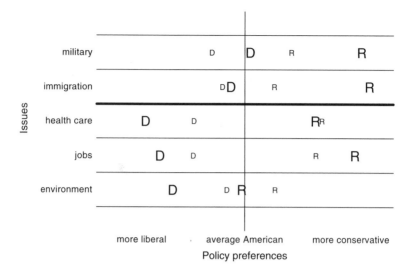

FIGURE 6.2. Issue importance and policy preferences, 2008.
Source: American National Election Studies.
Question wording: See this chapter's appendix.

American, which are indicated by the vertical line drawn in the middle of the figure – and thus literally represents the center of American opinion on these five issues. The two Republican-owned issues are listed first, followed by the three Democratic-owned issues. The mean policy preferences of those identifying as Democrats and Republicans are indicated on each issue with small Ds and Rs.[11] Not surprisingly, on each issue the average Democrat is to the left of the average American; the average Republican is to the right. Note that there is no discernible relationship between issue ownership and the distance between partisans and the average American on these five issues.

But a pattern does emerge when we separate out the responses of the partisans who say each of the issues is "extremely important," indicated in the figure by the large Ds and Rs. On all of the issues, partisans

---

[11] Those who "lean" toward one of the parties are included in the calculation of means.

in the owning party who care most about the issue are located further from the center than their co-partisans. But the exact opposite is generally true for partisans in the non-owning party: on four of the five issues – all except jobs – those in the non-owning party who care most about these issues have policy preferences that are actually closer to the center than their fellow partisans. So for example, Republicans for whom the issue of unauthorized immigration is extremely important hold views on immigration policy that are quite far to the right compared to the preferences of the typical American. But the opposite is true for Democrats: partisans who care most about the issue of unauthorized immigration are located close to the center – and in fact, they are actually slightly more moderate than their co-partisans. A similar arrangement of partisan preferences holds for the Democratic-owned issue of the environment. Democrats who care most about this issue hold views that are quite liberal compared to the views of the typical voter. By contrast, Republicans for whom the environment is extremely important have preferences located very close to the center.

These data suggest an addendum to the spatial model of issue ownership may be justified. As indicated by the gray arrows in Figure 6.1, the parties' ideal points may actually lie farther away from the center on the issues they own and toward the center on the issues they do not. Thus in the policy space diagrammed in Figure 6.1, the true locations of *D* and *R*'s ideal points may be further to the upper left than the equidistant locations on which the model is based. If this is true, then issue-owning parties should adopt platforms that are even less congruent and less responsive on the issues they own than under the original assumption that the parties' ideal points are equidistant from the typical voter on both issues.

ISSUE OWNERSHIP AND REPRESENTATION: EMPIRICAL ANALYSES

The spatial model of issue ownership generates sharp predictions about how issue ownership modifies the relationship between public opinion and public policy. The remainder of this chapter turns to two empirical analyses designed to assess the extent to which these theoretical expectations are borne out by actual public opinion and public policy data. The first analysis examines the relationship between key votes in Congress and constituency opinion; the second examines how federal spending responds to national opinion.

Although the spatial model provides theoretical predictions about both congruence and responsiveness, the focus here is largely limited to the latter of these two phenomena. Ideally, we would like to be able to assess both with empirical tests, but a limitation of the data typically leads scholars to focus on responsiveness: it is rare that opinion and policy making are measured in the same units, which is necessary for an analysis of congruence. This is particularly the case in the legislative context, where legislative records are derived from roll-call votes on many different topics. Analyses that focus on single roll-call votes can be subject to a fair amount of error in the measurement of a constituency's true preferences on the topic of the vote (Page and Shapiro 1983; Hagen, Lascher, and Comobreco 2001).[12] By contrast, differing units do not prevent us from assessing the slope of the relationship between opinion and policy making across districts: this can be done easily with techniques such as linear regression.

In addition, there is a substantive reason for refraining from focusing on congruence with regard to federal spending: it is not clear that Americans' collective answers to survey questions about spending accurately describe their true preferences – that is, the decisions they would actually make if they themselves were in policy-makers' shoes. Recall from Chapter 2 that in 2010, majorities of Americans simultaneously expressed support for increased federal spending on no fewer than eight consensus goals ranging from education to crime, while also calling for tax cuts – an unrealistic, budget-busting phenomenon regularly observed in surveys that include batteries of spending questions. These opinion data are therefore more accurately interpreted as indicating a broad consensus that federal funds should be spent on achieving certain national goals. A party that increased spending on all of these goals while simultaneously cutting taxes would indeed be congruent with Americans' expressed spending preferences in a literal sense. But such congruence does not seem in the spirit of how – either normatively or empirically – scholars of politics conceive of representation. Insight about the extent to which government responds

---

[12] Recent work that makes progress on the challenge of measurement error with regard to congruence includes Bafumi and Herron 2010, Jessee 2009, and Lax and Phillips 2012.

to Americans' budgetary preferences is thus more likely to be gained from an analysis of responsiveness to these preferences, which better reflects how shifts in the public's relative support for spending on different consensus goals affects the allocation of federal dollars.

Issue Ownership, Key Congressional Votes, and Constituency Opinion

The spatial model with issue ownership provides a straightforward prediction about the responsiveness of legislators to constituency opinion in the U.S. Congress: on any given issue, the relationship between constituency preferences and roll-call voting should be weaker for members of Congress (MCs) from the issue-owning party than from the other party. Here I explore these implications by examining the relationship between constituency opinion and the positions taken by members of Congress on eleven different issues.

Source of opinion data: the National Annenberg Election Survey. Constituency-level opinion on specific issues is obtained from the 2000 National Annenberg Election Survey (NAES) rolling cross-section study. The NAES interviewed a total of 58,254 American adults between December 1999 and January 2001. The survey included a battery of questions regarding a range of policies at the heart of the political debate during the 2000 presidential campaign. These include questions on controversies associated with five issues owned by the Republicans (crime, intervention in foreign civil wars, military spending, the missile defense shield, and taxes) and three questions on issues owned by the Democrats (education spending, the environment, and school vouchers). The NAES also fielded questions on three non-consensus issues: abortion, gay rights, and guns. These questions are included in the analysis to provide additional data that improve the precision of the estimates of interest.[13]

Although the NAES was designed to obtain a sample of the preferences of the nation as a whole, the random-digit dialing procedure used by the survey makes it possible to generate statistically unbiased estimates of opinion at the congressional district level. The survey included respondents from every congressional district in the United

---

[13] Results are robust to excluding these questions from the analysis.

States except those in Alaska and Hawaii, and averaged about 135 respondents per district. Not every policy question was asked of every respondent, but on the policy questions analyzed here the mean number of respondents per district ranged between 57 to 127 individuals, yielding relatively precise estimates of constituency opinion.[14] The size of the NAES sample, its breadth of policy questions, and its random-digit design make it a far superior resource than any academic study to date for generating estimates of constituency opinion at the congressional district level and studying its effect on Congress (Clinton 2006; see also Warshaw and Rodden 2012). Responses to all NAES questions were rescaled zero–one (liberal to conservative). Details on the questions may be found in this chapter's appendix.

Source of policy-making data: key roll-call votes in Congress, 1997–2002. The NAES was conducted between December 1999 and January 2001. To measure policy making I used votes cast in the House of Representatives from 1997 through 2002, the six years closest to the survey period that occurred before the redistricting following the 2000 Census. To identify roll-call votes appropriate for analysis, I consulted the annual lists of significant votes compiled by two highly regarded resources on Congress: *Congressional Quarterly* (which lists what it calls "key votes") (CQ Weekly 1997–2002) and the *National Journal* (which compiles a list to calculate annual "vote ratings" for each legislator) (Barone et al. 1999, 2001, 2003). Both sources limit their lists to votes of substantial import or controversy. In order to be considered for inclusion in my analysis, a roll-call vote had to be included on one of these two lists. To choose votes from this pool for analysis, I determined whether the subject matter of the vote could reasonably be deemed to be related to the subject matter of one of the issue domains under study. I did not use votes whose outcomes were lopsided in one direction or another. A total of 124 House votes on the eleven different issues were included in my analysis. A list of all of these votes and the issues to which they were assigned may be found in this chapter's appendix.

[14] Like many surveys, the NAES underrepresented younger Americans and racial minorities. Because sampling weights were not supplied with the NAES, I developed post-stratification weights on the basis of age, gender, and race using U.S. Census congressional district-level enumerations of these variables (specifically, data from the 2000 Census calculated for district lines in effect for the 106th Congress). I weighted the NAES sample accordingly.

To determine how these votes translated into records established by MCs on each of the eleven different issues, I estimated separate roll-call scores for each MC on each issue. This technique generates estimates of the location of each "aye" and "nay" vote in the roll-call analysis and, consequently, the location of each legislator in the issue space.[15] I generated estimates of the roll-call scores on the eleven different issues of all 528 representatives who served at least some time in the House between 1997 and 2002.[16] All roll-call records were rescaled zero–one (liberal to conservative).

Estimation strategy. The structure of these data and the question of whether responsiveness differs by issue ownership requires an estimation strategy that accounts for the considerable heterogeneity across districts and issues in the relationship between opinion and the roll-call records established by legislators. I therefore estimated the following multilevel mixed-effects linear model:

$$MC_i\text{'s position on issue}_j = \alpha + \beta_j \left(opinion\ on\ issue_j\ in\ district_i \right) + \gamma_i + \delta_j + \varepsilon_{ij},$$

where:

$$\beta_j = \eta_1 + \eta_2 \left(MC_i\text{'s party owns issue}_j \right) + \eta_3 \left(MC_i\ is\ a\ Democrat \right)$$
$$+ \eta_4 \left(MC_i\text{'s party owns issue}_j \times MC_i\ is\ a\ Democrat \right)$$
$$+ \eta_5 \left(neither\ party\ owns\ issue_j \right)$$
$$+ \eta_6 \left(neither\ party\ owns\ issue_j \times MC_i\ is\ a\ Democrat \right) + \upsilon_j$$
$$\gamma_i = \mu_0 + \zeta_i$$
$$\delta_j = \mu_1 + \zeta_j.$$

---

[15] I employed the ideal-point estimation technique developed by Clinton, Jackman, and Rivers (2004) as implemented by Martin, Quinn, and Park (2012) in the R statistical package. Note however, that I am not estimating MCs' ideal points as the term is used to describe the formal model earlier in this chapter. Rather, I am estimating the locations of public positions taken by MCs in each issue's space – which can be considered equivalent to the platforms in the model.

[16] The results presented here are robust to other estimation approaches. For example, I estimated legislators' positions on each policy as the scores derived from the first factor yielded by factor analyzing the roll-call votes in each policy domain. These alternative estimates are highly correlated with the estimates used in the present analysis and in fact produce results that more strongly support my theory than those reported here.

In this model, the parameters v and ζ are issue- and district-specific error terms: intercepts are assumed to vary at random by district (sub-scripted i) and by issue (j), and the effect of opinion on roll-call voting (that is, its slope) is also assumed to vary by issue. Of the most interest for our purposes is that the effect of opinion on roll-call voting for issue j is assumed to itself be affected by the party affiliation of the MC and which party owns the issue (the MC's party, the other party, or neither party), and the interaction of these variables.[17] The predictions from the spatial model of issue ownership are supported to the extent that the effect of a district's opinion on its MC's voting record is lower when the MC's party owns the issue than when it does not.[18]

Results: the responsiveness of legislators to district opinion. Estimates from the model are displayed in Table 6.2. The coefficients of interest are displayed at the top of the table: they are estimates of how district opinion and issue ownership affect roll-call votes, with separate estimates generated for Democratic and Republican members of Congress. Calculations from the table indicate that legislators from both parties – but particularly Republicans – are less responsive to dis-trict opinion on the issues their parties own compared to the issues they do not. Republican responsiveness on non-owned issues can be read off from the first coefficient listed on the table; it is .20. By contrast, Republican responsiveness on owned issues is .20 − .18 = .02: essen-tially, no responsiveness. Democratic responsiveness is found by sum-ming the relevant coefficients: on non-owned issues, it is .20 − .08 = .12; on owned issues it is the sum of all four coefficients listed in the top section of the table and thus just slightly less than zero.

These calculations are displayed in Figure 6.3, which plots the posi-tions taken by Republicans and Democrats on owned and non-owned issues across the policy space as predicted by the model. Here it can be plainly seen how responsiveness on owned issues (indicated by the solid lines in the figure) is dwarfed by responsiveness on non-owned issues (the

---

[17] This model is therefore an instance of a non-nested multilevel model with crossed random effects. See, e.g., Gelman and Hill (2007) and Rabe-Hesketh and Skrondal 2012). The error terms v_i and ζ_j are allowed to covary with one another in the esti-mated model.

[18] For easier interpretation, these estimates use the categorical measure of issue ownership rather than its interval-level measure. Estimates employing the interval-level measure returned substantively similar results. See this book's online appendix for details.

TABLE 6.2. *Responsiveness of members of congress (MCs)
to constituency opinion*

	DV: MC$_i$'s Estimated Position on Issue$_j$
tests of issue–ownership hypothesis	
district$_i$ opinion on issue$_j$	.20**
	(.07)
district$_i$ opinion × MC's party owns issue$_j$	−.18+
	(.09)
district$_i$ opinion × Democratic MC	−.08
	(.09)
district$_i$ opinion × MC's party owns issue$_j$ × Democratic MC	.05
	(.17)
MC$_i$'s party owns issue$_j$	.15**
	(.05)
MC$_i$'s party owns issue$_j$ × Democratic MC	−.24*
	(.10)
additional coefficients estimated in model	
district$_i$ opinion × neither party owns issue$_j$	.17+
	(.10)
district$_i$ opinion × neither party owns issue$_j$ × Democratic MC	.05
	(.10)
Democratic MC	−.38***
	(.06)
neither party owns issue$_j$	−.07
	(.06)
neither party owns issue$_j$ x Democratic MC	−.07
	(.06)
intercept	.64***
	(.04)
Standard deviations of:	
District intercepts	.11
Issue intercepts	.07
Issue opinion slopes	.10
N	5,808

Multilevel mixed-effects linear model estimated via restricted maximum likelihood. MC positions and district opinion scaled zero (liberal) to one (conservative) by issue. For additional details of model estimation, see text. Estimates significantly different from zero at $+p<.10$; $*p<.05$; $**p<.01$; $***p<.001$ (two–tailed tests).

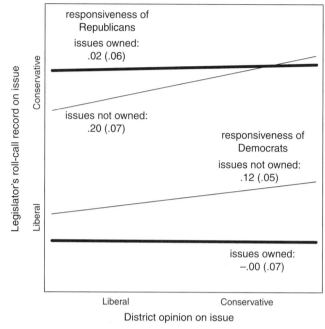

FIGURE 6.3. Responsiveness of congressional roll-call votes to district opinion.

Source: Predictions generated by model in Table 6.2.

thin lines). In fact, on owned issues, responsiveness to public opinion is essentially flat.[19] The figure also provides some circumstantial evidence for the spatial model's predictions regarding congruence, as legislators' roll-call records on non-owned issues are generally closer to the center than their positions on owned issues. As mentioned earlier, because roll-call records and district opinion are measured on different scales, this should be considered a suggestive finding rather than a definitive one.

Issue Ownership, Federal Spending, and National Opinion

Although the model developed at the beginning of this chapter is situated in a policy space, the same logic generates similar expectations

[19] When the records of both parties are considered together, overall responsiveness on non-owned issues is .16 with a standard error of .04; responsiveness on owned issues is .01 with a standard error of .04. The difference in responsiveness on the two types of issues is .15 with a standard error of .03, an estimate significantly greater than zero at $p < .001$.

about how the parties should respond to shifts in the priority space – that is, the public's relative prioritization of differing consensus goals. We can reenvision the diagram in Figure 6.1 as a priority space, where the x and y axes now represent the relative preferences of R, D, and V for prioritizing the consensus issues of health care and domestic security. The analogy to a policy space is not perfect, as the trade-offs among priorities are better represented with a budget constraint as they were portrayed earlier in this book (in Figure 3.3). But the implications of the model for prioritization are the same. To the extent that a party that cares more about a particular consensus goal (and thus owns the issue associated with that goal), we should expect it to be more likely to prioritize that goal with legislation and spending – even when the public's priorities shift away from the goal.

Here I test this hypothesis with data and estimation techniques similar to those employed in the rich body of scholarship exploring the relationship between the public's preferences over the federal budget and actual government spending. The most prominent work on this topic has been conducted by Christopher Wlezien and Stuart N. Soroka, who in a series of studies have found a consistent relationship between opinion and spending, whose strength can vary substantially by issue and by country (Wlezien 2004; Soroka and Wlezien 2005, 2010; other notable examples include Bartels 1991; Canes-Wrone and Shotts 2004; Hobolt and Klemmensen 2005, 2008). Wlezien has shown that this responsiveness takes place concurrently with the public's calibrating its preferences to account for changes in government policy in a "thermostat"-like fashion: as government dollars allocated toward a particular issue increase, public opinion shifts away from support for spending on the issue; the opposite takes place when spending is cut (Wlezien 1995). Where possible, I follow previous researchers' decisions with regard to selection of data and estimation techniques.

Data. I return to the opinion and federal outlays data presented earlier in this book. As discussed in Chapter 2, the General Social Survey (GSS) has been recording Americans' preferences for spending on a list of issues since the early 1970s.[20] And as shown in the

---

[20] Additional surveys on Americans' spending preferences using very similar question wording were conducted at times by the Roper Organization; these data are also included in the analysis. In years where both Roper and the GSS asked spending questions about the same issues, responses were averaged.

previous chapter, the percentage of federal outlays spent on various programs – including taxes, if coded in the opposite direction from spending – can be assigned in a straightforward fashion to many of these issues. I therefore merge these two datasets by time and by issue. The dataset includes three issues owned by the Republicans (crime, the military, and taxes) and six by the Democrats (education, energy, the environment, health care, poverty, and Social Security). To improve the precision of results, the analysis also includes six issues for which both opinion data and spending exist but for which we do not have hypotheses because they are either non-consensus issues (cities, foreign aid, and space) or not clearly owned by either party (parks, science, and transportation).[21] Federal outlays were assigned to issues by the subfunction to which they are categorized by the White House Office of Management and Budget as shown in this chapter's appendix; for additional details see the discussion in Chapter 5. Taken together, these issues come admirably close to being a complete representation of all government outlays: in a typical year, spending on these issues makes up 81 percent of all federal spending. Finally, as is done throughout this book, I consider cuts in taxation as "spending" on the issue of taxes. Thus decreases and increases in the annual sum of all of federal taxes as a share of federal spending serve as measures of, respectively, increases and decreases in spending on taxes.

For comparability with the results of previous scholarship on the relationship between public opinion and spending, the analysis here comports with that work in a number of ways. The dependent variable is annual change in issue-specific spending as a percentage of total federal outlays. The degree to which spending changes can vary widely by issue: as a percentage of all federal outlays, spending on issues such as the military and health care tends to change in a more dramatic fashion than spending on crime or the environment. Thus I measure change in spending in terms of standard deviations: that is, I divide the spending variable by the issue-specific standard deviation of spending change over the time period of analysis. (This is the approach taken by Soroka and Wlezien 2010: 97).

---

[21] The results presented here are robust to the exclusion of these issues from the analysis.

I also follow previous work in measuring aggregate public support for spending. Recall from Chapter 2 that the GSS assesses Americans' preferences by asking whether they think current levels of spending are "too much," "too little," or "about right." Aggregate support for spending on an issue is thus measured by subtracting the percentage of Americans saying too much is being spent on the issue from the percentage saying too little is being spent. I follow a nearly similar rule for calculating aggregate support for tax cuts. The GSS asks Americans whether their individual federal income taxes are "too high," "too low," or "about right." Not surprisingly, very few Americans profess that they pay too little in taxes; I therefore calculate the public's overall support for tax cuts by simply considering the percentage saying their taxes are "too high." I apply a one-year lag to all the opinion data to account for the fact that it can take time for outlays to adjust to the public's preferences, as is standard in previous research. Opinion data are centered by issue on the mean level of support for spending on the issue over the time period of analysis, which is also a common approach.

The time period analyzed here is the same as that examined in Chapter 5's analysis of federal outlays: it begins with federal fiscal year 1982 and ends in 2011. As noted in the previous chapter, federal fiscal year 1982 – which began on October 1, 1981 – is the first year in which budgetary control was completely in the hands of President Reagan and the divided Congress that came to power in the 1980 elections, and it is the point at which the relationship between issue ownership and federal spending began to come into full relief.

Estimation strategy. The issue-ownership hypothesis leads to quite straightforward expectations about responsiveness in this context: federal spending should be less affected by public opinion on issues owned by the party in control of the presidency and Congress. Furthermore, regardless of public opinion, we expect owning parties to direct federal dollars toward the issues they own more than the issues they do not. Before turning to a multiple regression approach, we can simply look at the data in Figure 6.4, which plots the relationship between opinion and spending found when the presidency and Congress are both controlled by the party owning the issue (dark

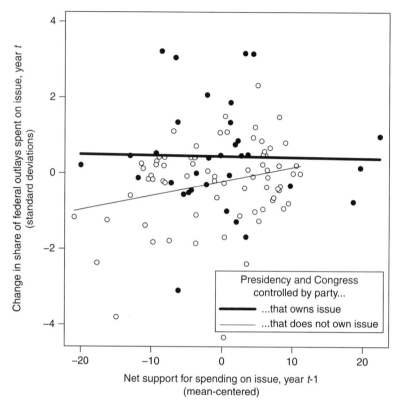

FIGURE 6.4. Responsiveness of federal outlays to national opinion.
Sources: See text.

circles) compared to the relationship when both branches are controlled by the party not owning the issue (hollow circles). Best linear
fit lines trace the two relationships, and they offer strong evidence for
both predictions from the issue-ownership hypothesis. The black line
is above zero and flat: on average, owning parties shift the federal budget toward their owned issues when they control the government, and
in doing so are completely unresponsive to the public's preferences.
By contrast, the gray line is generally below zero and positively sloped
(at .037 with a standard error of .015). This means that when a party
controls the government, it typically diverts spending away from the
issues it does not own – but it does so with a careful eye toward public
opinion by focusing these cuts on issues for which public support is
unusually low.

To more precisely assess the issue-ownership hypothesis, I estimate the following multilevel mixed-effects linear model.[22]

change in spending in year$_t$ on issue$_j$ as % of total federal outlays =

$$\alpha + \beta_j \left(\textit{national support for spending on issue}_j \textit{ in year}_{t-1} \right) + \gamma_t + \varepsilon_{tj},$$

where:

$$\beta_j = \eta_1 + \eta_2 \left(\textit{party of president in year}_{t-1} \textit{ owns issue}_j \right)$$
$$+ \eta_3 \left(\textit{Congress is controlled in year}_{t-1} \textit{ by party owning issue}_j \right)$$
$$+ \eta_4 \left(\textit{neither party owns issue}_j \right) + \upsilon_j$$
$$\gamma_t = \mu_0 + \zeta_t.$$

In this model, intercepts are assumed to vary at random by year, and the effect of opinion on national spending (its slope) is assumed to vary at random by issue.[23] This slope is in turn assumed to be affected by whether the president's party owns the issue, whether both houses of Congress are controlled by the party owning the issue, or by contrast whether neither party owns the issue.

Results: the responsiveness of federal spending to Americans' priorities. Estimates from the model are shown in Table 6.3. Once again, the coefficients of interest are displayed at the top of the table: they are estimates of how issue ownership affects the extent to which the president and Congress respond to opinion regarding federal spending. These coefficients confirm what was suggested by the raw data. The positive coefficients on ownership by the president and – particularly – Congress tell us that, all things being equal, when they control the government parties direct spending toward the issues they own. The negative coefficients on the interaction between ownership and preferences for the presidency and – again, particularly – Congress

---

[22] The results presented here are similar to those yielded by other estimation approaches, including those that explicitly account for the time-series nature of the data as well as estimates generated using the interval-level of measure issue ownership. See this book's online appendix for details.

[23] Because opinion is mean-centered by issue, issue-specific intercepts are not estimated in this model.

TABLE 6.3. *Responsiveness of federal outlays to national spending preferences*

	DV: change in % of all federal outlays spent on issue *j* in year *t* (standardized)
tests of issue-ownership hypothesis	
public's spending preferences in year$_{t-1}$ on issue$_j$	.031*
	(.016)
public's spending preferences$_j$ x president's party$_{t-1}$ owns issue$_j$	−.003
	(.018)
public's spending preferences$_j$ x Congress$_{t-1}$ is controlled by party owning issue$_j$	−.039*
	(.018)
president's party$_{t-1}$ owns issue$_j$	.164
	(.125)
Congress$_{t-1}$ is controlled by party owning issue$_j$	.311*
	(.137)
additional coefficients estimated in model	
neither party owns issue$_j$	.011
	(.126)
public's spending preferences$_j$ x neither party owns issue$_j$	−.016
	(.024)
intercept	−.171
	(.129)
Standard deviations of:	
Year intercepts	.446
Issue opinion slopes	.027
N	397

Multilevel mixed-effects linear model estimated via restricted maximum likelihood. For additional details of model estimation, see text. Estimates significantly different from zero at +p<.10; *p<.05; **p<.01; ***p<.001 (two-tailed tests).

confirm that the impact of preferences on spending is lower on issues owned by the party in power.

These differences in responsiveness can be quantified by generating estimates using the relevant coefficients. Consider the impact of a year-over-year shift of five percentage points in either direction in the public's net support for spending on a particular issue. (In the time period analyzed here, a shift of this size or larger occurred about one-fifth of the time.) If the issue is owned by the party in control of both Congress and the presidency, it responds to such a shift in the public's preferences by doing essentially nothing: the estimated change in spending is –.055 standard deviations with a standard error of .092. But if the issue is *not* owned by the party in control of the government, spending indeed shifts in a significant fashion in the direction of the public's preferences: an estimated .154 standard deviations with a standard error of .078.[24]

CONCLUSION

The findings in this chapter demonstrate that issue ownership offers a trade-off to American voters. Owning parties can be relied upon to devote attention and funds to addressing goals on which there exists a broad national consensus. Voters appreciate this, which is why they consistently say they trust parties to handle the issues they own. But the devotion associated with issue ownership comes with a price: a party's ideological extremism and rigidity on the issues it owns.

It is important to note that the theory developed here relies only on the fact that parties prioritize different sets of issues, as documented thoroughly in Chapter 5. It does not require that voters believe that an issue-owning party can deliver superior performance, for as Chapter 4 shows there is no empirical reason for voters to hold such beliefs. However, to the extent that voters do in fact deem owning parties to be more competent on the issues they own, the distortion between opinion and policy may be more profound. Voters might grant additional leeway to owning parties in exchange for greater competence (in a manner described by Krasa and Polborn 2010). It is also possible

---

[24] The difference between responsiveness on owned and non-owned issues is cally significant at $p = .08$ (two-tailed test).

that voters might be persuaded by an owning party that its policies on the issue are superior. In either case, the effect of public opinion on policy (measured empirically as the relationship between citizen preferences in one period and government action in the next) will be diminished even further.

Appendix to Chapter 6

Wording of Questions for ANES Policy Placement Scales

(source of data for Figure 6.2)

ISSUE	QUESTION WORDING
Environment	Next, we'd like to ask whether you favor, oppose, or neither favor nor oppose a series of ways that the federal government might try to reduce future global warming. Power plants put gases into the air that could cause global warming. Do you FAVOR, OPPOSE, or NEITHER FAVOR NOR OPPOSE the federal government lowering the amount of these gases that power plants are allowed to put into the air? [Do you favor that A GREAT DEAL, MODERATELY, or A LITTLE? / Do you oppose that A GREAT DEAL, MODERATELY, or A LITTLE?]
Health care	There is much concern about the rapid rise in medical and hospital costs. Some people feel there should be a government insurance plan which would cover all medical and hospital expenses for everyone ... Others feel that all medical expenses should be paid by individuals through private insurance plans like Blue Cross or other company paid plans ... Where would you place YOURSELF on this scale?

(continued)

ISSUE	QUESTION WORDING
Immigration	Citizens of other countries who have come to live in the United States without the permission of the U.S. government are called "illegal immigrants." Do you FAVOR, OPPOSE, or NEITHER FAVOR NOR OPPOSE allowing illegal immigrants to work in the United States for up to three years, after which they would have to go back to their home country? [Do you favor that A GREAT DEAL, MODERATELY, or A LITTLE? / Do you oppose that A GREAT DEAL, MODERATELY, or A LITTLE?]
Jobs	Some people feel the government in Washington should see to it that every person has a job and a good standard of living ... Others think the government should just let each person get ahead on their own ... Where would you place YOURSELF on this scale?
Military	Some people believe that we should spend much less money for defense ... Others feel that defense spending should be greatly increased ... Where would you place YOURSELF on this scale?

Wording of Questions from NAES Survey Used in Roll-Call Votes Analysis

ISSUE	QUESTION WORDING (with NAES variable ID)
Abortion	Make it harder for a woman to get an abortion – should the federal government do this or not? (BF02)
Crime	The number of criminals who are not punished enough – is this an extremely serious problem, serious, not too serious or not a problem at all? (BG12)
Education	Providing financial assistance to public elementary and secondary schools – should the federal government spend more money on this, the same as now, less or no money at all? (BD09)
Environment	Protecting the environment and natural resources – should the federal government do more about this, the same as now, less or nothing at all? (BS01)
Gay rights	Trying to stop job discrimination against homosexuals – should the federal government do more about this, the same as now, less or nothing at all? (BL05)
Guns	Restricting the kinds of guns that people can buy – should the federal government do more about this, the same as now, less or nothing at all? (BG06)

ISSUE	QUESTION WORDING (with NAES variable ID)
Intervention in civil wars	In your opinion, should the government use American military forces to stop civil wars in other countries or not? (BJo8)
Military	Maintaining a strong military defense – should the federal government spend more money on this, the same as now, less or no money at all? (BJo7)
Missile shield	How much money do you think the federal government should spend on developing a system that would defend the US against a nuclear missile attack? Should the federal government spend more money on this, the same as now, less or no money at all? (BJo3)
School vouchers	Give tax credits or vouchers to help parents send their children to private schools – should the federal government do this or not? (BDo2)
Taxes	The amount of money Americans pay in taxes – is this an extremely serious problem, serious, not too serious or not a problem at all? (BBo1)

Votes Included in Roll-Call Analysis

ISSUE	YEAR	ROLL CALL #	POLICY PROPOSAL
Abortion			
	1997	65	Ban late-term abortions
	1997	362	Lighten proposed ban on funds to aid orgs that provide abortions
	1998	325	Override partial-birth abortion veto
	1999	184	Permit abortions at overseas military hospitals
	1999	261	Criminalize interstate transportation of minor for abortion
	1999	301	Remove prohibitions on abortion coverage in federal health plans
	1999	349	Bar federal funds to foreign orgs that perform abortions
	1999	465	Make it a crime to injure or kill a human fetus
	2000	104	Ban late-term/partial-birth abortions
	2000	203	Allow abortions in military hospitals overseas

(continued)

ISSUE	YEAR	ROLL CALL #	POLICY PROPOSAL
	2000	318	End ban on abortions for federal prisoners
	2000	373	Prohibit FDA tests of RU486
	2000	396	Remove ban on federal funds to foreign orgs that perform abortions
	2000	422	Allow coverage for abortion in federal health plans
	2001	88	Federal crime to attack pregnant woman
	2001	89	Criminalize killing of fetus
	2001	115	Support restrictions to int'l agencies providing abortions
	2001	235	End ban on abortions for federal prisoners
	2001	357	Permit abortions at overseas military hospitals
	2002	97	Criminalize transport of minor for abortion
	2002	153	Permit abortions in military hospitals
	2002	342	Require late-term abortion bans to consider woman's health
	2002	343	Ban late-term abortions
	2002	411	Federal grantees cannot withhold abortion services
	2002	412	Prohibit discrimination against federal grantees that refuse abortions
Crime			
	1999	211	Increase juvenile gun penalties
	1999	215	Bar release of prisoners because of overcrowding
	1999	233	Authorize juvenile justice programs
	2000	115	Mandatory minimum sentences for using firearm in crimes
	2000	317	Reduce funding for truth-in-sentencing grants
	2001	242	Bar funds to deport aliens convicted of certain crimes
	2002	63	Require judges to file report when sentencing to life

ISSUE	YEAR	ROLL CALL #	POLICY PROPOSAL
	2002	64	Life imprisonment for repeat child molesters
Education			
	1999	319	Increase funds for teachers
	2001	143	Reduce increase in education aid to localities
	2001	238	Funding for disabled students
Environment			
	1997	108	Limit proposed waivers to Endangered Species Act
	2000	179	Use oil royalties to establish land conservation
	2000	280	Restrict designations of national monuments
	2000	305	Delay implementation of air quality standards
	2001	181	Bar offshore drilling near Florida
	2001	288	Bar delay of new arsenic standards
	2001	311	Increase CAFE standards for vehicles
	2001	317	Bar ANWR drilling
	2001	366	Reallocate farm subsidies to conservation
	2002	315	Prohibit funds for drilling off California coast
Gay rights			
	2000	471	Broaden coverage of federal hate crimes to include gays
	2001	352	Bar funds for domestic partner benefits of DC employees
	2001	354	Bar funds for DC to enforce antidiscrimination law against Boy Scouts
Guns			
	1999	234	Require background checks at gun shows w/in 24 hrs
	1999	235	Require certain gun show dealers to run background checks w/in 3 days
	1999	236	Ban gun sales without safety devices

(continued)

ISSUE	YEAR	ROLL CALL #	POLICY PROPOSAL
	1999	238	Ban juveniles from semiautomatic assault weapons
	1999	240	Repeal DC gun ban
	1999	244	Require background checks at gun shows
	2000	306	Block adding cities to HUD safe-guns program
	2000	324	Bar gun-safety agreement with Smith and Wesson
	2001	244	Bar funds to change FBI background checks on gun purchases
	2002	24	Exempt gun ads from campaign finance restrictions
	2002	292	Allow pilots to carry guns during flight
Intervention in Civil Wars			
	1997	233	Prohibit funds for Bosnia
	1998	58	Withdraw troops from Bosnia
	1999	49	Authorize Kosovo deployment
	1999	100	Prohibit ground forces in Kosovo without authorization
	1999	101	Remove U.S. forces from Kosovo
	1999	103	Authorize air operations in Kosovo
	1999	119	Bar funds for invasion of Kosovo by U.S. forces
	1999	183	Prohibit permanent Defense Department presence in Haiti
	1999	189	Strike provision to prohibit funding for Kosovo
	1999	266	Recognize achievement in Kosovo
	2000	89	Withhold funds for Kosovo
	2000	193	Require burden-sharing in Kosovo
	2001	246	Bar financial contributions to UN peacekeeping efforts
Military			
	1997	228	Cut funding for B-2 bombers
	1998	10	Override veto of defense construction spending
	1999	118	Reduce proposed supplemental defense spending increase
	2000	70	CBC budget resolution: defense to domestic spending

ISSUE	YEAR	ROLL CALL #	POLICY PROPOSAL
	2000	85	Increase supplemental defense spending
	2000	196	Terminate Trident II missile
	2001	172	Cut Air Force budget
	2002	141	Prohibit funding for nuclear earth-penetrator weapon
	2002	142	Repeal ban on developing low-yield nuclear weapons
	2002	158	Increase defense spending
	2002	194	Supplemental military appropriation
Missile shield			
	1999	58	Impose requirements on SDI
	1999	59	Support deployment of SDI
	2001	230	Praise success of SDI test
	2002	145	Prohibit SDI funding
	2002	157	Bar funds for nuclear SDI
	2002	214	Prohibit debate on ABM treaty
	2002	269	Cut funding for SDI missile silos
School vouchers			
	1997	569	Authorize states to use vouchers
	1999	521	Authorize voucher program for low-performing schools
	2001	135	Vouchers for students in poor-performing schools
Taxes			
	1997	148	Budget resolution cutting taxes, Medicaid and Medicare
	1997	245	Pass Clinton tax cuts
	1998	102	Constitutional amendment requiring 2/3 vote to raise taxes
	1999	90	Constitutional amendment requiring 2/3 vote to raise taxes
	1999	331	Substitute Democratic version of a proposed tax cut
	1999	333	Tax cuts, including estate tax phaseout
	1999	485	Provide tax breaks for medical savings accounts
	2000	15	Eliminate marriage penalty tax
	2000	73	Conservative budget resolution: larger tax cuts

(continued)

ISSUE	YEAR	ROLL CALL #	POLICY PROPOSAL
	2000	119	Constitutional amendment requiring 2/3 vote to raise taxes
	2000	127	Abolish the tax code
	2000	254	Repeal estate tax
	2000	450	Repeal tax increase on Social Security beneficiaries
	2000	458	Override veto of estate tax elimination
	2001	42	Democratic substitute tax cut
	2001	45	Tax cuts
	2001	66	Progressive Caucus budget resolution
	2001	68	GOP Study Group budget resolution
	2001	75	Reduce marriage penalty
	2001	84	Phase out estate and gift taxes
	2001	87	Constitutional amendment requiring 2/3 vote to raise taxes
	2001	104	Conference report on budget resolution
	2001	149	Approve conference report for tax cuts
	2001	404	Approve $100 billion in tax cuts
	2002	103	Make tax cuts permanent
	2002	219	Make estate tax cuts permanent
	2002	225	Constitutional amendment requiring 2/3 vote to raise taxes
	2002	229	Make marriage penalty tax cut permanent

Categorization of Government Spending Functions to Correspond with GSS Spending Preferences Items

Issue	GSS Variable Name*	OMB Function Codes, except where noted
Cities	NATCITY	451 Community development
Crime	NATCRIME	751 Federal law enforcement activities
		753 Federal correctional activities
		754 Criminal justice assistance
Education	NATEDUC	501 Elementary, secondary, and vocational education
		502 Higher education
		503 Research and general education aids
		702 Veterans' education, training and rehabilitation

Issue	GSS Variable Name*	OMB Function Codes, except where noted
Energy	NATENRGY	272 Energy conservation 274 Emergency energy preparedness 276 Energy information, policy, and regulation
Environment	NATENVIR	304 Pollution control and abatement
Foreign aid	NATAID	151 International development and humanitarian assistance 152 International security assistance
Health care	NATHEAL	551 Health care services 552 Health research and training 554 Consumer and occupational health and safety 571 Medicare 703 Hospital and medical care for veterans
Military	NATARMS	051 Department of Defense-Military 053 Atomic energy defense activities 054 Defense-related activities
Poverty	NATFAREY	451 Community development 452 Area and regional development 506 Social services 603 Unemployment compensation 604 Housing assistance 605 Food and nutrition assistance 609 Other income security 701 Income security for veterans
Science	NATSCI	251 General science and basic research
Social Security	NATSOC	651 Social security
Space	NATSPAC	252 Space flight, research, and supporting activities
Parks	NATPARK	303 Recreational resources
Taxes	TAX	all taxes collected by the federal government (includes income, corporate, estate, excise, and gift taxes)
Transportation	NATMASS	401 Ground transportation

* For some of the spending questions, the GSS uses two slightly different question word-ings; survey respondents are assigned at random to one of the two wordings. These wordings have the same substantive meanings and did not affect responses to a substan-tial degree. Thus they were averaged in the calculations of aggregate preferences. This table lists the simpler of the GSS mnemonic names associated with these variables.

7

Conclusion

The goal of this book has been to advance our scholarly understanding of the role issue ownership plays in American politics. Along the way, it has confirmed some previous findings, refined others, and explored heretofore uncharted territory. I began by making clear the kinds of issues for which we should expect the notion of issue ownership to be relevant: issues around which there exists a broad consensus about national goals and government's responsibility to pursue those goals. Where previous research has disagreed on the extent to which issue ownership can change over time, here I have shown that issue ownership is in fact relatively steady. For the vast majority of issues over the past four decades, the public's beliefs that one party is better than the other at handling a specific issue have been stable.

I have verified that issue ownership is meaningfully related to presidential election results, although ambiguity remains regarding the direction of causality. Voters may use issue ownership as a kind of heuristic to determine which party is likely to tackle the nation's most important problems. By contrast, it is also possible that they absorb the messages broadcast by the party winning a particular election that its owned issues are indeed important at the time. In either case, it is clear that the associations the public makes between the parties and particular consensus issues are beneficial to issue-owning parties.

Why do parties own issues in the first place? In this book, I have clarified the conceptual vagueness that has undermined previous work to demonstrate that issue ownership has its roots solely in the parties' priorities. Partisans sincerely care more about their parties' owned issues and they prioritize these issues with federal spending and legislation when they are in power in Washington. By contrast, I find no evidence that political parties either adopt more popular policies or render detectably superior performance on the issues they own. One way or another, the American public's consistent over-time assessments of the two parties' abilities to "handle" different sets of issues must have their origins in the parties' priorities.

Finally, I have unearthed the negative consequences of issue ownership for American politics. Because partisans care so much about their owned issues, a party's lawmakers are significantly more likely to ignore public opinion on these issues when crafting policy or making decisions about where to direct federal spending. Issue ownership therefore has the worrisome effect of dampening the relationship between citizen preferences and public policy. An overview of this book's main results may be found in Table 7.1.

Issue ownership thus has a double-headed impact on American politics and policy making; its benefits and costs to the nation go hand in hand. Over the past several decades, the Democrats and Republicans have generally been more likely to do something about the nation's most important problems on the issues that they own. Party activists – who care overwhelmingly more about their parties' owned issues than others – demand this kind of action. It is arguably their chief motivation for seeking power. But with this dedication to addressing owned issues comes an ideological zeal that can lead the parties to pursue purist, ideological policies on these issues and to continue to direct government resources toward them even when the public's concerns shift to other problems.

ISSUE OWNERSHIP, CAMPAIGNS, AND ELECTIONS

The concept of issue ownership plays a central role in how many political scientists understand campaigns and elections. Although this book has deliberately sidestepped any study of campaign strategy and messaging, the findings in these pages shed light on some of the scholarly debates in the field and suggest ways in which future research might be pursued. First, and perhaps most obviously, future work must rise above the conceptual imprecision and a lack of empirical

TABLE 7.1. *Partisan priorities: overview of findings and data*

Findings	Key to Figures and Tables	Datasets analyzed
CHAPTER 2		ANES, CF;
• Consensus issues make up a large share of the nation's issue agenda	Figure 2.1	Gallup 2004, 2008, 2012
• Consensus exists for federal spending on broad range of goals	Table 2.1	GSS, 2010
• Significant differences on spending priorities exist among partisans	Table 2.4	
• Trade-offs among spending priorities are of low salience among voters	Table 2.7	
• Consensus exists for government action on a broad range of goals	Table 2.2	Pew, 2011
• Significant differences on government priorities exist among partisans	Table 2.5	
• Trade-offs among government priorities are of low salience among voters	Table 2.8	
• Substantial shares of Americans disagree with the parties' policies while agreeing with their priorities	Table 2.6	GSS, 2010; ANES, 2008
CHAPTER 3		
• Issue ownership is significant and substantial in the United States; it was relatively stable over the 1970–2011 period	Table 3.2; Figure 3.4	IO dataset
• Parties perform better in presidential elections when their owned issues are salient, even after controlling for economic conditions and incumbency	Table 3.3; Figure 3.5	IO dataset; ANES, CF; Gallup 2004, 2008, 2012
CHAPTER 4		
• Parties owned highly salient issues in 1994 despite their advocacy of unpopular policies on these issues	Table 4.1	ANES, 1994
• There is no relationship between Americans' policy preferences on consensus issues and the positions parties take on these issues	Figure 4.1 Figure 4.2	ANES, 1970–2008
• There is a relationship between Americans' policy preferences on the non-consensus issue of abortion and ownership of the abortion issue	Table 4.2 Figure 4.3	NYT/CBS, 1989–2009; IO dataset

Findings	Key to Figures and Tables	Datasets analyzed
• Americans' perceptions of national conditions on crime and the economy are often incorrect	Table 4.4	Gallup, 1989–2010; NYT/CBS, 1992–2010; NC dataset
• National conditions on consensus issues do not move in tandem	Table 4.5	NC dataset
• National conditions are no more likely to improve under presidents on issues the president's party owns than on other issues	Table 4.6 Figure 4.5	NC dataset
CHAPTER 5		
• Party elites name their parties' owned issues as the nation's most important problems	Figure 5.1	Delegates, 1972–92; ANES, CF
• Party elites prioritize government spending on issues their parties own	Figure 5.3	
• Party voters prioritize government action on issues their parties own	Figure 5.2	Pew, 1994–2011;
• Party voters prioritize government spending on issues their parties own	Figure 5.3	GSS, CF
• Important legislation is more likely to be enacted on issues parties own when they control the presidency or Congress	Table 5.1 Figure 5.3	Mayhew dataset
• Federal spending increases are more likely on issues parties own when they control the presidency or Congress	Table 5.3 Figure 5.3	Outlays dataset
• Presidents' attempts to trespass on issues can cause a substantial – but only temporary – shift in issue ownership	Figure 5.4	IO dataset
CHAPTER 6		
• Partisans who care deeply about their parties' owned issues hold more extreme views than their counterparts in the other party	Figure 6.2	ANES, 2008
• Members of Congress are less responsive to district opinion on issues their parties' own than on other issues	Table 6.2 Figure 6.3	NAES, 2000 Roll-call dataset

(continued)

TABLE 7.1. *Partisan priorities: overview of findings and data (continued)*

Findings	Key to Figures and Tables	Datasets analyzed
• Federal spending is less responsive to shifts in national priorities on issues owned by the party controlling the presidency and Congress	Table 6.3 Figure 6.4	GSS, CF Outlays dataset

Key to Data sets

Survey data (CF = cumulative file)

ANES: American National Election Studies

Delegates: Convention delegate surveys (Herrera and Miller 1995; Jackson, Bostis, and Baer 1988; Jackson and Brown 1988; Miller et al, 1976; Miller and Jennings 1988, 1995).
Gallup: Gallup Poll
GSS: General Social Survey
NAES: National Annenberg Election Survey
NYT/CBS: *New York Times*/CBS News Poll
Pew: Pew Research Center
Lawmaking data
Mayhew: *Divided We Govern* dataset (Mayhew 2012)
Datasets created for *Partisan Priorities*
IO: Issue ownership dataset (collected from Roper Public Opinion Archives; see Chapter 3)
NC: National conditions dataset (see Chapter 4)
Outlays: Federal outlays by function, 1981–2010 (from OMB; see Chapter 5)
Roll-call: Key roll-call votes in Congress, 1997–2002 (see Chapter 6)

documentation regarding the meaning of issue ownership that has been the Achilles' heel of previous scholarship. In addition, despite the fair amount of attention previous work has devoted to the idea that issue ownership varies over time, scholars of campaigns would do well to acknowledge the remarkable constancy of the phenomenon and how it shapes candidate strategy. As they campaign for office, party-affiliated candidates are both bolstered and constrained by their parties' reputations. This would seem particularly the case for nonincumbent candidates, who have little opportunity to define themselves vis-à-vis these reputations. As he sought the presidency in 2000 with a proposal to privatize Social Security, Republican George W. Bush was fighting against the headwinds of nearly seventy years of his party's relative lack of prioritization of this issue. Similarly in

2004, Democrat John Kerry's critique of Bush's policies on domestic security and foreign affairs competed with the public's accurate sense that Democrats tended to rank these issues relatively low on their list of priorities. Issue ownership defines the public's images of candidates to a greater degree than individual candidates can substantively change the associations the public makes between issues and their parties.

The strategies pursued by Bush and Kerry also illustrate a possible explanation for "issue convergence." As discussed in Chapter 3, convergence describes the unexpected discovery by many scholars that presidential and congressional candidates tend to talk about the same issues – even when theory predicts they should stick to emphasizing their owned issues (Ansolabehere and Iyengar 1994; Damore 2004, 2005; Dulio and Trumbore 2009; Kaplan, Park, and Ridout 2006; Sides 2006; Sigelman and Buell 2004). The findings in this book indicate that part of the reason for convergence may be that the issue-owning candidate is emphasizing his party's traditional *priorities* on the issue while the other candidate is proposing a more popular *policy* on the issue. The debates among the presidential candidates on Social Security in 2000 and foreign affairs in 2004 followed this pattern. For example, a *Newsweek* poll conducted in June 2000 found American voters favoring the policy at the heart of Bush's proposal – "chang[ing] Social Security to allow workers to invest some of their Social Security payroll taxes in the stock market" – by 51 to 36 percent (Zogby et al. 2003). Similarly, an Annenberg survey conducted in April 2004 found Americans overwhelmingly agreeing with what would become one of Kerry's key critiques of Bush's foreign policies. When asked if the war in Iraq had "reduced" or "increased the risk of terrorism against the United States," 57 percent of Americans said "increased"; only 29 percent said "reduced." (Annenberg Public Policy Center 2004). In both campaigns, the strategy of the non-owning party's candidate was to propose a new policy that could be framed in a way to garner the support of a strong majority. In response, the owning party's candidate (Democrat Al Gore in 2000 and Republican Bush in 2004) called into question his opponent's sincerity and commitment to actually addressing the problem – that is to say, his opponent's priorities. The distinctions between policies and priorities help explain why these campaigns converged on the issues of Social Security and foreign affairs in ways not predicted by previous theories of issue ownership.

A final insight yielded by this book for the study of campaigns is that scholars should think twice before assigning ownership to non-consensus issues such as abortion, gay rights, or "traditional values." Unlike the case for consensus issues, broad disagreements exist among Americans on these issues regarding desired end states. Thus emphasizing a candidate's positions on issues such as these undoubtedly has at best a mixed effect compared to messaging that successfully associates the candidate with universal goals such as low taxes, good schools, or clean air. In fact, evidence is emerging that campaigns are pinpointing the segments of the electorate that agree with its candidate on non-consensus issues and targeting them – and only them – with messages about these issues (Hillygus and Shields 2008). Nevertheless, many prominent studies of issue ownership in campaigns have incorporated non-consensus issues in their analyses. The theoretical perspectives developed here suggest that such a decision only muddies the waters.

THE STUDY OF ISSUE OWNERSHIP: WAYS FORWARD

In this book, the analytical focus has largely been limited to issue ownership as (1) an aggregate phenomenon that occurs (2) across issues in (3) contemporary politics in (4) the United States. By narrowing the field of vision, these four choices have made it possible to achieve a deeper understanding of the phenomenon of issue ownership along these lines. But inevitably these decisions have left many mysteries unsolved. Here are a few that seem particularly interesting and important to be pursued in future research on issue ownership.

Issue Ownership as an Individual-Level Phenomenon

What, exactly, goes through voters' minds when they say one party can "handle" an issue better than the other? This book makes clear that in the aggregate, the ultimate sources of these judgments are the parties' priorities. But there are certainly many additional considerations in individuals' heads that shape their responses to these survey questions. Evidence is emerging that parties' policies, priorities or performance may all affect people's "handling" assessments and thus their vote choice (e.g., Borre 2001; Green and Hobolt 2008; Stubager and Slothuus 2012; Therriault 2012; van der Brug 2004; Walgrave, Lefevere, and Tresch 2012). An important gap that remains in our knowledge is how the parties' actions translate into citizens' assessments. Can parties persuade voters to adopt their policy positions on the issues they own? Do voters implicitly assume that prioritization is the same as competence? These important questions are difficult to answer with traditional cross-sectional surveys, which are rarely designed in ways that facilitate clean identification of cause and effect. Voters' assessments of the parties – particularly those about performance – can be heavily distorted by the lens of their own partisanship (Bartels 2002), and simply controlling for party identification in an individual-level model is unlikely to address the threat of bias. Experiments and panel surveys offer much more promise in this regard (Therriault 2012). In addition, the rich findings yielded by the aggregate-level analyses here suggest that advances may be made by triangulating aggregate measures and individual-level data – perhaps across time, states, or nations.

Foreign Affairs, the Military, and Domestic Security

Future work might look more closely at the dynamics of ownership on specific issues; of these, the interplay of the three issues of foreign affairs, the military, and domestic security are particularly complicated and important. As shown in Chapter 3, the Republican Party has been the undisputed owner of military and domestic security issues since at least the 1970s. But foreign affairs is one of the few issues that actually changed hands during this period, flipping from the Republicans to the Democrats during George W. Bush's presidency as Americans soured on the Iraq War (see also Goble and Holm 2008). These dynamics support John Petrocik's original categorization of foreign affairs as a "performance" issue that is owned by neither side. But because these three issues are all so closely related, further study is required to fully understand how and why the parties come to own these issues. Any future research will need to account for the fact that these are issues on which the interplay of priorities, policies, performance, and issue ownership is quite complex.

In some respects, the conditions would appear ripe for linking per-formance on foreign affairs with issue ownership. As the area of policy that is arguably under the most direct control of the president, the traceability chain between an incumbent's actions and ultimate results is relatively shorter than those on issues such as crime, education, or ille-gal immigration. During wartime, Americans get plenty of news about the incumbent's performance on foreign affairs. Counterbalancing this however, is that government may hold more sway over how this news is covered than in other policy domains (e.g., Bennett, Lawrence, and Livingston 2007; Mueller 2011), and the influence of public opinion with regard to foreign affairs is relatively weak compared to that of elites (Jacobs and Page 2005).

Further complicating matters is that with regard to priorities, Americans' preferences on military spending are among the most vola-tile of any of the issues analyzed in this book. As is the case for other consensus issues, firm majorities of Americans have supported keeping military spending at no less than current levels since the General Social Survey began asking questions about spending preferences in the early 1970s. However, over the past four decades, the public's net approval for military spending (i.e., the percentage favoring increases less the percentage favoring decreases) has risen to as high as 49 percent net support (in 1980) and sunk to as low as 33 percent net opposition (in 1993). This is a range simply not seen with regard to any other spending category. Nevertheless, in the era following the unprecedented nature of the September 11, 2001 terrorist attacks, Americans have consistently named the issues of domestic security and military pre-paredness as high priorities for the president and Congress even in the quite welcome absence of additional high-profile attacks. Adding to the complexity is the fact that Americans' policy preferences on foreign affairs are wrapped up intimately with their assessments of the nation's performance on this issue. Americans' beliefs about a war's success can be highly correlated with their attitudes about war policy, includ-ing whether more troops should be committed and whether the war is worth the cost in lives and resources (Gelpi, Feaver, and Reifler 2009).

In sum, foreign affairs, the military, and domestic security are issues on which Americans' priorities are relatively volatile, their perfor-mance evaluations well-informed (at least compared to many other consensus issues), and their policy preferences often strongly related to their evaluations of performance. One result of these complexities may be that foreign affairs is more than a pure "performance" issue: the Republican Party's firm reputation as caring more than the Democrats about domestic security and military issues may give the party a built-in advantage on foreign affairs – particularly in the wake of high-salience foreign policy events – that is bigger than merited by the parties' relative performance on this issue.

When Issue Ownership Changes Hands

How does issue ownership come to be transferred from one party to another, and what are the consequences? Unfortunately for analytical purposes, with the exception of the "performance" issues of foreign affairs and the economy such an event did not occur during the time period covered by this book – an interval constrained by the fact that issue-ownership questions on a wide range of topics did not appear regularly on surveys of Americans until the 1970s or later. Future research into this question will therefore likely require less reliance on quantitative data and more on qualitative analysis of the historical record. The theory developed here leads us to expect that issue ownership should change hands when there is a re-sorting of issue activists from one party to another and a subsequent shift in the priorities of party elites and voters. We would expect a corresponding pattern of partisan resistance to public opinion on these issues to follow suit. The surveys of party elites analyzed in Chapter 5 indicate that on the consensus issues covered in this book, this kind of sorting had already largely occurred – or was well under way – among elites by the mid-1970s.

One area of previous work that holds promise is scholarly research on partisan change with regard to *policies* on consensus issues, such as David Karol's in-depth investigation of position change on the issues of the military, taxes, and trade (Karol 2009). Karol's analysis of roll-call votes in Congress shows that the Democrats became the party of trade protectionism in the mid-1970s and the Republicans began championing military spending in the early 1960s and low taxes in the mid-1970s. One could certainly surmise how this kind of position change corresponded with a change in the parties' priorities. For example, Karol documents a shift in preferences for military spending among rank-and-file Democrats and Republicans occurring just after the parties' lawmakers appeared to change sides on the issue (Karol 2009: 161). Future work might assess whether the other elements of the issue ownership repertoire fell into place at the same time on these issues. One issue to keep an eye on in the near future is immigration, an issue on which activists in both parties place a high priority. As seen in Chapter 5, Republicans consistently view unauthorized immigration as a more important problem than do Democrats. But Latinos – many who are immigrants themselves, or the children or grandchildren of immigrants – make up an increasingly important part of the Democratic Party's coalition, giving the party a strong incentive to take action on the issue as well. The challenge for the Democrats is that (as discussed in Chapter 2) although unauthorized immigration is currently a consensus issue, immigration itself is not.

Issue Ownership across Democracies

Because its focus is limited to the United States, the generalizability of this book's theory and findings to other nations must be a matter of speculation rather than empirical corroboration. A long line of work has confirmed Budge and Farlie's original finding that issue ownership is an important feature of the political landscape across representative democracies (e.g., Bélanger 2003; Bélanger and Meguid 2008; Budge et al 2001; Budge, Robertson, and Hearl 1987; Green 2011; Green and Hobolt 2008; Meguid 2005). But the extent to which there are similar issue ownership dynamics in these nations – in particular, whether issue ownership's origins and its moderating effects on the linkage between opinion and policy are the same as in the United States – is not easily foreseen.

Conjectures about these questions are complicated by the effects of two institutional characteristics that vary across democracies. First, we might expect the role of issue ownership in politics and policy making to be affected by the extent to which voters can easily trace government action to the decisions made by one party or another. Such accountability may be particularly difficult to achieve in the United States because of the Constitution's division of powers between the president and Congress. But it would appear to be more feasible in

Westminster-style systems such as Canada and Great Britain, where the decision-making apparatus of the central government is typically under the control of only one party (or a like-minded coalition of parties) at any given time. Conceivably in these systems, voters might be able to more carefully monitor the parties' performance on a broader portfolio of issues – and thus tie issue ownership to performance – than in the United States. In addition, governments in countries with rules designed according to this "majoritarian vision" have been found to be more out of step with public opinion than those where parties typically share power in proportion to their strength in the electorate (Powell 2000). The implications of this fact for issue ownership are indeterminate. It could either magnify the parties' ignorance of public opinion on the issues they own, or by contrast make it possible for parties to disregard opinion on most issues, not just their owned issues.

A second factor that may influence the applicability of this book's findings to other nations is the degree to which new parties can effectively enter the system and thus compete for votes and power. Of particular interest is the ability of entry by "niche parties": those that "politicize sets of issues which were previously outside the dimensions of party competition" (Meguid 2005: 347; see also Adams et al 2006). In Europe, the two most prominent examples of niche parties over the past forty years have been those devoted to environmental issues (the "greens") and those arising in opposition to immigration. Bonnie Meguid's conceptualization of niche parties owning these issues is aligned with the framework developed here: parties own issues because they prioritize them. (The environmental goals prioritized by green parties appear to meet the criteria defining consensus issues. It is less clear whether similarly broad consensuses regarding immigration goals exist throughout Europe.) As Meguid shows, the emergence of these niche parties keeps these issues on the agenda and forces mainstream parties to respond. If a mainstream party adopts an accommodative strategy by incorporating the niche party's demands, issue ownership can be transferred to the mainstream party. Thus issue ownership may be more fluid in systems with electoral rules that ease the entry of new parties more than in the United States, where barriers to entry by third parties are particularly high.

ISSUE OWNERSHIP AND THEMES IN THE STUDY OF AMERICAN
POLITICS

Although the focus of this book has been squarely on the phenomenon of issue ownership, the discoveries here help illuminate several
broad themes of interest to scholars of American politics. I conclude
with some final thoughts about the relevance of my findings to current
debates and future research in these fields.

Political Parties

Whose political party? A lively conversation is taking place in the
scholarly literature on political parties between those who view the
parties as creatures under the firm control of politicians and those
who by contrast see parties and their politicians paying heed to
issue activists. The findings here will bolster the arguments of the
latter group, who conceive of parties as composed of coalitions of
"intense policy demanders" who use the party as a means to win legislation and federal dollars that benefit their group interests (Bawn et
al. 2006; Cohen et al. 2008; Karol 2009; Masket 2009). This book
suggests an additional axiom for this emerging theory of parties: a
party's intense policy demanders are more likely to be concentrated
on issues the party owns. So although there are certainly Democratic
activists who care about making the tax system more progressive, they
appear to wield nowhere the amount of influence in the Democratic
Party as Grover Norquist and his allies do in the Republican Party.
And although Republican activists do exist who are passionate about
market-oriented approaches to the nation's health care challenges,
they are almost certainly outnumbered by the ranks of health care
activists on the Democratic side. Documenting exactly how activists
in issue-owning parties successfully force their parties' politicians to
comply with their demands is a task for future research. With the
exceptions of the vignettes presented in Chapter 1, this book has little
to say on this topic. But these activists' fingerprints are all over the
findings presented in Chapters 5 and 6 that parties both prioritize their
owned issues and ignore public opinion on these issues.

  Less corroboration is found here for the idea that parties today
are "in service" to the needs of ambitious, office-seeking politicians

(Aldrich 1995). The obvious reading of this book's results is that politicians are instead either hemmed in by the ideological rigidity of issue activists or actually may consider themselves one of their number. Pennsylvania's current junior senator, Republican Pat Toomey, previously served as president of the Club for Growth. On the other side of the aisle, organized labor counts another Pennsylvanian as one of its own: former union leader and now Democratic congressman Robert Brady. Recent developments in the way campaigns are financed – in particular, the Supreme Court's *Citizens United* decision that legalized activists' ability to spend unlimited funds in support of their favored candidates for office – seem only to increase the pressure experienced by office-seeking politicians to heed the demands of those with intense policy preferences.

Insights on party polarization. As an explanation of how ideological rigidity can vary by issue and by party, issue ownership also yields new insights for another rich body of research on political parties: party polarization. Prominent works on polarization have documented the partisan divide on policy and ideology among voters, elites, and legislators (e.g., Brewer and Stonecash 2009; McCarty, Poole, and Rosenthal 2006; Levendusky 2009; Theriault 2008). The findings here make two contributions to our understanding of partisan polarization. First, this book demonstrates that in addition to being polarized on policy the parties are also polarized on the nation's priorities, with spending and legislation on each party's owned issues more likely to be observed when it is in power. The second point is that because polarization has occurred with regard to consensus goals, the consequences for Americans may be more disconcerting than polarization on non-consensus issues such as abortion or gay rights. We have seen that most Americans want government to deal with a broad range of problems, including an array of concerns traditionally identified as liberal or conservative. But if political parties increasingly focus only on the issues they own, national problems are more likely to be ignored depending on who is in power in Washington – a troubling development indeed.

There is one person, however, who has the incentive to go against this tide: the president. In order to be reelected, the president needs to both attract independent voters and point to a record of accomplishment in addressing the nation's most important problems. One way to satisfy these requirements is to champion policy initiatives – such as Clinton's crime bill or Bush's education law – that cut against the grain of issue ownership. (Arguably Obama took the same approach with his prioritization of the Republican-owned issue of the fight against terrorism, although he did not pursue this goal through high-profile legislation or increased spending.) The need for presidents to neutralize the other party's owned issues while continuing to satisfy their own party's "intense policy demanders" creates an important dynamic in our polarized era that deserves additional attention in the study of the relations between the executive and legislative branches.

Political Issues

The distinction between consensus and non-consensus issues. As discussed in Chapter 2, political scientists have long sought to classify issues in ways that facilitate insightful analysis. The distinction between consensus and non-consensus issues developed in this book may seem so obvious that some readers may be surprised that no one has come up with it until now. But they will search in vain for a previous approach that clearly delineates these kinds of issues from others. None of the previous classification schemes has set out the clear criteria presented here: that consensus issues are those on which Americans agree on ultimate goals and also agree that government bears responsibility for achieving them. In addition, unlike the approach here, previous scholars have been reluctant to group different aspects of the same issue together. This has made it difficult to understand the interplay between different aspects of issues, such as (to use Stokes's terminology) the "valence" and "position" politics of a particular issue.

The approach to categorizing issues that guides the analyses in this book is thus a fresh take on an old analytical problem. The findings yielded by this approach suggest a hypothesis deserving of testing in subsequent research: the politics of consensus issues are simply more complicated than the politics of other issues. Among these complications are the mysteries that voters (and for that matter, many policy makers!) can experience about which policies are most likely to achieve consensus goals. There is then the fact that voters can appreciate a party's record of devoting federal funds and legislation to a consensus issue even when they dislike its signature policies on the issue. And there is the difficulty of properly assigning credit or blame for the nation's conditions on the actions taken by elected officials on these issues. On top of it all is the fact that achieving consensus goals requires expending government resources and thus there are trade-offs among these goals – trade-offs that voters are rarely prompted to consider. Difficulties such as these are generally not found on non-consensus issues such as abortion, gay rights, school prayer, or guns. On these issues, the connections between policies and outcomes are more clear, the distinction between priorities and policies is essentially irrelevant, and changing policy requires little in the way of government resources. All of these observations suggest that consensus issues may be cognitively "harder" than other "easier" issues, and that the politics surrounding consensus issues may thus be more complex (Carmines and Stimson 1980).

The virtues of a multidimensional approach. As they seek clear explanations for the complicated events that can occur in the world of public affairs, scholars of politics are rightly guided by the principle of parsimony. Nearly thirty years ago, political scientists were given a powerful tool in their pursuit of a simple account of the nation's landscape of political issues: Keith T. Poole and Howard Rosenthal's pioneering technique for scaling congressional roll-call votes (Poole and Rosenthal 1985). Estimates generated with their method, NOMINATE, indicate that a single liberal–conservative dimension suffices for explaining how most members of Congress vote on most issues. In joint work with Nolan McCarty, Poole and Rosenthal show this is particularly true in our era of polarization, during which "other dimensions ... have largely vanished, as the coalitions on those issues have increasingly begun to match those of the liberal–conservative dimension" (McCarty, Poole, and Rosenthal 2006: 23).

For many purposes in the study of Congress and policy making, a reduction of all issues to one dimension has been – and will continue to be – tremendously valuable. But the findings here suggest that a multidimensional approach can bear fruit because the parties are not always perfect substitutes for one another. Rather, as Stefan Krasa and Mattias Polborn put it, in many contexts it is better to consider candidates and parties as "specialized" with regard to different issues (Krasa and Polborn 2010). All of the evidence in this book supports the notion that the parties are indeed specialized – not with regard expertise or capabilities – but to the extent that they care ᴐme issues more than others. Yes, in contemporary politics atic and Republican elected officials tend to take liberal and cᴏɴsᴇɪ vative positions, respectively, on just about every issue. But they face more pressure to adopt extreme positions on issues their parties own. Without taking a multidimensional perspective, both empirical analyses and theoretical models will be inadequate for understanding important phenomena such as issue ownership.

Citizens' Control of Government

Representation. The analyses here confirm scores of previous studies showing that public opinion has substantial influence on policy making and government spending. But this book shows that an important caveat must be added to this sunny conclusion: the effect of citizens' preferences on elected officials is significantly attenuated on issues their parties own. In fact, the two analyses presented in Chapter 6 suggest that issue ownership reduces the effect of opinion on policy to be effectively zero. Additional work is needed to see to what extent this pattern persists in different contexts and time periods, but what these findings speak to is the need for scholars of representation to analyze the opinion–policy relationship by party and by issue. Especially in our era of polarization, it is quite possible that responsiveness to citizen preferences varies on these dimensions in other important ways.

In addition, the findings here point to the need to think carefully about how the structure of different issues affects representation not only as an empirical phenomenon, but also how we should conceive of representation as a theoretical concept. For example, as discussed in Chapter 6, the notion of "congruence" does not appear to be an analytically useful way to conceive of the opinion–policy relationship with regard to spending preferences on consensus issues – at least not in the issue-by-issue way these preferences are typically recorded in sample surveys. The fact that year in and year out, aggre-
‑ᶠ⁓⁓ⁿᶜᵉˢ for increased spending on most consensus goals are e 50 percent should be read as endorsements of the ⱱⁿment should be pursuing these goals, rather than which to measure the congruence of elected officials ion.

Agenda setting. A rich line of literature – spearheaded by political scientists Frank R. Baumgartner and Bryan D. Jones – has documented how the agendas of America's governing institutions respond to public policy problems as they become salient among elites and the general public (Baumgartner and Jones 1993; Jones and Baumgartner 2005). This responsiveness is imperfect, however. Policy change tends to occur in a punctuated fashion, and an institution's responsiveness to the public's concerns declines to the extent that it has hurdles (or "institutional friction") in place that make change difficult (Jones, Larsen-Price, and Wilkerson 2009). The findings in this book indicate that partisanship is another factor that influences agenda setting. The political party that controls a particular institution is more likely to overcome institutional friction to address problems in the issue domains that it owns. This, in turn, suggests an explanation for why representative institutions respond to highly salient policy problems. Elections are more likely to be won by the party whose owned issues are salient, and thus institutions are more likely to be controlled by them. Parties use their control of institutions to address their owned issues with legislation and spending. Party labels attached to politicians are thus meaningful not just in terms of the policies they will pursue in office: they are also informative signals of the problems they will prioritize when governing. The analyses of elections and issue salience in Chapter 3 show only a correlation between issue salience and election results rather than demonstrating that the former affects the latter. But if future research should cleanly identify such a causal relationship, it will provide strong evidence that elections play an important role in linking the issue agendas of electorates with those pursued by representative governing institutions.

Accountability. Democratic elections are widely conceived to be a disciplining device. We expect poor performance by the incumbent party to be duly punished by voters and followed by the subsequent loss of office. Empirically, this is true in the United States with regard to two highly salient issues – the economy and (to a lesser extent) foreign affairs. Healthy economic conditions are of clear electoral benefit to incumbent presidents and their parties; poor economies tend to hurt them (for recent analyses see, e.g., Erikson and Wlezien 2012; Vavreck 2009). In addition, there is some – although certainly not as decisive – support for the idea that presidents' fortunes are tied to good and bad developments in foreign affairs, perhaps indirectly through their approval ratings (Mueller 1973; Fair 2009; for a discussion see Berinsky 2009: 178–206). But beyond these two issues, no empirical evidence for accountability exists. No matter how much the public claims to care about consensus issues such as education, crime, the environment, or the deficit – and how much these issues affect our lives as citizens – no relationships have been discovered between electoral success and national conditions on these issues.

Unfortunately, the findings in this book about parties and performance offer little consolation in this regard. The fact that there is no detectable relationship between parties' control of government and improvement on the issues the public says they are best able to "handle" leaves few reasons for optimism about accountability. As discussed in Chapter 4, the primary counterclaim is to argue that many of the parties' signature initiatives on their owned issues do improve national conditions; it is just that their effects occur too far in the future for even sophisticated time-series models to detect. The problem with this claim is that it requires an objective observer to make individual judgment calls on each piece of legislation's ultimate impact on the national problem it was designed to address. Has the USA PATRIOT Act deterred the terrorist threat? Did Reagan's 1984 crime bill reduce homicides? Did welfare reform alleviate poverty? Will the Affordable Care Act improve the nation's health? Given that it is rare that even the most scrupulously rigorous and nonpartisan experts reach consensuses about questions such as these, it is hard to surmise how ordinary Americans could do the same. Instead, when deciding which party is better able to handle a given issue, Americans appear to use the heuristic of equating effort with results. It is of course possible that in the long term, the former does lead to the latter. But relying on this proposition leaves our faith that democratic citizens can properly reward incumbents for improving the nation's welfare on a range of important issues on awfully shaky ground.

References

Achen, Christopher H. 1978. "Measuring Representation." *American Journal of Political Science* 22(3): 475–510.

Adams, Gregory D. 1997. "Abortion: Evidence of an Issue Evolution." *American Journal of Political Science* 41(3): 718–737.

Adams, James, Michael Clark, Lawrence Ezrow, and Garrett Glasgow. 2006. "Are Niche Parties Fundamentally Different from Mainstream Parties? The Causes and Electoral Consequences of Western European Parties' Policy Shifts, 1976–1998." *American Journal of Political Science* 50(3): 513–529.

Aldrich, John. 1995. *Why Parties? The Origin and Transformation of Political Parties in America.* Chicago: University of Chicago Press.

Aldrich, John, John L. Sullivan, and Eugene Borgida. 1989. "Foreign Affairs and Issue Voting: Do Presidential Candidates 'Waltz before a Blind Audience?'" *American Political Science Review* 83(1): 123–141.

Alesina, Alberto. 1988. "Credibility and Policy Convergence in a Two-Party System with Rational Voters." *American Economic Review* 78: 796–806.

Alesina, Alberto, and Howard Rosenthal. 1995. *Partisan Politics, Divided Government, and the Economy.* New York: Cambridge University Press.

Alesina, Alberto, and Jeffrey Sachs. 1988. "Political Parties and the Business Cycle in the United States, 1948–84." *Journal of Money, Credit and Banking* 20: 63–82.

Alt, James E. 1979. *The Politics of Economic Decline: Management and Political Behavior in Britain since 1964.* New York: Cambridge University Press.

American Presidency Project. 2012. "Walter F. Mondale Address Accepting the Presidential Nomination at the Democratic National Convention in San Francisco, July 19, 1984." http://www.presidency.ucsb.edu/nomination.php (accessed March 13, 2013).

Americans for Tax Reform. 2012. "The Taxpayer Protection Pledge Signers: 112th Congressional List." http://s3.amazonaws.com/atrfiles/files/files/12 0111-federalpledgesigners.pdf (accessed March 13, 2013).

Annenberg Public Policy Center. 2004. "Annenberg Polling Shows Dismay over Iraq Is Increasing; Public Supports Bush on Staying but Doubts He Has a Plan." April 16.

Ansolabehere, Stephen, and Shanto Iyengar. 1994. "Riding the Wave and Claiming Ownership over Issues: The Joint Effects of Advertising and News Coverage in Campaigns." *Public Opinion Quarterly* 58(3): 335–357.

Ansolabehere, Stephen, Jonathan Rodden, and James R. Snyder, Jr. 2008. "The Strength of Issues: Using Multiple Measures to Gauge Preference Stability, Ideological Constraint, and Issue Voting." *American Political Science Review* 102(2): 215–232.

Ansolabehere, Stephen, and James M. Snyder. 2000. "Valence Politics and Equilibrium in Spatial Election Models." *Public Choice* 103 (3–4): 327–336.

Aragones, Enriqueta, and Thomas R. Palfrey. 2002. "Mixed Equilibrium in a Downsian Model with a Favored Candidate." *Journal of Economic Theory* 103(1): 131–161.

Arnold, R. Douglas. 1990. *The Logic of Congressional Action*. New Haven, CT: Yale University Press.

1998. "The Politics of Reforming Social Security." *Political Science Quarterly* 113(2): 219–225.

Bafumi, Joseph, and Michael Herron. 2010. "Leapfrog Representation and Extremism: A Study of American Voters and Their Members in Congress." *American Political Science Review* 104(3): 519–542.

Bailey, Michael, Lee Sigelman, and Clyde Wilcox. 2003. "Presidential Persuasion on Social Issues: A Two-Way Street?" *Political Research Quarterly* 56(1): 49–58.

Barone, Michael, and Richard E. Cohen. 2003. *The Almanac of American Politics, 2004*. Chicago: University of Chicago Press.

Barone, Michael, Richard E. Cohen, and Charles E. Cook. 2001. *The Almanac of American Politics, 2002*. Washington, DC: National Journal.

Barone, Michael, Grant Ujifusa, and Richard E. Cohen. 1999. *The Almanac of American Politics, 2000*. Washington, DC: National Journal.

Bartels, Larry M. 1991. "Constituency Opinion and Congressional Policy Making: The Reagan Defense Buildup." *American Political Science Review* 85(2): 457–474.

2002. "Beyond the Running Tally: Partisan Bias in Political Perceptions." *Political Behavior* 24(2): 117–150.

2008. *Unequal Democracy: The Political Economy of the New Gilded Age*. Princeton, NJ: Princeton University Press.

Baumgartner, Frank R., and Bryan D. Jones. 1993. *Agendas and Instability in American Politics*. Chicago: University of Chicago Press.

Bawn, Kathleen, Seth Masket, Marty Cohen, David Karol, Hans Noel, and John Zaller. 2006. "A Theory of Political Parties." Paper given at the annual meeting of the American Political Science Association, Philadelphia.

Beck, Nathaniel. 1982. "Parties, Administrations, and American Macroeconomic Outcomes." *American Political Science Review* 76(1): 83–93.

Bélanger, Eric. 2003. "Issue Ownership by Canadian Political Parties, 1953–2001." *Canadian Journal of Political Science* 36(3): 539–558.

Bélanger, Eric, and Bonnie M. Meguid. 2008. "Issue Salience, Issue Ownership, and Issue-Based Vote Choice." *Electoral Studies* 27: 477–491.

Bennett, W. Lance, Regina G. Lawrence, and Steven Livingston. 2007. *When the Press Fails: Political Power and the News Media from Iraq to Katrina.* Chicago: University of Chicago Press.

Berelson, Bernard R., Paul F. Lazarsfeld, and William N. McPhee. 1954. *Voting: A Study of Opinion Formation in a Presidential Campaign.* Chicago: University of Chicago Press.

Berinsky, Adam. 2009. *In Time of War: Understanding American Public Opinion from World War II to Iraq.* Chicago: University of Chicago Press.

Berry, William D., Evan J. Ringquist, Richard C. Fording, and Russell L. Hanson. 1998. "Measuring Citizen and Government Ideology in the American States, 1960–93." *American Journal of Political Science* 42(1): 327–48.

Black, Duncan. 1948. "On the Rationale of Group Decision-Making." *The Journal of Political Economy* 56(1): 23–34.

Blais, Andre, Donald Blake, and Stephane Dion. 1993. "Do Parties Make a Difference? Parties and the Size of Government in Liberal Democracies." *American Journal of Political Science* 37(1): 40–62.

Borre, Ole. 2001. *Issue Voting: An Introduction.* Aarhus, Denmark: Aarhus University Press.

Bowman, Karlyn, and Andrew Rugg. 2010. "Public Opinion on Taxes." AEI Public Opinion Studies. April. http://www.aei.org/papers/politics-and-public-opinion/polls/public-opinion-on-taxes-2010/ (accessed March 13, 2013).

2012. "Attitudes about Abortion." AEI Public Opinion Studies. January. http://www.aei.org/files/2012/01/20/-attitudes-about-abortion-39-years-of-polling_131350993384.pdf (accessed March 13, 2012).

Bräuninger, Thomas. 2005. "A Partisan Model of Government Expenditure." *Public Choice* 125 (3/4): 409–429.

Brewer, Mark D., and Jeffrey M. Stonecash. 2009. *Dynamics of American Political Parties.* New York: Cambridge University Press.

Budge, Ian, and Dennis J. Farlie. 1983. *Explaining and Predicting Elections: Issue Effects and Party Strategies in Twenty-Three Democracies.* Boston: Allen and Unwin.

Budge, Ian, and Richard I. Hofferbert. 1990. "Mandates and Policy Outputs: U.S. Party Platforms and Federal Expenditures." *American Political Science Review* 84(1): 111–131.

Budge, Ian, Hans-Dieter Klingemann, Andrea Volkens, Judith Bara, Eric Tannenbaum, et al. 2001. *Mapping Policy Preferences: Estimates for Parties, Electors, and Governments 1945–1998*. Oxford: Oxford University Press.

Budge, Ian, David Robertson, and Derek Hearl. 1987. *Ideology, Strategy and Party Change: Spatial Analyses of Post-war Election Programmes in 19 Democracies*. Cambridge: Cambridge University Press.

Bullock, John G. 2011. "Elite Influence on Public Opinion in an Informed Electorate." *American Political Science Review* 105(3): 496–515.

Bureau of Economic Analysis. 2011. "Gross Domestic Product, Percent Change from Preceding Period." http://www.bea.gov/national/xls/gdp-chg.xls (accessed October 1, 2011).

Bureau of Labor Statistics. 2011a. "Consumer Price Index History Table." ftp://ftp.bls.gov/pub/special.requests/cpi/cpiai.txt (accessed October 1, 2011).

———. 2011b. "Employment Status of the Civilian Noninstitutional Population, 1940s to Date." ftp://ftp.bls.gov/pub/special.requests/lf/aat1.txt (accessed October 1, 2011).

Burstein, Paul. 2010. "Public Opinion, Public Policy, and Democracy." In *Handbook of Politics: State and Society in Global Perspective*, edited by Kevin T. Leicht and Craig J. Jenkins, 63–79. New York: Springer.

Campbell, Angus, Philip E. Converse, Warren E. Miller, and Donald E. Stokes. 1960. *The American Voter: Unabridged Edition*. New York: John Wiley and Sons.

Campbell, James E. 2011. "The Economic Records of the Presidents: Party Differences and Inherited Economic Conditions." *The Forum* MS# 1429.

Canes-Wrone, Brandice, and Kenneth W. Shotts. 2004. "The Conditional Nature of Presidential Responsiveness to Public Opinion." *American Journal of Political Science* 48(4): 690–706.

Carmines, Edward G., and James A. Stimson. 1980. "The Two Faces of Issue Voting." *American Political Science Review* 74(1): 78–91.

Carmines, Edward G., and James Woods. 2002. "The Role of Party Activists in the Evolution of the Abortion Issue." *Political Behavior* 24(4): 361–77.

Chappell, Henry W. Jr., and William R. Keech. 1988. "The Unemployment Rate Consequences of Partisan Monetary Policies." *Southern Economic Journal* 55(1): 107–122.

Clark, Adam, and Colby Itkowitz. 2012. "New Map Not Only Reason Tim Holden Lost." *The Morning Call*, April 25.

Clinton, Joshua D. 2006. "Representation in Congress: Constituents and Roll Calls in the 106th House." *Journal of Politics* 68(2): 397–409.

Clinton, Joshua, Simon S. Jackman, and Douglas Rivers. 2004. "The Statistical Analysis of Roll Call Data." *American Political Science Review* 98(2): 355–370.

Cohen, Marty, David Karol, Hans Noel, and John Zaller. 2008. *The Party Decides: Presidential Nominations before and after Reform*. Chicago: University of Chicago Press.

Cohen, Robin A., Diane M. Makuc, Amy B. Bernstein, Linda T. Bilheimer, and Eve Power-Griner. 2009. "Health Insurance Coverage Trends, 1959–2007: Estimates from the National Health Interview Survey." *Health Statistics Reports* 17 (July).

Congressional Progressive Caucus. 2011. "The People's Budget." http://grijalva.house.gov/uploads/The_CPC_FY2012_Budget.pdf (accessed July 3, 2012).

Congressional Quarterly. 1995. "Lawmakers Enact $30.2 Billion Anti-Crime Bill." *CQ Almanac 1994.* Washington, DC: CQ Press.

1997a. "Crime Bill, 1993–1994 Legislative Chronology." In *Congress and the Nation, 1993–1996,* Vol. 9: 683. Washington, DC: CQ Press.

1997b. "Health Care Reform, 1993–1994 Legislative Chronology." In *Congress and the Nation, 1993–1996,* Vol. 9: 513. Washington, DC: CQ Press.

2011. "GOP Wave Yields Control of House, Greater Numbers in the Senate." In *CQ Almanac 2010,* 66th ed., edited by Jan Austin, 11–3 to 11–5. Washington, DC: CQ-Roll Call Group, 2011 http://library.cqpress.com/cqalmanac/cqal10-1278-70365-2371719 (accessed April 17, 2013).

Converse, Philip E. 1964. "The Nature of Belief Systems in Mass Publics." In *Ideology and Discontent,* edited by David Apter. New York: The Free Press. 206–261.

Coughlin, Peter J. 1992. *Probabilistic Voting Theory.* New York: Cambridge University Press.

CQ Weekly. 1997. "Key Senate and House Votes." December 20. 3105–3119.

CQ Weekly. 1998. "Key House Votes." December 19. 3352–3358.

1999. "Key House Votes." December 4. 2944–2947.

2000. "Key House Votes." December 16. 2876–2882.

2001. "Key House Votes." December 22. 3106–3109.

2002. "Key House Votes." November 30. 3124–3130.

Dahl, Robert A. 1971. *Polyarchy: Participation and Opposition.* New Haven, CT: Yale University Press.

Damore, David F. 2004. "The Dynamics of Issue Ownership in Presidential Campaigns." *Political Research Quarterly* 57(3): 391–397.

Damore, David F. 2005. "Issue Convergence in Presidential Campaigns." *Political Behavior* 27(1): 71–97.

De Boef, Suzanna, and Luke Keele. 2008. "Taking Time Seriously." *American Journal of Political Science* 52(1): 184–200.

Dee, Thomas S., and Brian Jacob. 2011. "The Impact of No Child Left Behind on Student Achievement." *Journal of Policy Analysis and Management* 30(3): 418–446.

Delli Carpini, Michael X., and Scott Keeter. 1997. *What Americans Know about Politics and Why It Matters.* New Haven, CT: Yale University Press.

DeNavas-Walt, Carmen, Bernadette D. Proctor, and Jessica C. Smith. 2011. "Income, Poverty and Health Insurance Coverage in the United States: 2010." U.S. Census Bureau, P60–239. September.

Downs, Anthony. 1957. *An Economic Theory of Democracy*. New York: Harper and Row.

Druckman, James N., and Lawrence R. Jacobs. 2009. "Presidential Responsiveness to Public Opinion." In *The Oxford Handbook of the American Presidency*, edited by George C. Edwards III and William G. Howell, 160–181. Oxford, UK: Oxford University Press.

Druckman, James N., Martin J. Kifer, and Michael Parkin. 2009. "Campaign Communications in U.S. Congressional Elections." *American Political Science Review* 103(3): 343–366.

Duggan, John. 2012. "A Survey of Equilibrium Analysis in Spatial Models of Elections." Typescript. University of Rochester.

Dulio, David A., and Peter F. Trumbore. 2009. "Running on Iraq or Running from Iraq? Conditional Issue Ownership in the 2006 Midterm Elections." *Political Research Quarterly* 62(2): 230–243.

Egan, Patrick J. 2011. "Public Opinion, The Media, and Social Issues." In *The Oxford Handbook of American Public Opinion and the Media*, edited by Lawrence R. Jacobs and Robert Y. Shapiro, 622–638. New York: Oxford University Press.

Ellis, Christopher, and James A. Simson. 2012. *Ideology in America*. New York: Cambridge University Press.

Erikson, Robert S., and Kent L. Tedin. 2011. *American Public Opinion*, 8th ed. New York: Longman.

Erikson, Robert S., and Christopher Wlezien. 1999. "Presidential Polls as a Time Series: The Case of 1996." *Public Opinion Quarterly* 63(2): 163–177.

Erikson, Robert S., and Christopher Wlezien. 2008. "Leading Economic Indicators, the Polls and the Presidential Vote." *PS: Political Science and Politics* 41(4): 703–707.

2012. *The Timeline of Presidential Elections: How Campaigns Do (and Do Not) Matter*. Chicago: University of Chicago Press.

Erikson, Robert S., Gerald C. Wright, and John P. McIver. 1993. *Statehouse Democracy: Public Opinion and Policy in the American States*. New York: Cambridge University Press.

Fair, Ray C. 2009. "Presidential and Congressional Vote-Share Equations." *American Journal of Political Science* 53(1): 55–72.

Federal Bureau of Investigation. 2011. "Uniform Crime Reporting Statistics." http://www.ucrdatatool.gov/Search/Crime/State/TrendsInOneVar.cfm (accessed October 1, 2011).

Feld, Scott L., and Bernard Grofman. 2001. "Stuck in Space: The Neglected Importance of Issue Salience for Political Competition." Presented at Annual Meeting of the Public Choice Society, San Antonio, Texas.

Feldman, Stanley, and John Zaller. 1992. "The Political Culture of Ambivalence: Ideological Responses to the Welfare State." *American Journal of Political Science* 36(1): 268–307.

Fiorina, Morris P. 1981. *Retrospective Voting in American National Elections.* New Haven, CT: Yale University Press.

Fox, John. 2008. *Applied Regression Analysis and Generalized Linear Models,* 2nd ed. Los Angeles: Sage.

Gallup News Service. 2010. "Gallup Poll Social Series: Crime." http://www.gallup.com/poll/File/144782/Crime_Review_Nov_18_2010.pdf (accessed April 15, 2013).

Garand, James C. 1985. "Partisan Change and Shifting Expenditure Priorities in the American States, 1945–1978." *American Politics Quarterly* 13(4): 355–391.

Garand, James C., and Rebecca M. Hendrick. 1991. "Expenditure Tradeoffs in the American States: A Longitudinal Test, 1948–1984." *Western Political Quarterly* 44(4): 915–940.

Gartzke, Erik. 2006. "Codebook for the Affinity of Nations Index, 1946–2002. Version 4.0." March 10. http://dss.ucsd.edu/~egartzke/data/affinity_codebook_03102006.pdf (accessed July 5, 2012).

2010. "Mean Annual Affinity Scores between U.S. and other U.N. Members in Security Council Votes." http://dss.ucsd.edu/~egartzke/htmlpages/data.html (accessed November 1, 2011).

Gelman, Andrew, and Jennifer Hill. 2007. *Data Analysis Using Regression and Multilevel/Hierarchical Models.* New York: Cambridge University Press.

Gelpi, Christopher, Peter D. Feaver, and Jason Reifler. 2009. *Paying the Human Costs of War: American Public Opinion and Casualties in Military Conflicts.* Princeton, NJ: Princeton University Press.

Goble, Hannah, and Peter M. Holm. 2008. "Breaking Bonds? The Iraq War and the Loss of Republican Dominance in National Security." *Political Research Quarterly* 62(2): 215–229.

Goren, Paul. 1997. "Political Expertise and Issue Voting in Presidential Elections." *Political Research Quarterly* 50(2): 387–412.

Gravelle, Jane G., and Thomas L. Hungerford. 2012. "The Challenge of Individual Income Tax Reform: An Economic Analysis of Tax Base Broadening." Washington, DC: Congressional Research Service, Report R42435, March 22.

Green, Donald Bradley Palmquist, and Eric Schickler. 2004. *Partisan Hearts and Minds: Political Parties and the Social Identities of Voters.* New Haven, CT: Yale University Press.

Green, Jane. 2011. "A Test of Core Vote Theories: The British Conservatives, 1997–2005." *British Journal of Political Science* 41(4): 735–764.

Green, Jane, and Sara B. Hobolt. 2008. "Owning the Issue Agenda: Party Strategies and Vote Choices in British Elections." *Electoral Studies* 27(3): 460–476.

Green, Joshua. 2007. "The Rove Presidency." *The Atlantic Monthly,* September.

Greenstein, Robert. 2011. "A Framework for Deficit Reduction: Principles and Cautions." March 24. http://www.cbpp.org/files/3-24-11bud.pdf (accessed July 3, 2012).

Groseclose, Tim. 2001. "A Model of Candidate Location When One Candidate Has a Valence Advantage." *American Journal of Political Science* 45(4): 862–886.

Hagen, Michael G, Edward L. Lascher, and John F. Camobreco. 2001. "Response to Matsusaka: Estimating the Effect of Ballot Initiatives on Policy Responsiveness." *Journal of Politics* 63(4): 1257–1263.

Hammond, Thomas H., and Brian D. Humes. 1993. "'What This Campaign Is All about Is …': A Rational Choice Alternative to the Downsian Spatial Model of Elections." In *Information, Participation, and Choice*, edited by Bernard N. Grofman, 141–159. Ann Arbor: University of Michigan Press.

Hansen, John Mark. 1998. "Individuals, Institutions, and Public Preferences over Public Finance." *American Political Science Review* 92(3): 513–531.

Hayes, Danny. 2005. "Candidate Qualities through a Partisan Lens: A Theory of Trait Ownership." *American Journal of Political Science* 49(4): 908–923.

2008. "Party Reputations, Journalistic Expectations: How Issue Ownership Influences Election News." *Political Communication* 25(4): 377–400.

Herrera, Richard, and Warren E. Miller. 1995. "Convention Delegate Study, 1992: United States." Ann Arbor, MI: Inter-university Consortium for Political and Social Research (Study # 6353).

Hibbs, Douglas A., Jr. 1977. "Political Parties and Macroeconomic Policy." *American Political Science Review* 71(4): 1467–1487.

1987. *The American Political Economy: Macroeconomics and Electoral Politics*. Cambridge, MA: Harvard University Press.

Hibbs , Douglas A. , Jr. and Christopher Dennis. 1988. "Income Distribution in the United States." *American Political Science Review* 82: 467–490.

Hillygus, D. Sunshine, and Todd G. Shields. 2008. *The Persuadable Voter: Wedge Issues in Presidential Campaigns*. Princeton, NJ: Princeton University Press.

Hobolt, Sara Binzer, and Robert Klemmensen. 2005. "Responsive Government? Public Opinion and Policy Preferences in Britain and Denmark." *Political Studies* 53(2): 379–402.

2008. "Government Responsiveness and Political Competition in Comparative Perspective." *Comparative Political Studies* 41(3): 309–337.

Hofferbert, Richard, and Ian Budge. 1992. "The Party Mandate and the Westminster Model: Election Programmes and Government Spending in Britain, 1948–1985." *British Journal of Political Science* 22(2): 151–182.

Hoffman, Catherine. 2009. "National Health Insurance – A Brief History of Reform Efforts in the U.S." Kaiser Family Foundation Publication 7871. http://www.kff.org/healthreform/upload/7871.pdf (accessed July 3, 2012).

Holian, David B. 2004. "He's Stealing My Issues! Clinton's Crime Rhetoric and the Dynamics of Issue Ownership." *Political Behavior* 26(2): 95–124.

Hotelling, Harold. 1929. "Stability in Competition." *The Economic Journal* 39: 41–57.

House Budget Committee. 2012. "The Path to Prosperity: A Blueprint for American Renewal." http://budget.house.gov/UploadedFiles/ Pathtoprosperity2013.pdf (accessed July 3, 2012).

Iyengar, Shanto, and Donald Kinder. 1987. *News That Matters: Television and American Opinion*. Chicago: University of Chicago Press.

Jackson, John S., III, and Barbara Leavitt Brown. 1988. "Party Elites in the United States, 1980: Republican and Democratic Party Leaders." Ann Arbor, MI: Inter-university Consortium for Political and Social Research (Study # 8209).

Jackson, John S., III, David Bostis, and Denise Baer. 1988. "Party Elites in the United States, 1984: Republican and Democratic Party Leaders." Ann Arbor, MI: Inter-university Consortium for Political and Social Research (Study # 8617).

Jacob, Brian A. 2005. "Accountability, Incentives and Behavior: Evidence from School Reform in Chicago." *Journal of Public Economics* 89(5-6): 761–796.

Jacobs, Lawrence R., and Benjamin I. Page. 2005. "Who Influences U.S. Foreign Policy?" *American Political Science Review* 99(1): 107–123.

Jacoby, William G. 2000. "Issue Framing and Public Opinion on Government Spending." *American Journal of Political Science* 44(4): 750–767.

Jacoby, William G., and Saundra K. Schneider. 2001. "Variability in State Policy Priorities: An Empirical Analysis." *Journal of Politics* 63(2): 544–568.

2009. "A New Measure of Policy Spending Priorities in the American States." *Political Analysis* 17(1): 1–24.

Jennings, Will, and Christopher Wlezien. 2011. "Distinguishing between Most Important Problems and Issues." *Public Opinion Quarterly* 75(3): 545–555.

Jessee, Stephen A. 2009. "Spatial Voting in the 2004 Presidential Election." *American Political Science Review* 103(1): 59–81.

Jones, Bryan D., and Frank R. Baumgartner. 2005. *The Politics of Attention: How Government Prioritizes Problems*. Chicago: University of Chicago Press.

Jones, Bryan D., Heather Larsen-Price, and John Wilkerson. 2009. "Representation and American Governing Institutions." *Journal of Politics* 71(1): 277–290.

Jones, Rachel K., and Kathryn Kooistra. 2011. "Abortion Incidence and Access to Services in the United States, 2008." *Perspectives on Sexual and Reproductive Health* 43(1): 41–50.

Kandel, William A. 2011. "The U.S. Foreign-Born Population: Trends and Selected Characteristics." Washington, DC: Congressional Research Service, Report R41592, January 18.

Kaplan, Noah, David K. Park, and Travis N. Ridout. 2006. "Dialogue in American Political Campaigns? An Examination of Issue Convergence in

Candidate Television Advertising." *American Journal of Political Science* 50(3): 724–736.

Karol, David. 2009. *Party Position Change in American Politics: Coalition Management*. New York: Cambridge University Press.

Kaufmann, Karen M. 2004. "Disaggregating and Reexamining Issue Ownership and Voter Choice." *Polity* 36(2): 283–299.

Kenworthy, Lane. 2010. "How Much Do Presidents Influence Income Inequality?" *Challenge* 53(2): 90–112.

Key, V. O. 1942. *Politics, Parties and Pressure Groups*. New York: Thomas Y. Crowell.

Kinder, Donald R. 1998. "Opinion and Action in the Realm of Politics." In *The Handbook of Social Psychology*, 4th ed., edited by Daniel T. Gilbert, Susan T. Fiske, and Gardner Lindzey, 778–867. New York: McGraw-Hill.

King, Gary, Michael Laver, Richard I. Hofferbert, Ian Budge, and Michael D. McDonald. 1993. "Party Platforms, Mandates, and Government Spending." *American Political Science Review* 87(3): 744–750.

Klingman, David, and William W. Lammers. 1984. "The 'General Policy Liberalism' Factor in American State Politics." *American Journal of Political Science* 28(3): 598–610.

Kramer, Gerald H. 1971. "Short-Term Fluctuations in U.S. Voting Behavior, 1896–1964." *American Political Science Review* 65(1): 131–143.

Krasa, Stefan, and Mattias Polborn. 2010. "Competition between Specialized Candidates." *American Political Science Review* 104(4): 745–765.

Lacy, Dean. 2001. "A Theory of Nonseparable Preferences in Survey Responses." *American Journal of Political Science* 45(2): 239–258.

Lax, Jeffrey R. and Justin H. Phillips. 2012. "The Democratic Deficit in the States." *American Journal of Political Science* 56(1): 148–166.

Layman, Geoffrey C., and Thomas M. Carsey. 2002. "Party Polarization and 'Conflict Extension' in the American Electorate." *American Journal of Political Science* 46(4): 786–802.

Layman, Geoffrey C., Thomas M. Carsey, John C. Green, Richard Herrera, and Rosalyn Cooperman. 2010. "Activists and Conflict Extension in American Party Politics." *American Political Science Review* 104(2): 324–346.

Lenz, Gabriel. 2009. "Learning and Opinion Change, Not Priming: Reconsidering the Priming Hypothesis." *American Journal of Political Science* 53(4): 821–837.

Levendusky, Matthew. 2009. *The Partisan Sort: How Liberals Became Democrats and Conservatives Became Republicans*. Chicago: University of Chicago Press.

Light, Paul. 1998. *The President's Agenda*, 3rd ed.. Baltimore: Johns Hopkins University Press.

Lindbeck, Assar, and Jörgen W. Weibull. 1987. "Balanced-Budget Redistribution as the Outcome of Political Competition." *Public Choice* 52(3): 273–297.

——. 1993. "A Model of Political Equilibrium in a Representative Democracy." *Journal of Public Economics* 51(2): 195–209.

Litvan, Laura. 2012. "Anti-Tax Advocate Norquist Endorses Lugar's Opponent." *Bloomberg Businessweek*, May 2. http://www.businessweek.com/news/2012-05-01/anti-tax-advocate-norquist-said-to-endorse-lugar-opponent (accessed July 3, 2012).

Los Angeles Times Poll. 2001. March. Retrieved March 25, 2012 from the iPOLL Databank, The Roper Center for Public Opinion Research, University of Connecticut.

Lowi, Theodore J. 1964. "American Business, Public Policy, Case-Studies, and Political Theory." *World Politics* 16(4): 677–715.

Luks, Samantha, and Michael Salamone. 2008. "Abortion." In *Public Opinion and Constitutional Controversy*, edited by Nathaniel Persily, Jack Citrin, and Patrick J. Egan, 80–107. New York: Oxford University Press.

Maher, Kris. 2012. "Veteran Keystone Democrats Are Ousted." *The Wall Street Journal*, April 25, A4.

Marist College Institute for Public Opinion Poll. 2005. February. Retrieved March 26, 2012 from the iPOLL Databank, The Roper Center for Public Opinion Research, University of Connecticut.

Martin, Andrew, Kevin Quinn, and Yong Hee Park. 2012. "Package MCMCpack." http://mcmcpack.wustl.edu/. Version 1.2–7.

Masket, Seth E. 2009. *No Middle Ground: How Informal Party Organizations Control Nominations and Polarize Legislatures.* Ann Arbor: University of Michigan Press.

Mayhew, David R. 1991. *Divided We Govern: Party Control, Lawmaking, and Investigations, 1946–1990.* New Haven, CT: Yale University Press.

——. 2012. "Datasets for *Divided We Govern*." http://pantheon.yale.edu/~dmayhew/data3.html (accessed July 5, 2012).

McCarty, Nolan, Keith T. Poole, and Howard Rosenthal. 2006. *Polarized America: The Dance of Ideology and Unequal Riches.* Cambridge, MA: MIT Press.

Meguid, Bonnie M. 2005. "Competition between Unequals: The Role of Mainstream Party Strategy in Niche Party Success." *American Political Science Review* 99(3): 347–359.

Miller, Joanne M., and Jon A. Krosnick. 2000. "News Media Impact on the Ingredients of Presidential Evaluations: Politically Knowledgeable Citizens Are Guided by a Trusted Source." *American Journal of Political Science* 44(2): 295–309.

Miller, Warren E., Elizabeth Douvan, William J. Crotty, and Jeane Kirkpatrick. 1976. "Convention Delegate Study of 1972: Women in Politics." Ann

Arbor, MI: Inter-university Consortium for Political and Social Research (Study # 7287).

Miller, Warren E., and M. Kent Jennings. 1988. "Convention Delegate Study, 1984: United States." Ann Arbor, MI: Inter-university Consortium for Political and Social Research (Study # 8967).

——— 1995. "Convention Delegate Study, 1988: United States." Ann Arbor, MI: Inter-university Consortium for Political and Social Research (Study # 6366).

Miller, Warren E., and J. Merrill Shanks. 1996. *The New American Voter*. Cambridge, MA: Harvard University Press.

Miller, Warren E., and Donald E. Stokes. 1963. "Constituency Influence in Congress." *American Political Science Review* 57(1): 45–56.

Mueller, Dennis C. 2003. *Public Choice* III. New York: Cambridge University Press.

Mueller, John T. 1973. *War, Presidents and Public Opinion*. New York: Wiley and Sons.

——— 2011. "Public Opinion, The Media, and War." In *The Oxford Handbook of American Public Opinion and the Media*, edited by Lawrence R. Jacobs and Robert Y. Shapiro, 675–689. New York: Oxford University Press.

National Election Pool Exit Poll. 2010. iPOLL Databank, The Roper Center for Public Opinion Research, University of Connecticut. http://www.roper-center.uconn.edu/data_access/ipoll/ipoll.html (accessed July 3, 2012).

Neal, Derek, and Diane Whitmore Schanzenbach. 2010. "Left Behind by Design: Proficiency Counts and Test-Based Accountability." *The Review of Economics and Statistics* 92(2): 263–283.

New York Times/CBS News Poll. 2012. February 8–13. http://s3.document cloud.org/documents/292755/feb12poll.pdf (accessed April 15, 2013).

Norpoth, Helmut, and Bruce Buchanan. 1992. "Wanted: The Education President. Issue Trespassing by Political Candidates." *Public Opinion Quarterly* 56(1): 87–99.

OED Online. 2011. "handle, v.1". Oxford University Press. December. http://www.oed.com/view/Entry/83880 (accessed January 31, 2012).

Oritz, Jon. 2008. "SEIU Donations to Obama, against McCain Exceed $16.5 Million." *sacbee.com*, October 27. http://blogs.sacbee.com/the_state_worker/2008/10/column-extra-your-money-and-pr.html (accessed July 3, 2012).

Page, Benjamin I. 1978. *Choices and Echoes in Presidential Elections: Rational Man and Electoral Democracy*. Chicago: University of Chicago Press.

Page, Benjamin I., and Robert Y. Shapiro. 1983. "Effects of Public Opinion on Policy." *American Political Science Review* 77(1): 175–190.

Peterson, Paul E. 1995. *The Price of Federalism*. Washington, DC: The Brookings Institution.

Petrocik, John R. 1996. "Issue Ownership in Presidential Elections, with a 1980 Case Study." *American Journal of Political Science* 40(3): 825–850.

Petrocik, John R., William L. Benoit, and Glenn J. Hansen. 2003. "Issue Ownership and Presidential Campaigning, 1952–2000." *Political Science Quarterly* 118(4): 599–626.

Pétry, François. 1995. "The Party Agenda Model: Election Programmes and Government Spending in Canada." *Canadian Journal of Political Science* 28(1): 51–84.

Pew Global Attitudes Project. 2003. "Views of a Changing World." June. http://www.people-press.org/files/legacy-pdf/185.pdf (accessed July 3, 2012).

Pew Hispanic Center. 2011. "Unauthorized Immigrant Population: National and State Trends, 2010." February 1, http://pewhispanic.org/files/reports/133.pdf (accessed July 5, 2012).

Ponnuru, Ramesh. 2012. "Grover Norquist's Endless Campaign." Bloomberg.com, June 18. http://www.bloomberg.com/news/2012-06-18/grover-norquist-isn-t-losing-the-no-tax-battle.html (accessed July 3, 2012).

Poole, Keith T., and Howard Rosenthal. 1985. "A Spatial Model for Legislative Roll Call Analysis." *American Journal of Political Science* 29(2): 357–84.

Pope, Jeremy C., and Jonathan Woon. 2009. "Measuring Changes in American Party Reputations, 1939–2004." *Political Research Quarterly* 62 (4):653–661.

Powell, G. Bingham, Jr. 2000. *Elections as Instruments of Democracy: Majoritarian and Proportional Visions*. New Haven, CT: Yale University Press.

Princeton Survey Research Associates International/*Newsweek* Poll. 2005. February. Retrieved March 26, 2012 from the iPOLL Databank, The Roper Center for Public Opinion Research, University of Connecticut.

PSRA/*Newsweek* Poll. 2001. February. Retrieved March 25, 2012 from the iPOLL Databank, The Roper Center for Public Opinion Research, University of Connecticut.

Rabe-Hesketh, Sophia and Anders Skrondal. 2012. *Multilevel and Longitudinal Modeling Using Stata*, 3rd ed. College Station, TX: Stata Press.

RePass, David E. 1971. "Issue Salience and Party Choice." *American Political Science Review* 65(2): 389–400.

Riker, William H. 1983. *The Strategy of Rhetoric: Campaigning for the American Constitution*. New Haven, CT: Yale University Press.

1986. *The Art of Political Manipulation*. New Haven, CT: Yale University Press.

Roemer, John E. 2001. *Political Competition: Theory and Applications*. Cambridge, MA: Harvard University Press.

Roth, Bennett. 1995. "Dole Says He Wants Four Agencies Closed to Balance Budget." *Houston Chronicle*, March 11, A2.

Schattschneider, E. E. 1935. *Politics, Pressures, and the Tarriff*. New York: Prentice-Hall.

Sears, David O., and Jack Citrin. 1982. *Tax Revolt: Something for Nothing in California*. Cambridge, MA: Harvard University Press.

Sellers, Patrick J. 1998. "Strategy and Background in Congressional Campaigns." *American Political Science Review* 92(1): 159–171.

Shapiro, Robert Y. 2011. "Public Opinion and American Democracy." *Public Opinion Quarterly*, 75(5): 982–1017.

Sharkansky, Ira, and Richard I. Hofferbert. 1969. "Dimensions of State Politics, Economics, and Public Policy." *American Political Science Review* 63(3): 867–879.

Sides, John. 2006. "The Origins of Campaign Agendas." *British Journal of Political Science* 36(3): 407–436.

2007. "The Consequences of Campaign Agendas." *American Politics Research* 35(4): 465–488.

Sigelman, Lee, and Emmett H. Buell. 2004. "Avoidance or Engagement? Issue Convergence in U.S. Presidential Campaigns, 1960–2000." *American Journal of Political Science* 48(4): 650–661.

Simon, Adam F. 2002. *The Winning Message: Candidate Behavior, Campaign Discourse, and Democracy.* New York: Cambridge University Press.

Soroka, Stuart N., and Christopher Wlezien. 2005. "Opinion–Policy Dynamics: Public Preferences and Public Expenditure in the United Kingdom." *British Journal of Political Science* 35(4): 665–689.

2010. *Degrees of Democracy: Politics, Public Opinion, and Policy.* New York: Cambridge University Press.

Spiliotes, Constantine J., and Lynn Vavreck. 2002. "Campaign Advertising: Partisan Convergence or Divergence?" *Journal of Politics* 64(1): 249–261.

Stimson, James. A. 2004. *Tides of Consent: How Public Opinion Shapes American Politics.* New York: Cambridge University Press.

Stokes, Donald E. 1963. "Spatial Models of Party Competition." *American Political Science Review* 57(2): 368–377.

Stolberg, Sheryl Gay, Jeff Zeleny, and Carl Hulse. 2010. "Health Vote Caps a Journey Back from the Brink." *New York Times*, March 21, A1.

Stubager, Rune, and Rune Slothuus. 2012. "What Are the Sources of Political Parties' Issue Ownership? Testing Four Explanations at the Individual Level." *Political Behavior*, online publication June 19. doi:10.1007/s11109-012-9204-2 (July 6, 2012).

Sulkin, Tracy. 2005. *Issue Politics in Congress.* New York: Cambridge University Press.

Sunlight Foundation. 2012. "Outside Spending by Race: Indiana Senate." http://reporting.sunlightfoundation.com/outside-spending/race_detail/S/IN/00/ (accessed July 3, 2012).

Tax Policy Center. 2011. "Historial Federal Income Tax Rates for a Family of Four." http://www.taxpolicycenter.org/taxfacts/Content/Excel/family_inc_rates_hist.xls (accessed October 1, 2011).

Theriault, Sean M. 2008. *Party Polarization in Congress.* New York: Cambridge University Press.

Therriault, Andrew. 2012. "Whose Issue Is It Anyway? A New Look at Party Reputations and Candidate Evaluations." Typescript, Vanderbilt University.

Thome, Helmut. 1999. "Party Mandate Theory and Time-Series Analysis: A Methodological Comment." *Electoral Studies* 18(4): 569–585.

Toder, Eric, and Daniel Baneman. 2012. "Distributional Effects of Individual Income Tax Expenditures: An Update." Washington, DC: Tax Policy Center, February 2.

Tufte, Edward R. 1978. *Political Control of the Economy*. Princeton, NJ: Princeton University Press.

Tumulty, Karen, and Philip Rucker. 2012. "Can Romney Find a Way to Connect with GOP Voters?" *Washington Post*, February 17.

U.S. Census Bureau Foreign Trade Division. 2012. "U.S. Trade in Goods and Services – Balance of Payments (BOP) Basis." June 8. http://www.census.gov/foreign-trade/statistics/historical/gands.txt (accessed July 5, 2012).

U.S. Department of Education. 2010a. "Table 128. Percentage of Students at or above Selected Reading Score Levels, by Age, Sex, and Race/Ethnicity: Selected Years, 1971 through 2008." *Digest of Education Statistics*, Institute of Education Sciences. http://nces.ed.gov/programs/digest/d10/tables/xls/tabn128.xls (accessed October 1, 2011).

2010b. "Table 8. Percentage of Persons Age 25 and over and 25 to 29, by Race/Ethnicity, Years of School Completed, and Sex: Selected Years, 1910 through 2010." *Digest of Education Statistics*, Institute of Education Sciences. http://nces.ed.gov/programs/digest/d10/tables/xls/tabn008.xls (accessed October 1, 2011).

U.S. Energy Information Administration. 2011. "Annual Energy Review, Table 3.3: Consumer Price Estimates for Energy by Source, 1970–2009." October 19. http://www.eia.gov/totalenergy/data/annual/index.cfm (accessed November 1, 2011).

U.S. Environmental Protection Agency. 2011a. "EPA National Emissions Inventory (NEI) Air Pollutant Emissions Trends Data: Current Emissions Trends Summaries from the NEI 1970–2011, Average Annual Emissions, All Criteria Pollutants." http://www.epa.gov/ttnchie1/trends (accessed October 1, 2011).

2011b. "Inventory of U.S. Greenhouse Gas Emissions and Sinks: 1990–2009, Table 2–1: Recent Trends in U.S. Greenhouse Gas Emissions and Sinks." http://epa.gov/climatechange/emissions/usinventoryreport.html (accessed October 1, 2011).

U.S. Immigration and Naturalization Service. n.d. "Estimates of the Unauthorized Immigrant Population Residing in the United States: 1990 to 2000." http://www.dhs.gov/xlibrary/assets/statistics/publications/Ill_Report_1211.pdf (accessed April 10, 2013).

Vavreck, Lynn. 2009. *The Message Matters: The Economy and Presidential Campaigns*. Princeton, NJ: Princeton University Press.

Viser, Matt. 2009. "Brown: Health Care Bill Hurts Mass." *Boston. com*, December 28. http://www.boston.com/news/local/breaking_ news/2009/12/brown_health_ca.html (accessed July 3, 2012).

Walgrave, Stefaan, Jonas LeFevere, and Anke Tresch. 2012. "The Associative Dimension of Issue Ownership." *Public Opinion Quarterly*, online publication June 5. doi:10.1093/Public Opinion Quarterly/nfs023 (accessed July 6, 2012).

Warshaw, Christopher, and Jonathan Rodden. 2012. "How Should We Measure District-Level Public Opinion on Individual Issues?" *Journal of Politics* 74(1): 203–219.

Weisman, Jonathan. 2012. "Two House Democrats Defeated after Opposing Health Law." *New York Times*, April 26, A1.

White House Office of Management and Budget. 2012a. *Historical Tables.* http://www.whitehouse.gov/omb/budget/Historicals (accessed July 3, 2012).

  2012b. *Fiscal Year 2013 Budget of the U.S. Government.* Washington, DC: U.S. Government Printing Office.

Wilson, James Q. 1973. *Political Organizations.* New York: Basic Books.

Winters, Marcus A., Julie R. Trivitt, and Jay P. Greene. 2008. "The Impact of High-Stakes Testing on Student Proficiency in Low-Stakes Subjects: Evidence from Florida's Elementary Science Exam." *Economics of Education Review* 29(1): 138–146.

Wlezien, Christopher. 1995. "The Public as Thermostat: Dynamics of Preferences for Spending." *American Journal of Political Science* 39(4): 981–1000.

  2004. "Patterns of Representation: Dynamics of Public Preferences and Policy." *Journal of Politics* 66(1): 1–24.

  2005. "On the Salience of Political Issues: The Problem with 'Most Important Problem.'" *Electoral Studies* 24(4): 555–579.

Wlezien, Christopher, and Stuart Soroka. "The Relationship between Public Opinion and Policy." In *The Oxford Handbook of Political Behavior*, edited by Russell J. Dalton and Hans-Dieter Klingemann. Oxford: Oxford University Press, 2007.

Zaller, John. 1992. *The Nature and Origins of Mass Opinion.* New York: Cambridge University Press.

Zogby, John, Regina Bonacci, John Bruce, Will Daley, and Rebecca Wittman. 2003. "Public Opinion and Private Accounts: Measuring Risk and Confidence in Rethinking Social Security." Cato Project on Social Security Choice. January 6.

Index